Portraits of the Artist
in Contemporary Fiction

Lee T. Lemon

Portraits of the Artist
in Contemporary Fiction

University of Nebraska Press
Lincoln and London

The paper in this book meets the
guidelines for permanence and durability
of the Committee on Production Guidelines
for Book Longevity of the
Council on Library Resources.

Library of Congress
Cataloging in Publication Data

Lemon, Lee T.
Portraits of the artist
in contemporary fiction.
Bibliography: p.
Includes index.
1. English fiction—20th century—
History and criticism.
2. Artists in literature. I. title.
PR888.A78L45 1985
823'.914'093527 84-22005
ISBN 0-8032-2868-6 (alk. paper)

For Maria, my best reader

Contents

Preface

Between the generation of James Joyce and the generation of
John Fowles, the fictional portrait of the artist changed notably. Essentially, the Byronic gave way to the Wordsworthian.
In the years before World War II, our best novelists saw their
artists as isolated rebels. Stephen Dedalus "flies the nets of
nationality, religion, language," defiantly abandoning country,
church, friends, and family in an effort to attain the godlike
purity and freedom he thinks is the artist's right. In their own
ways, Thomas Wolfe's hyperactive protagonists, Timothy Hazard in Walter Van Tilburg Clark's *The City of Trembling
Leaves*, and Thurs Wraldson in Feike Feikema's World's Wan-

derer Trilogy fall into the Byronic mold. Each is larger than life; each has drives that lesser mortals cannot fathom and dare not imitate; each sees himself tragically alone, a Gulliver among pygmies, a magnificent soul tormented by a society that refuses not only reverence and awe but sometimes even food and shelter. The main differences among Stephen Dedalus and the artist heroes of Dreiser and others are in the ways they express their contempt for the ordinary world in which people go to work, fall in love, raise families, and create communities; it ranges from the agonized arrogance of the young Dedalus to the agonized rage of Eugene Gant and his spiritual brothers.

Whether the Byronic artists of the novels before World War II saw themselves as a kind of John the Baptist preparing the way for the coming of Truth and Beauty and, perhaps, Goodness, or as a Nietzschean *Übermensch*, the next step up the evolutionary ladder, the enemy was the philistine. Essentially, the philistine is the rule-follower; he is the hollow man, the man in the gray flannel or three-piece suit and the red-white-and-blue mind, and he is evil because he cherishes the conditions that keep the artist enchained. He establishes the schools that try to force the artist into mindless conformity; he infiltrates the world of art either to destroy the integrity of the artist's vision or to attempt to block the creator's work; he oversees an economic system that makes it difficult for the artist to preserve his integrity and fill his stomach; he enforces a moral system that attempts to deny the artist's experience, to prevent the recording of that experience, and to punish anything beyond conformity to a mass norm that denies all individuality and vision.

Such is the enemy of the Byronic artist, who knows that within himself is a vision he must express, if not exclusively for his own sake, then for the sake of pulling the world from the quagmire in which it rots.

The typical Byronic artists of the novels of the first half of this century also have a bit of Shelley in them. Sometimes, like the young Dedalus or D. H. Lawrence's Paul Morel, they are, initially at least, sensitive plants. If they become monsters of selfishness, it is because they have so often been injured. They can preserve their spiritual sensitivity only by growing spiritual calluses. Two other aspects of the Byronic artist, as I'm using the phrase here, should be highlighted. The arrogance is in part the outgrowth of an unflinching sense of mission and a faith that the artist's gift neither can nor should be rationally defended or explained, that rationality is essentially a connivance of the philistines, and that the gift transcends rationality. Shelley, in a Byronic moment, wanted to become the West Wind, that impetuous force that sweeps the world and brings change; the nature of the change is less important than the confidence that any change, so long as it is from the heart, is good. To try to assess the value of what it sweeps away, or even the value of the act of sweeping, is blasphemous, as blasphemous as would be an attempt to fight the will of God or to pretend to comprehend its motivation. If one is a Byronic artist, both the message and the messenger are sacred; the only proper response for the nonartist is to "weave a circle round him thrice," for he has been touched by divinity and has become its sacred vessel.

I do not know precisely what led to the death of the fictional Byronic artist-hero. I suspect there is a kind of natural life span to the stereotypes we create to help us understand our world. In the hands of a Joyce, a Lawrence, a Dreiser—even in the hands of a Wolfe, a Clark, or a Feikema—the explanatory stereotype was presented with sufficient intensity and fullness that it did in fact help us understand better the peculiar situation of the artist—his development, his struggle with the world, with his own self, with his art. A young stereotype, a stereotype in the process of being developed, is after all not a stereotype but what Wimsatt and Beardsley called a "concrete universal," an incarnation of a body of traits that gives a new name, a new concept, to some aspect of our world. By the 1940s and 1950s, Dreiser's Genius had become Cornel Wilde as Chopin—simultaneously kissing George Sand and dashing off a concerto, just as Wolfe's Eugene Gant had become Ayn Rand's Howard Roark. The stereotype that once enabled us to think a bit more sharply now threatened to lead us to think more dully.

On another level, it is perhaps impossible for an age that does not take God seriously to take God's self-proclaimed oracles seriously. One hundred years earlier, in Matthew Arnold's vision, culture was to replace religion; the artist was to be the new evangelist and prophet, and literature the sacred books. Despite Arnold's hope, the ensuing generations of literary evangelists and prophets gave no clear call, no coherent sense of purpose for the believers in culture. The gospels according to George Eliot, Thomas Hardy, William Butler Yeats, James Joyce, Virginia Woolf, D. H. Lawrence—to mention just some of the major British writers—presented mutually incompatible testaments. If there were some source of inspiration beyond the individual consciousness of the artist, even some principle of awareness, it certainly spoke with forked tongues. After a hundred years of waiting, the kind of reader likely to take serious fiction seriously was in general not willing to take seriously the artist's claim to know the one truth. If the nineteenth century discovered the death of God, it took intellectuals almost a hundred years to realize that a dead God cannot send messages to his prophets. If we can no longer believe that the artist is the translator of absolute truth and beauty and goodness, Byronic arrogance becomes boorish posturing and Byronic contempt becomes itself contemptible.

Until the wheel turns again, and we once more need to be reminded of the specialness of the artist, Thomas Mann's *Doctor Faustus* will probably remain the grand obituary of the Byronic artist. Early in the century, Freud had argued that what passed as divine inspiration was apt to be suppressed glandular secretions, that "the lunatic, the lover, and the poet" are closer kin than even Shakespeare dared imagine. Edmund Wilson expanded the story of Philoctetes into the archetype of the artist, suggesting that although only the artist can give society the waking dreams it so desperately needs, society must shun the artist because his power is inextricably linked to his repugnantly festering wounds. For Mann's Adrian Leverkühn, the wound is untreated syphilis, a disease which, to use Verlaine's phrase, "deregulates the senses" and thereby creates that essential difference that separates the individual from the philistines, that creates at least the possibility of lifting the artist above the masses. Mann's diseased Byronic hero may create beauty, but it is no longer absolute and is certainly no longer either true or good. Stephen Dedalus's flight—however abortive—to godlike freedom is symbolized by his acceptance of his carnality, his hitherto forbidden self, in the vision of the girl on the beach; his full acceptance of what has been somewhat ruthlessly suppressed within him is an act of rebellious vision. Leverkühn's later and similar but more complete rebellion is a deliberate bargain with the devil, for there is no godlike power to serve, and the Byronic artist may serve anything but the philistine.

The Wordsworthian artist—the figure that dominates the *Künstlerroman* during the past forty years—is, in the sense in which I use the term, primarily an ordinary human being trying to live in a world peopled with individuals as important as himself. The artist is likely to have a sense of what he is doing but, unlike the historical Wordsworth, is also likely to recognize his own fuzziness about the place his work occupies in the grand scheme of things. If the artist does become an absolutist, like Lessing's Anna Wulf, the condition is never permanent. There are too many doubts, both about the existence or even the desirability of the absolute and, somewhat more frequently, about the worthiness of the artist-hero as spokesperson for whatever that vision might be. Compared to the Byronic artist, the artist-hero of most contemporary fiction is very much an anti-artist, in the same sense in which many contemporary fictional protagonists are anti-heroes. The exemplary heroes of past fictions seem, according to the current critical clichés, to have been replaced by bumblers. (Actually, heroes in serious fiction are less numerous than we usually assume. Our best novels supply a rather steady stream of Tris-

tram Shandys, Dobbins, Pips, and Judes; our heroic figures
have most often come either from our myths or from our popular fictions.)

The Byronic version of artistic development emphasizes
discontinuity—the goal is to pass from worm to butterfly as
quickly as possible and, after the alteration, to retain a minimum of features from the earlier stage. Ideally, the Byronic
artist would like to avoid the worm stage, is likely to resist it
while it occurs, and will either deny it or boast of it afterwards. The Wordsworthian pattern stresses continuity. Most
of the protagonists who appear in the following pages must
learn—and sometimes slowly and painfully, that the artist
cannot be more than human without being at least human. A
part of Anna Wulf's writer's block is her unwillingness to act
unless she can do so with more than human authority and her
refusal to accept the condition of most humanity, to accept the
role of "boulder pusher"; in Patrick White's *The Vivesector*,
Hurtle Duffield's best paintings result from his feelings of profound kinship with his subject. Durrell gives Darley more potential as an artist than Pursewarden precisely because Darley
cannot, despite his misguided attempt to imagine himself as a
Byronic lover, separate his concerns from those of the persons
around him. The storyline of the typical pre–World War II
Künstlerroman may be described as the protagonist's gathering of strength to enable him to glory in his differences from
others; the storyline of the more recent *Künstlerroman* is
more likely to show the protagonist's gathering of sufficient
strength to feel compassion for fellow humans and to endure
the pain of that compassion.

The term *"Künstlerroman"* is itself a curious legacy of what
I have called the Byronic conception of art. It suggests somehow that the development of the artist and attendant themes
can be neatly separated from broader issues, that there is
something so transcendent about art, that art has such intrinsic value, that it ought be presented in isolation. To the extent
that nonartistic themes appear in the *Künstlerroman*, they appear as distractions, as the nets which the young Dedalus

must flee. Rather than isolating the aesthetic, most of the works looked at in the following pages attempt to incorporate it in a larger view, in some cases implicitly, in others explicitly.

I have, therefore, tried to preserve a delicate balance between the narrowing claims of my topic and the much broader concerns of the fictions. The chapters on the individual writers—Lawrence Durrell, Doris Lessing, John Fowles, Patrick White, and John Barth—first place the aesthetic themes of the novels within the social, ethical, and philosophical contexts which give them their peculiar resonance; each chapter then moves on to explore the individual author's handling of more narrowly traditional aesthetic problems—the nature of the artistic gift, problems of technique and form, the purpose of art, and so on.

What emerges is a reading of the fictions of the five writers that attempts to articulate, in both senses of that word, their views on the one subject they know best, their craft. I have been concerned more with their fictions than with their direct comments about art because I believe that the best and deepest thought of an artist is more likely to be shown in the art than in casual interviews and essays, although the latter are often invaluable for corroboration and clarification.

Translating a writer's fictions about a subject into an explication of views is always risky; the factors that distance an author from a work, the distortions and accommodations that are made as the author translates values into drama and the critic retranslates the drama into ideas are as well known as they are real. I have tried to avoid such traps by assuming that the writers are rather stable human beings whose ideas might change from time to time, but whose values remain fairly constant. Doris Lessing's flirtations with Communism, Jungian and Laingian psychology, and Sufi mysticism illustrate the point splendidly. Her shifting doctrinal adhesions lead to quite different kinds of fictions, quite different vocabularies, quite different styles. But her values have remained constant. At each stage of her career, her writing shows immense concern for the maximum realization of human potential, and a sense that that realization will not arise through ever-growing individualism but through some sort of communal sharing. Although the instrument for sharing changes from the social to the psychic, the value of sharing is a constant. The assumption of that kind of consistency of values guides my interpretations of individual works.

There are, of course, a great number of other novels and novelists I could have considered; our age, as students of it keep reminding us, has produced much art about art, and studies of metafiction and of the self-reflexive novel abound. The novels I have chosen to consider are those which support my thesis about the presence of humanistic concerns in the portrayal of art and artists in fiction. Alternative theses—of the death of art generally and of the novel in particular, of the impossibility of art being about anything but art, of the general exhaustion of our culture and our imagination, of the alienation of author and text, of the highest art as silence—these are so dominant that it is often difficult to remember that very good novels still get written, and that some novels still move some readers, and that among the determinants of any particular text is an individual human being through whose sensibilities the very powerful forces of language, intertextuality, genre, and what have you, are filtered. The novelists I have selected do, however, represent a very broad spectrum. The somewhat arbitrary rules for inclusions were publication of at least one major work with an artist as hero, the achievement of a major reputation after World War II, and acceptance as a major writer by a fair number of those who watch such things with care. The concern with fictions written in English is regrettably provincial, but it is expedient; it permits me to side-step the very intricate and interesting problems of cross-cultural traits. The writers included are quite diverse; techniques and styles range from the rather nineteenth-century structures of Patrick White to the metafictions of John Barth, whose works replay old games with such fervor and depth that they become new. World views range from the social mysticism of Lessing to the hard-headed reinterpretation of Darwin by Fowles, from White's profound mysticism to Barth's equally profound scepticism.

Despite the diversity, common themes emerge. In one way or another, each believes that the world is ineffable, that the best the artist can do is to wage an honest and life-long fight to come as close to the truth as possible. The realization that what must be expressed is precisely that which cannot be expressed adequately is what humbles the artists-protagonists. With some there is the doubt, with others the certainty, that there may be no truth to express. Without the privilege the Byronic artist claimed, they must learn to accept their humanity, for ultimately that may be more valuable than their art; it is certainly the basis of their art. If they are to be "wonderful," to use Barth's word, they must learn to see themselves not as the demigods the Byronic spirit made of artists, but as the humans they are; and, to quote Barth again, "self-knowledge is always bad news"—at least at first. More often than not, it leads to an awareness of likenesses to others rather than of differences from them—a sense that artists are no wiser, no more compassionate, no more deserving of love, than the common lot of humanity. And from that, if one also has the technical skill, and the drive, and the courage, may come sufficient caring about the other—whether it be other individuals, society as a whole, chairs, stones, whatever—that is the essential gift of any human who would be more than an isolated individual. When Joyce imagines his quintessential artist, it is as a disinterested God paring his fingernails. When White imagines his, it is the drunken, semiliterate Alf Dubbo, kneeling in a gutter and transported out of his alcoholic stupor by his wonder at the motion of water as it runs along a curb, and by his fear that he will never have the ability to capture that motion in a painting. The two visions are emblematic of the artist in the two periods.

Portraits of the Artist
in Contemporary Fiction

Chapter 1

Lawrence Durrell

The Uses of Uncertainty

Somewhere in the heart of experience there is an order and a coherence which we might surprise if we were attentive enough, loving enough, or patient enough. Will there be time?[1]

Pursewarden, in one of those aphorisms in which he seems to speak for Durrell, remarks that the only thing worth fighting for is variety. Although it is the kind of quip that delights those who argue that Durrell's more complex works are excursions into a kind of precious aesthetic or sexual decadence, it is for Durrell a very serious statement of just what might be the only attitude toward the world that acknowledges the dazzling richness of experience. The work of the artist is somehow to capture that richness, to stimulate his readers to an awareness of it; the purpose of being human is to be able to live fully with that richness, to accept joyously the variety the world offers.

Perhaps that is what is most unusual about Durrell's "message" in his serious novels, and why they require such intricate forms. Practically every other novelist—serious or popular, traditional or avant-garde—writes of men and women who either settle comfortably into a pattern or who fail to do so. The leading players in the works of Richardson, Fielding, Austen, Dickens, Thackeray, George Eliot, Hardy, Conrad, Lawrence, Joyce, Bellow (the list could be extended indefinitely) are essentially human beings who attempt to cozy into a niche. Generally, in the eighteenth- and nineteenth-century novels (and their thematic descendants in the twentieth century), the fiction ends happily if the leading characters are stabilized in a situation approved of by society in general (usually a good marriage and a better-than-average income) and sadly if the protagonist fails to secure such stability. Even though later novelists concentrated more on the failures (e.g., Hardy or Conrad) or made their niches apart from the approval of society (Joyce and Lawrence), the pattern changes little. Lady Chatterley and Mellors settle into a relationship just as surely as do Elizabeth and Darcy; Stephen Dedalus is as anxious to find an occupation and a father as Joseph Andrews is. Even as complex a novelist as Faulkner suggests, in those works that show most awareness of the richness of experience, that humankind's best hopes are a kind of proudly impervious stoicism (Dilsey) or a kind of monumentally blithe lack of awareness (Lena Grove).

I do not want to belabor the point, but there is a kind of awesome stability about reality suggested in even the most turbulent modern fiction. After the horrors of rape, murder, and castration, Faulkner's Lena Grove and Byron Bunch ride off into the sunset; after almost suicidal despair, Lawrence's Paul Morel walks toward the light and his destiny as an artist; Bellows's complex Herzog finds happiness with the simple life. Stephen Dedalus, like Darley, feels inspired, but only after he has cut himself off from much of experience. Most novels, that is, seem to be based on the assumption that times are only temporarily out of joint and so end either when they are again in joint (Dedalus acknowledges his calling or Morel turns to life), or when the protagonist can no longer struggle (Lord Jim and Jude die). Durrell seems to feel that either pattern is an affront to the plenitude of our world and to the potential within us.

Durrell has suggested repeatedly that what is most modern about the modern artist is a

> new reality, which disrupted language and lives wholesale, was grasped, conceived, and assimilated at the turn of the century. After 1900 the artist seems to regain authority over his medium. . . . It is tempting to suggest that the discoveries of Freud and Einstein helped him, by their firm conceptual treatment of the unknown, and by the uncompromising honesty with which they dealt with the two universes—the universe outside man and the universe inside.[2]

How precisely Durrell understood either Freud or Einstein is one of those interesting questions that misses the point; what Durrell certainly understands, and what it is greatly more important for an artist to understand, is the effects of their discoveries on human beings. If culture is, as Durrell defines it, "the sum, at any time, of all the efforts man is making to interpret the universe about him," including all the arts and sciences, any artist attempting to chart the human condition must recognize the role played by the scientific ideas that dominate the period (*Key,* p. 1). After Freud and Einstein, we have become aware of what may have always been true, that art is concerned not "with explaining reality, but with teaching us how to accommodate ourselves to it" (*Key,* p. 44). Consequently, for Durrell, truth is recognized "by one quality— its *poignance.*"[3] It is significant that Durrell's grasp of the "poignance" of the theories of relativity and of the unconscious is both firmer and more encompassing in his fiction than in his criticism.

The criticism, especially *Key to Modern British Poetry,*

suggests that the effects of Freud and Einstein were almost immediately liberating, so that

> after 1900 the artist seems to gain an authority over his medium without having to pay the price of madness. . . . The artist, you feel, has no right any more to cast himself bodily into the breach, to sacrifice his reason in order to grasp reality. (*Key,* p. 40)

Yet, almost thirty years after Durrell's pivotal date, Hemingway's heroes long for the consolations of an absolute faith and, still later, Sartre describes the nausea brought by an experience of reality. The pervasive theme of much of the serious fiction of the twentieth century is, in fact, that the old truths are gone and that without them we are lost and lonely. In the later fictions, as we shall see, Durrell is quite sensitive to the hunger for the certainty that Freud and Einstein helped destroy. Among the major concerns of The Quartet and of The Avignon Quintet are the nature of that uncertainty and how, not whether, we can live with it.

The fifties and sixties produced libraries of literature detailing the roles of Freud and Einstein in creating our Age of Anxiety; there is no need to review that in detail. The charge was, simply, that Einstein's insights, reenforced by Heisenberg's, left us with no certainty about the nature of the physical reality in which we must live; Wittgenstein told us that our conceptual tools are sadly deficient—that our most inspired flights of reason are but linguistically wing-clipped flutterings within arbitrary universes of discourse; Freud seemed to tell us that our moral values are dependent upon conditioning beyond our control, dependent upon accidents of potty training and misunderstandings stemming from infantile sexuality. The result, so the argument ran, was inevitably the existential man, the terrified creature who must make particular choices in a world in which no particular choice has any discernible justification. Hence, in part, the rebellious but different individualisms of Joyce and Lawrence, the stoicism of Hemingway, and the passivity of Faulkner. Hence also the invitations to suicide and insanity issued by the European existentialists.

By some accident of genius or character, Durrell saw the Freud-Einstein world as a world of infinite possibility. Looked at from Durrell's perspective, the old truths provided the security of a cage; as Pursewarden says, " 'If things were always what they seemed, how impoverished would be the imagination of man!' " (*Balthazar*, p. 23). Durrell understands the exciting beauty of the relativist perspective; an absolutist understanding of the world subordinates all truths to one and denies what it cannot subordinate, the relativistic understanding need exclude nothing. There is no single reason, no single determinate, for example, behind Pursewarden's suicide. There are, however, reasons—the desire to free his sister from the memory of their incestuous love, chagrin at his mistaken judgment of the political situation in Alexandria, concern about his position as a writer, jealousy of Mountolive, even professional jealousy of the potential he sees in Darley. If The Quartet went on, I am confident that there would be still other reasons offered. If we read carefully, we both do and do not understand Pursewarden's suicide. We do not understand it in the sense that we can point to a cause and say "that's it"—as we can, say, with Elizabeth Bennett's decision not to marry Darcy. But we can say that the motives are certainly understandable and that, given the particular concatenation of events, Pursewarden's suicide makes a kind of *ex post facto* sense—which is to leave open the possibility that it is as ultimately unpredictable as Da Capo's resurrection. As Hippo remarks in *Tunc*, " 'There seem to be a hundred reasons to account for every act. Finally one hesitates to ascribe any of them to the act. Life gets more and more mysterious, not less.' "[4] But unlike most of his terrified contemporaries, Durrell finds this mystery, this flexibility of reality, exhilarating.

It is exhilarating not only because it is intellectually challenging (and, Durrell would say, reflects the way the world is), but also because it liberates the imagination; to an extent, it permits us to remake our reality. Leila Hosnani takes a promising but somewhat shallow Mountolive and imagines him into a cultivated man of the world; Amaril imagines and creates a nose for his beloved; Justine frees herself from a trauma caused by a childhood rape because Pursewarden goads her into reimagining it. "What I call life," Durrell remarked on "The Kneller Tape," "I see as an act of the imagination" (*World*, p. 163).

This is not to imply that all individual truths are equally significant, that all individual acts of the imagination are equally valuable. As we shall see, this is one of the lessons Darley must learn. He cannot be whole so long as he accepts only a single imagining of reality, nor so long as he is merely confused by alternate versions, nor even so long as he feels it is possible to arrive at Truth. He says in a dream, "'I must know *everything* in order to be at last delivered from the city.'" Shortly afterwards, he remembers the wiser Balthazar saying, "'Truth is what most contradicts itself in time'" (*Balthazar*, pp. 22–23). A large part of Darley's education consists of his learning to come to terms with a world that is too complex for either simple truths or complete knowledge.

What Einstein did for external nature, Freud and his followers—including Durrell's favorite, Groddeck—did for internal nature. At the very least, they offered another facet of reality for the imagination of man to work upon, another of a series of sets of motivations and explanations of human conduct that, while not completely true, contribute a useful piece to the picture. Arnatuti's recreation of Justine in *Mouers* is almost totally a Freudian creature; his version errs not because it is wrong but because it is only one portrait of her. Moreover, the perspective Freud has given makes paramount the significance of memory; and memory is but the humanized experience of time—that fourth aspect of relativity. Before Freud, memory was thought to have been a consciousness of the past, a solace for age and loneliness, a source of regret; after Freud it becomes the often commanding voice of the past. A pre-Freudian Darley on his island, attempting to recall his experience in Alexandria, would be indulging in mere nostalgia; a post-Freudian Darley in the same situation is literally attempting to, as he puts it, "heal myself" (*Justine*, p. 13), to understand his present disquietude by making himself conscious of his past.

Much of Darley's problem—to get neatly back to relativity—is that not only are there layers of memory, with each layer coloring the truth a bit differently, but there are also different memories. Darley cannot know what happened to him in Alexandria until he is able to assimilate Balthazar's memories—and Pursewarden's, and Clea's, and Justine's. Balthazar's version of the events, Durrell wants us to realize, is no more true than Darley's (consider, for example, how little Balthazar knows of Pursewarden). Even toward the end of *Clea*, at a point where Darley should surely know Pursewarden, Durrell works a magnificent bit of sleight of hand. After reading Pursewarden's letters to his sister, Darley becomes a devout member of the Pursewarden cult, almost in awe at the sublimity of soul of the older novelist. Just as the reader thinks he understands the essential Pursewarden, Durrell reintroduces Keats—a journalist who has just recently felt the nudge, who at that point is one of the chosen—who talks about the pettiness and meanness of Pursewarden's letters to his wife. Memory contradicts memory, but the contradictions in Durrell's world seldom cancel out, nor does a later memory very often prove the first untrue. Rather, the contradictions in this relativistic universe are additive, each presenting a peculiar facet of the character, of the event, of the situation. Truth is not a matter of exclusion, but of inclusion.

Perhaps this also helps to account for one of the most winning features of Durrell's work: it is almost totally nonjudgmental. The novels are in part what Balthazar called "'the perpetual reservation of judgment and the perpetual choosing'" (*Balthazar*, p. 226). With perhaps the exception of Memlik (and I suspect that if Durrell had written more about him he would not be an exception), every character, even the worst, is eventually presented sympathetically. Only the most hard-hearted of readers cannot sympathize with the old Co-hen, the sleazy furrier who dies wishing to make amends to Melissa; or with the violent Narouz, a murderer, deformed, passionately yet hopelessly in love with Clea, defender of the family honor, visionary mystic. To understand fully enough (one never understands fully in Durrell's world) is at the very least to feel the beginnings of compassion. And that, for Dur-rell, is the start of being human.

To return to Pursewarden's quip, ultimately variety is the only thing worth fighting for because without an acceptance of and perhaps even a thirst for variety, we cannot know enough of our world, or of ourselves as individuals and as a species. Not to accept variety—to deny or even to prejudge the mys-ticism of Narouz or the pragmatism of Maskelyne, the anguish of Justine or her selfishness, the foolishness of Scobie or his saintliness, or even the alchemy of DaCapo—is wilfully to exclude oneself from knowledge of the world in which we must live. It is to base our lives on partial truths, as if we were content to use but one of our five senses. It is to confine human imagination and human compassion only to that which one's consciousness, formed by whatever accident or purpose, accepts.

Durrell's rather strange statement that after Freud and Einstein "the artist . . . has no right any more to cast himself bodily into the breach, to sacrifice his reason in order to grasp reality" (*Key*, p. 40) begins to make more sense. If, as Durrell believes, the artist is the see-er, the visionary, the Cyrano whose eloquence charms us into a love affair with life, then the artist must be free to see more things in heaven and on earth than are dreamed of in Horatio's or anyone else's philos-ophy; he must be free to suggest to his audience that there are more things in heaven and on earth than dreamed of even in his own philosophy. And in a sense, these are precisely the humanistic, if not the technical, implications of the insights of both Freud and Einstein. Freud and his followers have, if we take the optimistic interpretation, told us that we are almost infinitely more varied, more complex, and therefore more laden with potential, than we had ever believed ourselves. And Einstein has told us that there is always another perspective, another variable, another way of expressing our relationship to external reality. For an optimist like Durrell, the work of Freud and Einstein does in reality give the modern artist a "nudge" from the universe.

As might be expected, Durrell generally avoids definitive statements about the nature of the artist and his art, and when he does make such statements, they are likely to be quite general. The critic attempting to formulate Durrell's aesthetic is in much the same position as Darley trying to reformulate his past; there are somewhat different versions represented in different works, and often the different versions depend upon different points of view, different universes of discourse. Judged within any narrowly one-positional framework, the versions will be contradictory; judged from a more complex perspective, the versions are complementary or nonexclusive presentations of the same topic—in much the same way that it is true that Justine marries Nessim because he offers her a full part in his political life and equally true that she marries him because he has the means to support the search for her lost child. Like Darley, the critic has to rework the material, refusing either to settle for a simple version or to despair of finding enough of the truth. At one point Clea accuses Darley of having "'a mania for exactitude and an impatience with partial knowledge which is . . . well, unfair to knowledge itself. How can it be anything but imperfect'" (*Clea*, p. 119). The difficulty of working with Durrell's thought is our hunger "for exactitude"; the joy of working with it comes from our sense that the inexactitude is not carelessness but rather a respect for the complexity and intricacy of his subject—whether it be art or love.

For Durrell the mature artist—as distinct from the developing artist and those popularizers or critical successes who make things that resemble art—is first and foremost a relatively complete human being who has broken through his own ego and who is creative. We aren't, Durrell remarks in

"The Kneller Tape," "born human; I should say that the meaning of life is to make us become so, earn the price of admission
so to speak. Most people live vegetable lives . . . Lots of
poets among them, alas" (*World*, pp. 164–65). The point is
important partly because it insists upon the humanity of the
artist, and therefore on the humanity of the vision, and because it refuses to set the artist apart as a special kind of person, not subject to the concerns and the limitations, whether
internal or external, of less specifically gifted human beings.
Nor is the artist essentially different from the inventor.
Julian's description of the genius applies as much to the artist
as to the scientist:

> "But when a link is broken those rare men address themselves
> to the problem. What we call genius occurs when a gifted man
> sees a relation between two or more fields of thought which
> had up till then been believed to be irreconcilable. He joins
> the contradictory fields in an act of intellectual harmony and
> the chain begins to hold once more. The so-called genius of
> the matter is merely the intuitive act of joining irreconcilables.
> There is nothing added, how could there be? . . . The ka-
> leidoscope must be given a jolt, that is all."[5]

Darley collecting his perspectives on Alexandria and Pursewarden dancing to the right and left of an object are simply
gathering the irreconcilables which, as artists, they will
eventually join.

From *The Black Book* on, Durrell has kept reminding us
that, if anything, the creative person is charged with the difficult responsibility of being more human than others; only
when he is able to be more sympathetic, more sensitive, more
understanding, is the creativity meaningful. Tarquin (a kind of
Balthazar seen perhaps before Durrell himself has matured
creatively) is one of the most unpleasant characters in *The
Black Book* and one of the few characters in all his fiction
whom Durrell seems to judge negatively; it is typical of Tarquin that "in the music he made . . . there was no love."[6]
Charlock, the inventor in *Tunc-Nunquam* who " 'would have

liked to achieve in my line whatever would correspond to a work of art—which my friend Koepgen has defined as an act of disciplined insubordination'" (*Tunc*, p. 175), is merely a clever technician until he destroys the records of the Merlin Corporation—a kind of vast scientific-industrial complex that seems to control the entire world. Even Amaril, the handsome surgeon whom everyone likes and all women desire, becomes fully creative and fully satisfied only under the humanizing influence of love, only when he falls irrevocably in love with the noseless Semira and must dedicate himself to creating the perfect nose for her.

It is not an over-generalization to note that the characters in Durrell's serious works achieve stature in direct proportion to the depth and breadth of what an older psychology would call their sympathetic imagination, that faculty which was said to be the basis of morality by its function of making the self aware of the other. Narouz, the barbarously cruel brother of Nessim, achieves dignity largely through two acts—his sympathetic understanding of his father's feelings as the latter tolerates an affair between his wife and Mountolive, and his refusal (until he is near death) to intrude upon Clea's feelings despite his passion for her. Justine's finest moment occurs when she accepts Nessim's marriage proposal in part because she senses his need of her; the bumbling transvestite Scobie is loveable partly because he loves—his imagination, for example, will not let him tolerate the suffering caused by the circumcision of young girls in Alexandria. Even Da Capo becomes less of a villain and more of a mere amusement when he is off on an imaginative pursuit of an alchemical adventure. And Leila is at her finest as she uses her imagination to create a Mountolive more cultured, even more imaginative himself, than would have been possible without her guidance.

Yet these, and others, are only partial victories of the imagination. To be fully human, fully creative, requires more; within The Quartet only Keats, Pursewarden (perhaps), Clea, and Darley achieve it. It requires a total breakthrough, a birth that, although painful, is within the reach of all. Durrell's fullest statement of what that second birth entails is given by Pursewarden in his "Imaginary Conversations with Brother Ass," his name for Darley:

> Brother Ass, the so-called act of living is really an act of the imagination. The world—which we always visualise as "the outside" World—yields only to self-exploration! Faced by this cruel, yet necessary paradox, the poet finds himself growing gills and a tail, the better to swim against the currents of un-enlightenment. . . . (Yes, but it *hurts* to realise!) If he were to abandon his rôle all hope of gaining a purchase on the slippery surface of reality would be lost, and everything in nature would disappear! But this act, the poetic act, will cease to be necessary when everyone can perform it for himself. What hinders them, you ask? Well, we are all naturally afraid to sur-render our own pitifully rationalised morality—and the poetic jump I'm predicating lies on the other side of it. . . . Whoever makes this enigmatic leap into the heraldic reality of the poetic life discovers that truth has its own built-in morality! . . . In-side the penumbra of this sort of truth morality can be dis-regarded because it is a donnée, an inhibition. It is there to be lived out and not thought out! . . .
> . . . The heraldic reality can strike from any point, above or below: it is not particular. But without it the enigma will re-main. You may travel round the world and colonise the ends of the earth with your lines and yet never hear the singing your-self. (*Clea*, pp. 153–54)

But before the heraldic reality strikes ("Heraldic reality" is Durrell's phrase for a kind of complete, almost intuitive yet earned understanding, much like Coleridge's notion of the seer's ability to read nature as "God's mighty alphabet"), what does the artist do? Durrell's answer is as simple as it is proba-bly true: he lives and learns. In a letter to Henry Miller, Dur-rell mentions that he cannot permanently live at the intensity required to write fully; he needs to keep his hand in, to relax by writing his travel books and what Graham Greene called "entertainments."[7] Although Durrell's letters are generally quite impersonal in many ways, they suggest—with some important disclaimers—a Durrell not unlike Darley in some ways, Pursewarden in others. As Durrell noted in his interview with Marc Alyn, a large part of the difference between what is lived and what is written is "The scale! We describe giants and freaks in order to illustrate the instincts and inclinations that are infinitely more attenuated in real life. But the monsters exist in every one of us." Alyn adds, "Lawrence Durrell, or the aesthetics of Enlargement?" and Durrell replies, "Excellent!"[8] Durrell's letters tell of soaking up atmosphere, of becoming involved in the lives of the people around him, of excitement when things are going well and despair when they are going badly. The sexuality of Alexandria, the political situation, the babel of tongues and cultures has left him probably less stunned and less melodramatic than Darley, and with less surface cynicism than Pursewarden, but certainly with as much to understand. So between nudges, between lightning strikes of the heraldic reality, Durrell, like Darley, enjoys and suffers his way through life and practices his craft—living not too differently from those incomplete artists who have never felt the nudge. Like Arnauti's *Moeurs*, Clea's abstractions, or Darley's *Justine*, their works just miss the point—which is not to say that they are uninteresting or without value, but it is to say, in Pursewarden's phrase, that they give the impression that the artist has not yet heard the "singing" himself.

Although we do not know much about Clea's abstractions, we do know enough about *Moeurs* and *Justine* to describe them in part as ego-dominated failures of imagination. Both are attempts to explain, to make a kind of rational sense, out of a series of events seen through the ego of the author. In a sense, both Arnauti and Darley are attempting to explain not only their experience of Justine, but—more egoistically—to rationalize their failures with her. Arnauti, proud of his psychological tools, assembles a nymphomaniac Justine whose love is unattainable because of "the Check," an emotional cutoff brought about by a childhood rape. The explanation permits Arnauti to write a fashionable case history disguised as a fiction, to display his patience in dealing with a "sick" wife, and to explain to his readers that, given Justine's "check," no other man could have done better. Darley's version in *Justine* is equally self-serving, and therefore unimaginative. His particular ego demands an explanation that permits Justine to love him, so he minimizes the "check" and replaces it with a husband who is sporadically insanely jealous. It is, to use the word with which Pursewarden described Darley, the explanation of a "sentimentalist." Although the point will be returned to later, it is worth noting in passing that part of Darley's nudge, at least a condition of it, comes because he is forced, partly by Balthazar's "Interlinear," to see the affair non-egoistically. Not only was Justine not in love with him, she used him to get information for her husband and to conceal her love for Pursewarden. It is difficult to imagine two reasons for an affair that would be more damaging to a sentimentalist's ego.

It is important to repeat that neither Arnauti's *Moeurs* nor Darley's *Justine* is worthless, despite their authors' immaturity. *Justine*, and the parts we have of *Moeurs*, read like somewhat better-than-average but not exceptional fictions; they interest, they shed a different light on their subjects, without wholly satisfying. For their readers they are a part of Pursewarden's relativity dance, those steps to the right and to the left that one must take to view the subject adequately. And, albeit ego-based, they are the beginnings of imaginative effort, of the attempt to understand what is outside one's self. In terms of imagination, if not of immediate sympathy, the effort of each to make an extended fiction from his memories of his beloved carries him far beyond, say, Narouz's intense but narrow vision of Clea.

Between nudges, or while waiting for the first nudge, the artist must also practice his craft. One cannot will the special kind of truth Durrell demands of himself, but one must nevertheless "practice at the nets and so on, but once the game begins you forget all about technique; an effortless automatism replaces conscious intention" (*World*, p. 165). Or, as Pursewarden would put it,

> Nor do I mean that it is useless to master and continuously practice your craft. No. A good writer should be able to write anything. But a great writer is the servant of compulsions which are ordained by the very structure of the psyche and cannot be disregarded. (*Clea*, p. 136)

Given the development of artists in Durrell's works and his own practices, it seems clear that he is not saying that the great writer is not also a good writer. "Any professional writer . . . must," according to Fraser,

> salute first of all in Durrell a Protean quality, a versatility and virtuosity that has, however, something very solid behind it. There is in Durrell an honest journeyman of letters, a craftsman who will have a shot at almost anything, and create occasionally something major or spectacular but always a workmanlike job. The range is very wide. . . .
> In Durrell's later life, there is a bewildering intermixture of works of high ambition and what might be called honest potboilers.[9]

Although Durrell considers himself a romantic (*Supposer*, p. 28), he has none of that naive romanticism which sees the artist as a version of the inspired mutant who almost from birth paints or writes superbly. Even the wise Clea must serve her technical apprenticeship painting realistic portraits of disease for Balthazar, and Keats earns his way with words through years of commonplace journalism. In Durrell's world, lightning does strike, and the artist is not complete until stricken, but he had also better be ready for it.

Thus far I have said little directly about the suffering of the artist. The notion is a loaded one; it generally implies that the artist is abused by the world around him, that his sensibilities are assaulted by philistines and their works, that his vision is not shared, and that he is not fed while snapping at the hand that tries to feed. Like Durrell himself, his fictional artists do suffer—from Lawrence Lucifer in *The Black Book* through Nero in *Acte;* through Keats, Clea, Pursewarden and Darley in The Quartet; through Charlock in *Tunc-Nunquam,* and Blanford in The Avignon Quintet. In each case, however, the suffering has about the same explanatory power as does Arnauti's theory of Justine's "check." Undoubtedly none of the artists would be what they are were it not for their suffering, but what they suffer—whether it be the agonies of incestuous love or physical mutilation—may be and has been shared by Durrell's non-artists. Pursewarden's incestuous involvement with his sister is no more intense and no more character-forming than Julian's with Benedicta in *Tunc-Nunquam;* Clea's loss of a hand and Scobie's loss of an eye create widely divergent effects. One is tempted to say that for Durrell suffering is merely a part of the human condition for artist and non-artist alike, but the implications of that are much too pessimistic. Although there are exceptions (notably Julian), suffering does not so much define character as give it an impetus toward some oblique development. It may alter the ego; it does not determine it.

We have already seen that Darley's ego must be shattered before he can feel the nudge. Not only must he learn that Justine never loved him, at least not in the way he thought, he must also learn that Melissa preferred Cohen as a lover, and that the Pursewarden whom he so admired thought of him as "Brother Ass"—albeit affectionately. Even in *Justine* Darley feels that he has failed "in art, in religion, and in people" (p. 196). Reading Pursewarden's letters, he sheds " 'tears of exasperation. . . . I just realised that I am not an artist at all. There is not a shred of hope in my ever being one' " (*Clea,* p. 178). At one point, he sinks so low as to tell Clea that he might turn to criticism! (as Durrell himself did at an especially low point in his life, when he was away from his beloved Mediterranean and lecturing in Argentina); the result, *A Key to Modern British Poetry,* is an unusually perceptive and wide-ranging account of what is rather grandiosely known as the "modern mind."

Even Keats, within The Quartet the least fully described of those who have felt the nudge, undergoes his personal agony. The pre-nudge Keats was almost the caricature of the journalist, smelling

> slightly of perspiration. . . . Once he had wanted to be a writer but took the wrong turning, and now his profession had so trained him to stay on the superficies of real life (acts and facts about acts) that he had developed the typical journalist's neurosis . . . namely that Something has happened, or is about to happen, in the next street. . . . There was nothing wrong with John except the level on which he had chosen to live his life— but you could say the same about his famous namesake, could you not? (*Balthazar*, pp. 25–26)

When Darley meets Keats later, in *Clea*, he expects a muckraking journalist, dragging "his trail of slime" (p. 178) and anxious to write a best-selling exposé of the notorious Pursewarden. But Keats has been through a war. He tells Darley:

> "When I look around that . . . battlefield at night, I stand in an ecstasy of shame, revelling at the coloured lights, the flares wallpapering the sky, and I say: 'All this had to be brought about so that poor Johnny Keats could grow into a man.' . . . No other way would have helped me because I was too damned *stupid*. . . . " (*Clea*, p. 182)

Because we see so little of Keats, it is perhaps an exaggeration to speak of his suffering, but the terrors of war and the recognition of one's own stupidity certainly make that suffering implicit, if not overtly dramatized.

Pursewarden is, of course, much more fully developed. Read narrowly enough, his is the classic case of Freudian sublimation. Left at an early age with a beautiful but blind sister, he entertains her by creating tales of other worlds (much as the Brontës did); they fall tenderly in love and conceive a blind child who soon dies. Their love is as star-crossed as that of any young lovers of tragedy. As Darley learns, Pursewarden's ironic mask hides a tenderness born of deep suffering. Noted as a savage ironist whose last work is a trilogy entitled *God Is a Humorist*, he is seen by Clea "'quite simply'" as "'a man *tortured beyond endurance by the lack of tenderness in the world*'" (*Justine*, p. 244). Perhaps it is no wonder that in his notes he writes: "All great books are excursions into pity" (*Mountolive*, p. 166).

Clea endures what, in its suddenness and savagery, must be a terribly debilitating blow to a painter. In what Durrell himself has called a rebirth scene (*World*, pp. 166–67), Clea loses her hand in an underwater accident. Even before the loss of the hand, Clea, always one of the most mature, the most stable, of the characters in The Quartet, has told Darley that her "old self-sufficient life has transformed itself into something a little hollow, a little empty'" (*Justine*, p. 244). In one of its phases, her art is little different from the journalism of Keats: she paints realistic pictures of wounds for Balthazar's medical records. In a later phase she tries abstractions, which dissatisfy her, but which she feels are a stage through which she must go—her "practice at the nets." But after the loss of the hand her paintings suddenly come alive; the hand has proved itself

> "almost more competent than an ordinary flesh-and-blood member! In fact its powers are so comprehensive that I am a little frightened of it. . . . But most important of all—ah! Darley I tremble as I write the words—IT can *paint!*
>
> "I have crossed the border and entered into the possession of my kingdom, thanks to the Hand. . . . All roads have opened before me, everything seems now possible for the first time." (*Clea*, pp. 278–79)

And so Clea's nudge comes as a result of a painful, disfiguring accident (much as Leila's ability to realize, in the full sense of that word, a cultivated Mountolive comes after her disfiguring smallpox).

Apparently, in Durrell's world the artist does not reach maturity without some kind of blow. Even for Blanford in The

Avignon Quintet, the artist is stimulated by a loveless childhood and by taunts that lead him to create a fictitious character to hide behind in his notebooks.[10] Perhaps what dis-
tinguishes the suffering of Durrell's artists from that of artists
created by earlier novelists is that it is never an angry suffering and that it is always seen as simply part of the process of
becoming a human being. The non-artist Mountolive's reaction could be that of any of Durrell's artists: "It was unpleasant to be forced to grow. It was thrilling to grow. He gravitated
between fear and grotesque elation" (*Mountolive*, p. 28).

The lack of anger is a bit more complex and equally important. The young artists of Joyce, Dreiser, Thomas Wolfe, Cary,
and others all use anger and hurt as a springboard. They see
the world as a hopelessly corrupt, insanely and culpably ignorant scene which they must either change or flee. For Durrell's artists—the only exception is the insane Nero of *Acte*,
demented because his art has not changed the world—the
response to suffering is not anger but an attempt at understanding, often through introspection and recollection. Although Darley, at the beginning of *Justine*, has fled Alexandria
as surely as Stephen Dedalus has fled Dublin, his mood (even
allowing for the egoism) is based upon a sense that he must
understand—not reject—his past. And Durrell, unlike
Darley at the time, knows that to understand he must suffer
the humiliation of learning that his initial beliefs were hid-
eously incomplete.

From another perspective, the lack of anger of his artists
has two further ramifications: it conditions the nature of the
struggle and the nature of the victory by internalizing both.
This is not to say that there is not abundant external action in
Durrell's novels—there are rapes, killings, disappearances,
torture, mutilation, foreign intrigue, romance—but rather
that it forms the backdrop against which the artist develops
rather than determines his development. It is what Kenneth
Burke would call "scene" rather than "agent" or "act." In the
last half of *The Portrait of the Artist as a Young Man*, for instance, Joyce carefully arranges a set of "fights" for Stephen

against very carefully graded opponents, each representing one of the nets Stephen must flee. Stephen's development is shown and his superiority proved as he wins each fight. Darley, on the other hand, is put through his paces, not so that he can out-argue, say, Pursewarden and prove that he is not Brother Ass, but so that he can internalize the points of view of Pursewarden, Clea, Justine, Melissa, Balthazar, and others, and so attain some mastery over himself. The result is an especially meaningful victory because it is both positive and definitive. He does not have to defeat the equivalents of Lynch, Davitt, and Cranly because he has assimilated them; through his recreation of his past he has included them and is justifiably confident of his growth.

As Durrell reminds his reader quite often, self-knowledge is both a result of and a condition for courage, the special kind of courage an artist must have. In a rather curious but thoroughly consistent character sketch, Durrell tells the reader that Nessim wanted to paint. "He thought and suffered a good deal but he lacked the resolution to dare—the first requisite of a practitioner" (*Justine*, p. 28). It is curious because, vis-à-vis the external world, Nessim is a man of extraordinary daring: he organizes a political plot that could mean the ruin of the family fortunes and his own death, coolly confronts the police terrorist Memlik, and even orders the execution of his own brother, yet he lacks the special daring necessary to become an artist. Because—with the exceptions of his occasional jealousy, greatly exaggerated by Darley—his conflicts are external, he suffers without attaining self-knowledge. Although Durrell never judges his characters, there is a terrible sense of loss of potential when we discover that, despite all Nessim (and Justine) have been through, at the end of *Clea* he is picking up where he left off—like a Buddhist who has learned so little in one incarnation that he must relive his experiences in the next.

Perhaps Campion, the painter in *The Dark Labyrinth*, best explains the necessity of courage. He tells Fearmax, the mystic, that

"Painting by the power of the hand and the eye is one thing. Painting with the lust of the soul is quite another. I am spinning a myth about myself in a series of canvases. It is so lucid and clear that it scares me. I am not troubled by what I might be unable to say. I am troubled by what I shall, unknown to myself, reveal. And yet the process is irresistible."[11]

Pursewarden is not quite so dramatic, although at one point he does tell Darley, in a bit of advice he contradicts later, "'force it a bit and tell yourself that you don't give a damn if you *do* go mad, and you'll find it comes quicker, you'll break the barrier'" (*Balthazar*, p. 17). And in another mood:

"First you have to know and understand intellectually what you want to do—then you have to sleep-walk a little to reach it. The real obstacle is oneself. I believe that artists are composed of vanity, indolence and self-regard. Work-blocks are caused by the swelling-up of the ego on one or all of these fronts. You get a bit scared about the imaginary importance of what you are doing! Mirror-worship. My solution would be to slap a poultice on the inflamed parts—tell your ego to go to hell and not make a misery of what should be essentially *fun, joy*." (*Clea*, p. 110)

This is probably a part of the meaning implicit in Clea's artistry after she loses her hand: she is no longer frightened at the importance of what she is doing (or perhaps even of self-revelation), for it is the hand, an incarnation of Groddeck's IT, which paints.

Without such courage, the works produced are at least partial failures. We know very little of Darley's work before the nudge; the only description we have of it is Pursewarden's comment to Balthazar, a comment that infuriates Darley:

"'These books have a curious and rather forbidding streak of cruelty—a lack of humanity which puzzled me at first. But it is simply the way a sentimentalist would disguise his weakness. Cruelty here is the obverse of sentimentality. He wounds because he is afraid of going squashy.'" (*Balthazar*, pp. 109–10)

In passing, it is interesting to compare this with one of Durrell's less enthusiastic statements about *The Black Book:*

> I feel a fraud, really. *The Black Book* is epileptic, a fit. WHY? Was I a monster? I tried to say what I was, but of course with my talent for covering myself in confetti made a hell of an epic. I wanted to write myself so miserable and wormy and frightened as I was. (*Correspondence*, p. 91)

Pursewarden's description of Darley's work also seems to be consistent with the descriptions we have of Pursewarden's own writing. I think, however, that we can accept Pursewarden's judgment of Darley's work; certainly *Justine* is a sentimentalist's view of an affair, albeit a sentimentalist who has gone beyond overcompensation for his own sentimentality.

There is also another aspect of courage necessary for the artist; it can be seen either linguistically or epistemologically, and probably is best seen both ways. John Keats, who seems surely to have told his "ego to go to hell and not make a misery out of what should be essentially *fun, joy*," describes it as an ability to continue despite the inadequacies of language and as a condition of describing the richness of the world. The pre-nudge Keats lived in a quite simple reality, what Durrell called "act-fact-act," and seemed reasonably content as a bustling describer of surfaces. After the nudge, he learns that

> "Truth is double-bladed. . . . There is no way to express it in terms of language, this strange bifurcated medium with its basic duality! Language! What is the writer's struggle except a struggle to use a medium as precisely as possible, but knowing fully its basic imprecision? A hopeless task, but none the less rewarding for being hopeless." (*Clea*, p. 184)

The medium may be the message, but it is not the reality (or, in the more extreme contemporary jargon, the sign does not represent the thing, but the trace of the thing). Epistemologically, there is simply too much in the world, too many points of view, too many interwoven stories, too many conflicting emotions for the mind of even the mature artist ever to apprehend it all, to say nothing of embodying it in a single construct. This discrepancy between the awesome plenitude of reality and the limited capacity of man and his media may be seen either as a curse or as a challenge. In Doris Lessing's *Golden Notebook*, it is the former, a major reason for Anna Wulf's writer's block (although certainly not the sole cause of her breakdown); Durrell, always more optimistic, sees it as an opportunity, an opening of limitless possibilities, because "somewhere in the heart of experience there is an order and a coherence which we might experience if we were attentive enough, loving enough, or patient enough" (*Justine,* p. 211).

Durrell leaves the nature of the nudge, the strike by the heraldic reality, the "great inkling," deliberately vague; even the terms he uses suggest an unwillingness to deal with it too directly. Perhaps the closest he has come in his critical writing is in a short critique of Sartrean existentialism:

> A propos the existentialists—there is, it seems to me, one terrible metaphysical flaw in the whole Sartre thesis. The lack of CRISIS. The only justification for the art of *stasis* which in the XXth century art is in the precipitation of crisis. The crisis in the audience—and thus the cathartic principle of change of stance—the reborn self. This is missing in these boys, I think. (*Correspondence,* p. 224)

The nudge, the crisis, is for Durrell the great turning point, not only for the artist but also for the audience (a point that will be considered later). But there is no prescription for it; one of the reasons Durrell includes so many artists within The Quartet is presumably because he wants to make it clear that the state of grace can be attained in various ways. Although at one point Pursewarden tells Darley that he should " 'force it a bit,' " he later rescinds the advice. After accusing Darley of being "lazy of spirit," he continues,

But then, why struggle? If it is to happen to you it will happen
of its own accord. You may be quite right to hang about like
this, waiting. I was too proud. I felt I must take it by the
horns, this vital question of my birthright. For me it was
grounded in an act of will. So for people like me I would say:
"Force the lock, batter down the door. Outface, defy, disprove
the Oracle in order to become the poet, the darer!"

But I am aware the test may come under any guise. . . . the
heraldic reality can strike from any point, above or below.
(*Clea*, p. 154)

The nudge comes unexpectedly, but not undeservedly; it may
be years in preparation, and its effects seem as permanent as
birth. It is, I suspect, the feeling that Durrell himself experienced as a result of Miller's praise of an early version of *The
Black Book*. Durrell wrote Alan G. Thomas:

I'm starting out now in a more splendid curve than you would
ever have imagined possible of me, with all your infectious
faith and gaiety and loyalty. . . . I HAVE BEGUN TO BE A REAL
WRITER. There is no one else on the horizon in England who
seems to me to be developing into the same kind of faun. At
the best, brilliant literary practitioners, which is on a level
with cabinet-making—any poor fool can learn it at the poly-
technik. . . . By degree I may be lesser [than the Walpoles,
the Morgans, etc.]: by genius I belong to another race. . . . I
am my own kind, I haven't begun. Beside Lawrence, beside
Miller, beside Blake. Yes, I am humble, I have hardly started.
BUT I AM ON THE SAME TRAM. [12]

In another letter, he tells Henry Miller:

anything positive I have as a writer I owe to your books—my
stance, a new emotional attitude, the way I hold my gloves at
the world. As for the wisdom—my God—it is all a question of
induction, convection, you might say contagion. (*Letters*, p.
82)

For Durrell, the nudge does not imply that whatever comes after is high art; we have seen that he deliberately relaxes with a variety of quite good journeyman works—a spy story, travel books, humor, criticism. Durrell is wise enough to know that to live constantly in the heat of inspiration is to explode into the kind of monster or freak he admits creating in his fiction— the exaggeration, the enlargement of tendencies that in normal human beings are more "attenuated." Even Pursewarden writes doggerel; and although Darley believes that the older novelist is at his literary best in his letters to his sister, Keats reminds us that there are other, less noble letters.

Perhaps the greatest gift of the nudge, the one which makes possible all the others (and even adds a new dimension to the artist's courage), is self-confidence. It shows itself in Durrell's recognition that the artist has no need to prove himself in each of his works; like a self-confident Homer, he is willing to nod in public. But the self-confidence has at least two other important effects: it is the basis for the joy and for the compassion that is at the heart of Durrell's best work. If one can believe, with Keats, that the purpose of a war is to turn one into a writer, or with Darley that the "whole universe" has given him a nudge (*Clea*, p. 282), the world is surely a place that merits loving attention, that merits the kind of tenderly precise description that runs through Durrell's poems and travel books and novels. And it is certainly not a fearful place—which does not mean that the artist is never frightened, or that fearful things do not happen. It is, rather, a place of opportunity, if, and only if, the artist recognizes that "the mutability of all truth" ought encourage rather than hamper the artist. What more could the artist ask for than a world in which

"each fact can have a thousand motivations, all equally valid, and each fact a thousand faces. So many truths which have little to do with fact! Your duty is to hunt them down. At each moment of time all multiplicity waits at your elbow. Why,

Darley, this should thrill you and give your writing the curves
of a pregnant woman." (*Clea*, pp. 72–73)

This recognition of the "mutability of all truth" permits Pursewarden, for example, to do what psychiatrists and a less gifted
artist could not do—rid Justine of the Check. He does it by
the simple expedient of forcing a crisis, of forcing her to see it
from a perspective as seemingly cruel as it is effective. He
points out that she probably enjoyed the rape and certainly
has enjoyed the notoriety and the pampering it has permitted
her. The point is not whether Pursewarden's diagnosis is or is
not accurate; it is rather that it is one possible perspective, a
crisis-forcing perspective, that compels Justine to recognize
the absurdity of building a life upon a single response to a
single event seen from a single point of view. As Barth pointed
out in *The Floating Opera*, in an absurd universe in which it
makes no difference whether one lives or dies, one might as
well live; in a universe in which there is no rational basis for
choosing anything, one certainly is under no obligation to
choose misery. A part of the effect of the nudge seems to be to
give the self-confidence required to accept joy.

The compassion in Durrell's work has been seen in other
contexts; it is truly remarkable. Fraser notes that the characters in The Quartet

> are immoral by conventional standards, but they do not treat
> each other as objects. The need for distance or separateness,
> even in the most intimate relationship, the need to respect the
> otherness of the other, is something which Lawrence felt, but
> which Durrell feels even more deeply. (*Critical Study*, p. 17)

The characters are also cruel by conventional standards, but
(with the exception of the early Tarquin and an occasional
minor character whose cruelty is a necessary function of the
tale) Durrell never seems to judge them. There is almost always that other side of the character—the tenderness and loyalty of Narouz, the anguish of Justin's castration, Pursewarden's ultimate and radical idealism, Maskelyn's quiet

dignity and loneliness, Cohen's love for Melissa—a side that does not so much justify the cruelty or selfishness as it reminds the reader that this, too, is a human worth caring for. I suspect that the artist, like the rest of us, can feel that universal sympathy, that willingness to accept the "otherness of the other," only if there is an immense reservoir of self-assurance, a certainty that one has enough strength to withstand whatever the world has to offer. It is both quite clear and quite important that our feelings toward Pursewarden are supposed to become more favorable as we learn that his attitude toward Darley includes not only the superior chiding we get early, but the genuinely concerned, genuinely felt recognition of Darley's worth as a person and as an artist that we get late. Even Darley's growth in maturity can be charted reasonably accurately by his growing lack of envy of Pursewarden, by his recognition of the fact that Pursewarden's significance lies precisely in his otherness, and that that otherness is an opportunity for Darley, rather than a threat. Perhaps the most dramatic example of the power of the nudge to induce enough self-confidence to generate compassion comes from the change in Keats. Darley expects Keats (and we as readers have no reason to disagree with Darley) to be anxious to publish a rather nasty best-selling biography of Pursewarden; the post-nudge Keats is too mature even to consider the idea. Although he does not seem to like Pursewarden, he recognizes a significance in the man that a journalistic retelling of the facts could not do justice to. Great books, Pursewarden said, "are excursions into pity" (*Mountolive*, p. 166)—and it seems clear that Keats is ready to write a great book.

It is worth noting, by the way, what happens to the artist who remains fearful of the world. In *Acte* Durrell imagines a rather unusual Nero, an emperor distraught by the realization that his art has not immediately perfected Rome; shaken by his powerlessness to make the world conform to his vision, he caters to his ego by elaborately destroying the city and torturing its inhabitants. His cruelty is a result of his fear that the world will not be endurable unless he imposes his will upon it.

For Durrell, the artist as artist has three areas of responsibility: to preserve the continuity of art, to help pass on the artistic succession, and to help his audience appreciate that "mutability of all truth." The last gives importance to the first two; for Durrell, it is a highly serious, even religious mission. From his early letters to Miller through "The Kneller Tape," he repeats his insistence that the purpose of art is quite significant indeed. In February of 1937 he tells Miller that "ALL ART IN THE GERM IS CURATIVE!" (*Correspondence*, pp. 65–66). Two months later, he writes Miller that he believes "in artists as healers" (*Correspondence*, p. 90); in 1949 Durrell rebuts the puritanical protestations against Miller's growing reputation in England with the remark, "As if we weren't *religious* writers!" (*Correspondence*, p. 258). Nevertheless, art must work indirectly because morality

> should not have an explicit place in an art context; to the artist everyone is primally good, however bad or ignorant their actions. If art preaches, it isn't in terms of ethics or tabus or behaviors. It inspirits and urges people to wake up by giving them the vicarious feel of the poetic illumination; this "takes them out of themselves as we say," which is an important notion after all. It doesn't read sermons, but teaches by example. (*World*, p. 163)

Even though Durrell uses the phrase "take them out of themselves" with a slight apology, it is perhaps the perfect way to describe it briefly. We've seen that the nudge comes only after the budding artist is taken out of himself—although we don't know how it came to Pursewarden, Keats must be transmogrified by a war, Clea by an injury which leaves her with an "IT" that paints impersonally, and Darley—whose progress we follow most fully—must repeatedly be taken out of his own experience and forced to live it vicariously, through the eyes of Balthazar, Arnauti, Clea, Justine, and others. The great work, the work done with "pity" (I'd prefer "compassion" to Pursewarden's word) makes us vicariously experience the otherness of the other.

That kind of experience involves, for Durrell, not the presentation of particular insights into the nature of individuals or of society, but rather an awareness of the complexities of human nature, of the fact that "human beings are really walking question marks, how's and why's and perhapses" (*World*, p. 164). When a novel does attempt to embody a particular insight, a particular ideological explanation of reality, it is both thin and a distortion of the reality—like Arnauti's study of Justine. A Freudian—or, I am sure Durrell would say, a Marxist, or Catholic, or behaviorist, or whatever—interpretation of anything so complex as a person is as reductive as, say, a strictly Freudian explanation of World War II. And, of course, it is impossible to avoid being judgmental if we feel that we have the answers or that we have been given all the relevant data within the work.

If this is true, the games Durrell plays in The Quartet are more than brilliantly successful narrative hooks; they are essential parts of a plan to lead the reader through a series of double takes, of revisions and reassessments of situations that originally seemed comprehensible. Cohen's love for Melissa, Clea's love for Amaril, Narouz's gift of inspired oratory, Da Capo's return to life—such surprises are both the jolts that keep reader interest high and lessons to Darley and to the reader that things are seldom what they seem.

Yet the point of the change of stance is more than just recognition of the confusion or complexity of reality; it is a rebirth. In some moods, as in "The Kneller Tape," Durrell would even write of it as if it were a first birth:

> No, I wouldn't say we were born human; I should say that the meaning of life is to make us become so, earn the price of admission so to speak. Most people lead vegetable lives, taking everything on trust. (*World*, pp. 164–65)

Compassion, courage, optimism—those products of the great nudge—are as available to the audience as to the artist. Pursewarden rhapsodizes on what he calls "the miracle of Pursewarden's Ideal Commonwealth":

I believe in this miracle. Our very existence as artists affirms it! It is the act of yea-saying about which the old poet of the city [Cavafy] speaks in a poem you once showed me in translation. The *fact* of an artist being born affirms and reaffirms this in every generation. The miracle is there, on ice so to speak. One fine day it will blossom: then the artist suddenly grows up and accepts the full responsibility for his origins in the people, and when *simultaneously* the people recognise his peculiar significance and value, and greet him as the unborn child in themselves, the infant Joy! . . . The new society—so different from anything we can imagine now—will be born around the small strict white temple of infant Joy! . . . Nothing stands in the way of this Ideal Commonwealth, save that in every generation the vanity and laziness of the artist has always matched the self-indulgent blindness of the people. But prepare, prepare! It is on the way. It is here, there, nowhere!

The great schools of love will arise, and sensual and intellectual knowledge will draw impetus from each other. The human animal will be uncaged, all his dirty cultural straw and coprolitic refuse of belief cleaned out. . . . (*Clea*, p. 140)

The Utopian vision seems, at first thought, uncharacteristic of so unpolitical a writer as Durrell and certainly more appropriate for a Lessing or a Burgess. Durrell would, I think, like Pursewarden, remind the doubting critic that, although art is not obliged to deal in politics, it must deal in values.

Specifically—and what is radical here is not the idea but the insistence and complete conviction with which Durrell expresses it—the function of art is to educate the imagination, for

man is simply a box labelled personality. He peers out of the box through five slits, the senses. On this earth he is permitted access to three dimensions of space and one of time. Only in his imagination can he inhabit the whole—a reality which is beyond the reach of intellectual qualification: a reality which even the greatest art is incapable of rendering in its full grandeur. It is a ridiculous and humiliating situation but we must accept it, and be content with our provisional truths, our short-range raids on this greater territory which permeates our inner lives—and which we try to avoid realizing behind the barriers of habit and laziness. If art has any message it must be this: to remind us that we are dying without having properly lived. (*Key*, p. 5)

It might be added, although Durrell has not taken up the point specifically, that art is to educate the imagination precisely as experience educates the imagination; it is to supplement experience, adding an intensity and a variety unavailable in the life of the average reader. The function is vital because, as we are told in countless ways in The Quartet, " 'there are only as many realities' " as we " 'care to imagine' " (*Balthazar*, p. 152). Or, as Balthazar puts it, " 'We become what we dream. . . . We achieve in reality, in substance, only the pictures of the imagination' " (*Clea*, p. 64). Much of The Quartet is devoted to convincing readers that this is literally true, despite the vanity which makes us wish otherwise. Not only are we told that Clea and Darley could not have become lovers unless they had first imagined it, Leila's imagination creates a more substantial Mountolive, Amaril's imagination of a beautiful Semira creates a beautiful Semira, the popular imagination of the Muslims creates a Saint Scobie.

Durrell makes it quite clear that imagination is not simply a plan, a vision, a dream. Those characters who have only a plan for reality fare badly. Arnauti never understands Justine, despite his obvious intelligence and sensitivity; Justine and Nessim seem perpetually trapped within a plan that shapes their lives so completely they have no will to imagine alternatives. Imagination does not chart courses, it opens possibilities.

That is why, perhaps, the quality of the imagination is so vitally important. The diseased imagination—that of a Nero or of a Petronius as Durrell creates them in *Acte*—will enact suffering as surely as the healthy imagination will enact joy. Only in our imaginations are we able to "inhabit the whole," to accept Art's message "that we are dying without having properly lived" (*Key*, p. 5). And, Durrell might have added, to make the possibility of having properly lived so joyous that we choose it.

The "whole" that Durrell refers to is, most likely, what he elsewhere calls the Heraldic Universe. It is a difficult concept to discuss in Durrell's work because it is ineffable in its nature and because it seems to be, for Durrell, an article of faith so basic that it is not—within either his fictions or his critical writings—subjected to the same degree of testing as his other ideas. His fullest description comes in a letter to Miller; it is one of those exuberant statements that is more of an announcement to a friend of a "great Inkling" than a reasoned presentation.

THE MINUS SIDE	THE PLUS SIDE: PURE FORMS

THE ONE

I II III IV

All human searching for perfection as strain or disease, all concepts from Tao to Descartes, from Plato to Whitehead aim at one thing: the establishment of a non-conscious, continual STATE or stasis: a point of cooperation with time. In order to nourish conceptual apparatus, moralities, forms, you imply a deficit in the self. Alors all this WORK or STRIVING—even Yoga—aims at finding Rest or relaxation in time. It aims at the ONE.

WHAT HAPPENS AFTER THAT IN THE FIELD OF PURE REPOSE?

You enter a field or laboratory of the consciousness which is not dangerous because it is based on repose. It does not strain you because having passed through the impurities of the ONENESS of EVERYTHING, you are included in Time. NOW FORMS EMERGE. Because 'contemptible' numbers are the only way to label them, you can say 1st State, 2nd State, 3rd State, like an etching. This is what I have called THE HERALDIC UNIVERSE. You cannot define these forms except by ideogram: this is 'non-assertive' form.

THE HERALDIC UNIVERSE.

(*Correspondence*, pp. 202–3)

Actually, as Durrell seems to recognize, several variations on a major ethical system, and a major aesthetic, have been

based on ideas quite similar to these. The notion is similar to
that of various Neoplatonists (and of a number of Oriental
thinkers) that the life of material experience is illusory, and
that the primary effort in being fully human is to break
through the perception of matter to the perception of pure
form. In a religious context, of course, the realm of pure form
is for the Christian, heaven; for the Hindu or Buddhist, nir-
vana. It is the realm in which the individual becomes aware of
the underlying, eternal principles of things (not principles in a
rationalistic sense: the knowledge is intuitive, synthetic rather
than analytic).[13] For Durrell, who has admitted a life-long af-
finity for Taoism,[14] a philosophy which teaches harmony in an
essentially dualistic universe, it is the realm that he sometimes
describes as the realm of symbols, the realm where there is no
straining of ego, no separation of I and it, no veil between self
and reality. And it must be added that philosophically "forms"
have potential for realization in manifold varieties. To the extent that one has a full understanding of the form of the novel,
for example, one has an understanding of all possible individuations, all possible novels subsumed under that form. To
the egoistic imagination which works only with material things,
life is a war between the will of the individual and brute matter,
the former ever attempting to impose its limiting pattern, the
latter ever subject to its evolutionary inertia. To the imagination that can perceive the heraldic universe, life is a merging of
the potential of the individual with the potentials inherent in
the relevant forms. Clea, for example, after her nudge, no
longer attempts to replicate the clinical color or to search out
the abstract pattern. As she says, " 'IT can paint!' " Darley no
longer searches his memory for an interpretation of events that
will satisfy his restless pride; he instead begins with the oldest
and least egocentric, least personal of all beginnings, "Once
upon a time . . . " (*Clea*, p. 282). From that beginning, all possibilities are open.

Durrell is not (to coin a phrase which I hope does not catch
on) an aesthetic chauvinist; we have seen that he considers art
and science partners in our attempt to understand our world.

Yet, understandably, the emphasis in his work is upon the artist as the person most likely to be able to lead others to the heraldic universe. Pursewarden's vision of the Ideal Commonwealth, minus the dramatic overstatement, is Durrell's. But both Pursewarden and Durrell are realistic enough to know that it will not come until artists are no longer vain and lazy and audiences no longer blind and self-indulgent. In the meanwhile, the task of the artist is to pass on his vision to other artists, to act as a kind of exemplum-stimulus, as Lawrence does for Pursewarden, and Pursewarden does for Keats, Darley, and Clea. Durrell's conviction of the importance of this function of the artist is probably a result of personal experience; Henry Miller and T. S. Eliot were, in quite different ways, Durrell's mentors. He writes of Miller's work with a kind of ecstasy; he worries about what Miller will think of his novels and poems; he praises Miller for passing on to him the vision and courage that let him dare *The Black Book*. He praises Eliot for patience, understanding, calmness, advice, and insistence on perfection.

The concern with the relation of artists to other artists extends through Durrell's career. Gregory, in *The Black Book*, writes that

> in order to write one must first be convinced that every book ever written was made for one to borrow from. The art is in paying back the loans with interest. (P. 143)

Darley, near despair and from a different angle, describes the relationship differently:

> We artists form one of those pathetic human chains which human beings form to pass buckets of water up to a fire, or to bring in a lifeboat. An uninterrupted chain of humans born to explore the inward riches of the solitary life on behalf of the unheeding unforgiving community; manacled together by the same gift. (*Clea*, p. 177)

As Durrell expresses it in his own voice in "The Kneller Tape," "this is the continuity of literature" (*World*, p. 165). It is also our best hope of keeping alive the vision of our potential until we are worthy to realize it.

Despite the romantic exuberance of his vision of the artist as a kind of preserver of the imagination and legislator of the world, there is a very hard-headed side to Durrell's conception of the role of the artist. If the artist is vitally important, what he creates must be worthily made. He can write of craft quite deprecatingly, comparing the artist to a masseuse who massages the aches and pains of the players. In a typically Durrellian comment, he reminds us that we "should never forget that poetry, like life, is altogether too serious not to be taken lightly" (*Key*, p. 90). Both sides of Durrell's feelings about art are shown splendidly in a little scene from *Dark Labyrinth*. Mrs. Truman asks the artist Campion, "How do artists happen?" He replies:

> "Do you really want to know? Or are you wasting my time?"
> . . . "It's easy," he said at last. "When they're babies you drop them on their heads or neglect them, so they are driven to try to recapture something; so they learn a skill; then those as are bad artists are content to go on copying Nature, while those as are good—something very funny happens to them. . . ."
> "They begin to make love to the object."
> "How?"
> "In paint. This face of yours is so lovely. I am in a sort of sense making love to it with every brush-stroke."

Later that evening, Mrs. Truman hears Campion talking to a friend:

> "Of course . . . if you get the massive butt of the nose, the sort of way the root thickens into the frontal lobe, the whole face falls into shape." (*Labyrinth*, pp. 135–36)

For Durrell both aspects of the artist—the lover of what Ransom called the "precious object" and the technician who sees a woman's nose as a "massive butt joining the frontal lobe"— are equally important. For the artist, although not for the human being, all the love of the object one is capable of will be ineffective unless one solves that technical problem; and to solve the technical problem without love is to create portraits equivalent to Keats's journalism or Clea's brilliantly realistic clinical sketches.

If Durrell writes much more of the love of the artist for his subject than he does of the technical and formal matters, it is, I suspect, because the former is vastly more interesting. Yet Durrell's and Miller's letters include a kind of running argument over the importance of form, and his novels are certainly as completely and self-consciously crafted as those of any contemporary writer. His characters, especially those in The Quartet and in The Avignon Quintet, discuss form as seriously and as extensively as they discuss human passion; more often than not, the forms they discuss are very like those in which they are enveloped. Even Justine, near the beginning of The Quartet, remarks while looking into a set of mirrors that such a multiple version of reality would surely be the proper form of the modern novel (*Justine*, p. 27); Balthazar repeatedly suggests much the same, even using the palimpsest metaphor; and, of course, Pursewarden is not only working on a trilogy at the time of his death, he suggests to Darley that they collaborate on a quartet of novels. In the later Avignon Quintet, Blanford goes a step further. Blanford is one of the narrators of the series, an elderly novelist who conducts conversations with the ghosts of his characters and his friends. He is talking to Sutcliffe, probably his favorite and most useful creation, a novelist and an alter-ego (who claims to be Blanford's creator), about a quintet:

"The relationship between our books will be incestuous then, I take it? They will be encysted in each other, not com-

plementary. There would be room for everything, poem, autobiography, short story and so on,"

"Yes," said his creator [Blanford] softly. "I suppose you have
heard of that peculiar medical phenomenon called the tera-
toma? It is literally a bag full of unfinished spare parts—
nails and hair and half-grown teeth—which is lodged like a
benign growth somewhere in a human body. . . ."

"A short story lodged in a book?" (*Livia*, p. 17)

Like the descriptions of contemporary form given within The
Quartet, this description within The Avignon Quintet may be
a fair prediction of what the series may grow into. The description of the encysted stories adequately characterizes the
four volumes we do have—set up most interestingly by the
strange narrative of "Monsieur," Blanford's story that turns
out to be a novel-within-a-novel.

The constant experimentation with form—including the
"double-decker," The Revolt of Aphrodite, published sepa-
rately as *Tunc* and *Nunquam*—is Durrell's attempt to capture
what, in the opening note to *Balthazar*, he has called the
"classical" form "for our time." It is that form which assumes a
relativistic universe in which truth is approximated only by
constantly shifting perspectives. Although this is certainly an
oversimplification, in a sense The Quartet is an attempt to get
at the "truth" of a situation; The Avignon Quintet seems, at
this stage, an attempt to get at the truth of character or, more
precisely, our understanding of character. Blanford, contemplating his proposed quintet, muses that

by a singular paradox (perhaps inherent in all writing?) the
passages that he knew would be regarded as overtheatrical or
unreal ("people don't behave like that") would be the truth,
and the rest which rang somehow true, the purest fabrication.
He wondered if in the next book about these people he could
not cut down a layer or two to reveal the invisible larval forms,
the root forms which had given him these projections?[15]

In a very real sense, this is precisely what Durrell does as he takes us from the end of the strange but conventional "Monsieur" to Blanford's musings about it, and later to Blanford and Sutcliffe's imagined conversations about the relationship between the characters they knew and those they created. The problem is not only that memory, the storehouse from which the artist's imagination draws, is defective, but also that the human personality itself is immensely complex and protean. In "The Kneller Tape" Durrell describes the "personality" as "an illusion . . . in thinking of it as a stable thing we are trying to put a lid on a box with no sides" (*World,* p. 163). Durrell lets Blanford comment specifically on the problem that complexity poses for the novelist:

> "What always bothered me was the question of a stable ego—did such a thing exist? The old notion of such an animal was rather primitive, particularly for novelists with an itch to explain this action or that. . . . The human psyche is almost infinitely various—so various that it can afford to be contradictory even as regards itself. How poor is the pathetic little typology of our modern psychology. . . . That is why our novels, yours and mine, Robin [Sutcliffe], are also poor. There are many Livias, some whom I love and will love until my dying day; others fell off me and dried up like dead leeches. Others were just larval forms in the sense of Paraclesus." (*Livia,* pp. 37–38)

Within this protean concept of character, it is no wonder that Durrell found the traditional form of the novel inadequate. The old cause-and-effect report on the stages of the protagonist's development simply did not allow for contradictory possibilities, for those warring multiplicities of each individual's character. The "act-fact-act" form in which Magwich helps Pip because Pip helped Magwich—the form in which Pip's character at any point in *Great Expectations* is a direct result of the latest stimulus—simply does not do justice to our recently enriched understanding of human nature.

Yet, despite the structural complexity of Durrell's major

novels, they are amazingly old-fashioned in many ways. His claim that The Quartet is a boy-meets-girl story is absolutely true; The Quartet also has enough suspense and action to keep a novel twice its length going. It even has a typically Victorian ending—with, of course, a Durrellian touch. In the closing pages of *Clea*, the reader is given, almost in the manner of Dickens, a sketch of the current status and prospects of most of the major characters, and all loose ends are neatly sewn up—until the workpoints, in which Durrell reminds us that the stories will go on, that there are things we do not know and that presumably Darley does not yet know. Even The Avignon Quintet manages a quite successful use of some of the older narrative hooks. The narrative within a narrative begins with one of the more familiar conventions, a sensitive man compelled to tell a strange tale; the tale itself involves ritual assassination, mysticism, exotic settings, historical speculation, the titillation of a hinted menage à trois. Once past "Monsieur" and into another layer of reality, the reader discovers that Blanford is awaiting the same kind of ritual assassination that played a role in his novel. What I am suggesting, of course, is that Durrell has a remarkable ability to combine what he calls the classic form of our age with the elementary but fundamental tricks that made the older fictions work.

Durrell seldom discusses technical problems—small scale matters as distinct from large scale formal concerns—except to mention occasionally in a letter that he has a great love of words, that he is working on a new style for The Quartet, that he is immensely grateful to Eliot for technical advice. Yet the craftsmanship of his work shows a high respect for detail, a consciousness that even the most loving portrait is made up of brushstrokes.

The concern for detail carries from the level of the sentence to the construction of scenes. Few modern writers can match the careful craftsmanship of Durrell's sentences, or their variety; his aphorisms are as memorable as Pope's, his descriptive passages lush and rolling where appropriate, or sparse and

bristly where that is most fitting. Individual scenes are wonderfully put together bits that somehow both stand out and fit
in. Justine's first meeting with her prospective mother-in-law,
Leila, is typical. The women are antagonists—both strong,
both beautiful, both sophisticated—meeting in a situation in
which each must appear both polite and friendly. With the
utmost dignity, they feed each other a kind of candy each instinctively knows the other detests. Or there is a scene in
which Mountolive, by this time almost a paragon of diplomatic and cosmopolitan suavity, learns of his promotion to an
ambassadorship. He bargains for his superior's old uniform in
a way that, by its pettiness, transforms a paragon into a
human. Such bits, always building to a new insight but doing
so with the immense precision and timing of a first-rate come-
dian, are characteristic of much of The Quartet and not un-
typical of Durrell's better work. They show, in Durrell's
words, a great deal of "practice at the net."

There is a temptation, especially when one knows of the
tremendous speed with which The Quartet was written and
the suddenness of Durrell's reputation, to assume that he is
the stereotypical romantic artist—one who has lived in exotic,
often dangerous surroundings and who unexpectedly feels the
lightning strike of inspiration. Actually, few literary careers
have developed as consistently and deliberately as Durrell's.
The themes and the techniques of *The Black Book* reappear in
The Quartet, in *Tunc-Nunquam*, and in The Avignon Quintet
with a frequency that shows a strong character possessed by a
particular set of concerns, and a pointedness that tells the
reader that Durrell wants the overlappings noted. The author's note at the end of *Tunc* informs "attentive readers" that
the "odd echo from *The Alexandria Quartet* and even from
The Black Book . . . is intentional!" Although The Avignon
Quintet lacks such a note as yet, the fact that Sutcliffe is
caught reading Pursewarden's essays is but one of a series of
forceful reminders of the interconnectedness of Durrell's major novels.

Parallels of theme and character are much too extensive to

enumerate, nor is there space to discuss individual instances fully; I shall have to point to only a few. The gaunt, seemingly ageless Balthazar (intelligent, homosexual, concerned about his appearance) is a version of *The Black Book's* Tarquin; Nessim and Narouz, the handsome brother who goes out into the world and the ugly one who remains at home, are precursors of Julian and Jocas from *Tunc-Nunquam;* Pursewarden's incestuous love for his sister, which is partly responsible for his brilliance, his irony, his agony, and his suicide, is another version of Julian's incestuous love for Benedicta.

Technical and thematic elements are similarly repeated and varied. *The Black Book* includes another perspective on the writer's life in the form of "The Diary of Death George"; its melodramatic sentimentality provides a counter-melody not unlike Darley's sentimentality; the narrator, Lawrence Lucifer, shares first names with both Darley and Durrell; the impetus of the narrator to write is a desire to remember fully, like Darley's impetus. And near the end of *The Black Book,* the narrator speculates on what he might think about, might write, might do, leaving a kind of open-endedness and optimism that suggests, on the one hand, the workpoints at the end of *Clea* and, on the other, Darley's sudden confidence. The workpoints theme and technique is used again in *Monsieur,* in the form of a series of aphorisms from Sutcliffe.

In a lesser writer, or a writer whom one does not admire, such repetitions indicate a paucity of imagination, a return to the same bag of tricks. In Durrell, as in other great writers, it indicates rather a persistence of vision, an enduring concern with a select set of human experiences that leads to a compulsion to reexamine, to test nuances, to observe variations. Jane Austen seems to have had an almost obsessive interest in the fortunes of bright and honest young ladies forced to live in a society composed of their inferiors in common sense; Dickens constantly returns to the helpless in a world peopled mostly by the disinterested and the cruel, with just enough of the kindly to make happy endings possible; Hemingway creates a monohero whose name and age change from novel to novel, but who is most often surrounded by the same cast of stock players. Durrell is different because he is more self-conscious of his obsession, and because the ideas he holds make such repetitions with variation thematically functional.

We have already seen some evidence of the self-consciousness in the note to *Tunc* and the mention of Pursewarden's essays in *Monsieur*. Durrell's plans to write an apparently related series of novels goes back at least to April of 1937, when he tells Miller that he has "planned AN AGON, A PATHOS, AN ANAGNORSIS. If I wrote them they should be The Black Book, The Book of Miracles, The Book of the Dead" (*Correspondence*, p. 83). By July he has changed the order, reversing the last two titles. Nine years later he writes Miller that he is at work on The Book of the Dead; it begins to appear only in 1957 as The Alexandria Quartet. The Book of Miracles would certainly describe The Avignon Quintet. Durrell's "odd echoes" of earlier works are more than literary games.

Although I do not want to overemphasize the notion, Durrell's relativistic world view does lend an extra function to the varied repetitions of character types, ideas, techniques, scenes, and so on. The relativist knows that he never has it right, that the only real question is Blanford's question to his cat: "How real is reality?" (*Monsieur*, p. 292). For the relativist, the persistent variation of the same materials is neither a failure of the imagination nor obliviousness to alternative versions of reality; it is, rather, the only means by which reality may be understood.

Because in Durrell's world nothing—except the need for compassion, for belief in the universe, for openness to all interpretations of experience—is ever final, the appropriate ending for this study of his portraits of artists is not a summary, but a series of workpoints:

Groddeck, the IT, and Clea

Sutcliffe's letter to Pursewarden about his Essays, in particular on the limitations of irony

Lawrence Lucifer's conversations with Darley, Pursewarden, and Blanford on the effect of the "English Death" on artists

Julian and Blanford discuss the creation of character from technological and aesthetic standpoints

Darley's move to Southern France, and the effect of the landscape on his outlook and style

Arnauti, Blanford, and Pursewarden discuss sex as both a hook for readers and as a subject that provides the sharpest insight into character

Mountolive's meeting with Akkad; his conversion to Gnosticism

Chapter 2

Doris Lessing

From Fragmentation to Wholeness

> *The true novel wrestles on the edge of understanding, lying about on all sides desperately, for every sort of experience, pressing into use every flash of intuition or correspondence, trying to fuse together the crudest of materials, and the humblest, which the higher arts can't include. But it is precisely here, where the writer fights with the raw, the intractable, that poetry is born. Poetry, that is, of the novel: appropriate to it.*[1]

To explore the fictional worlds of Doris Lessing, hoping to follow a single path through their rich diversity, is to violate both the spirit of her work and its expressed intent. Perhaps more than any other writer in our century, she has insisted upon wholeness of vision, upon an integration of each aspect of our human nature into a more than human perfection. Fragmentation, for Lessing, is evil: it appears when an idealistic young African communist must choose between party discipline and humanitarian instincts; it appears when any one of several of her women must choose one role over another; it appears when an artist must incarnate the welter of somehow we must try to come to grips with our experience by "letting the words proliferate," by fragmenting a bit of experience, splitting it off from the whole, and examining it.

Lessing's vision of the artist is a part of her vision of humanity as a whole. Humanity is, Lessing says over and over again, almost ready to undergo some mutation, some evolutionary change which will alter both our consciousness and our social structures. "We all stand," she writes in *A Small Personal Voice*,

> at an open door, and . . . there is a new man about to be born, who has never been twisted by drudgery; a man whose pride as a man will not be measured by his capacity to shoulder work and responsibilities which he detests, which bore him, which are too small for what he could be; a man whose strength will not be gauged by the values of the mystique of suffering. . . .
>
> There are only two choices: that we force ourselves into the effort of imagination necessary to become what we are capable of being; or that we submit to being ruled by the office boys of big business, or the socialist bureaucrats who have forgotten that socialism means a desire for goodness and compassion— and the end of submission is that we shall blow ourselves up. (Pp. 8–9)

In several of her works Lessing has given us her version of both the new person and of alternatives to the new person. In both *Memoirs of a Survivor* and *The Four-Gated City* things simply stop working; men and women refuse to "shoulder work and responsibilities which . . . [they] detest," and so the gadgets they make that keep our civilization on its course are made carelessly and break down quickly. In *Memoirs*, small gangs prowl the city with no thought beyond their individual survival as their society dies of its own inertia—of, to remember Frost, ice; in *The Four-Gated City*, civilization dies of fire, of a holocaust. But the difference in feel between the two novels is due to something else, to the fact that not only has the new person emerged in *The Four-Gated City*, it seems in at least precarious control of what is left of the world.

reality into a single set of words; it appears when one see
as a series of discrete stages; it appears when one tries t
capture one's past, only to realize that all that can be r
tured is *a* past. The peculiar curse of humanity—and for
ing it is necessary to add "of humanity in its current sta
development"—is that we can be sane only when our vis
of the whole, but that our minds are so constituted tha
can work only with parts. When thought begins, it

> *works like this. Thought comes into mind. If consci*
> *thought is in words. If not, if ordinary association-thou*
> *then it isn't words. Words are when one stands back to*
> *This first word then sprouts into other words and ideas l*
> *flash of lightning. No, like water suddenly lifting limp br*
> *off sea bottom. Words proliferate so fast you can't catch*
> *A word: then an idea suggested by that word (Who sugg*
> *the word?) You think: My idea? Whose?*[2]

And so we are off, letting the words build their pseudo
shored up by bits of the whole and terrorized because
ize that they are bits.

There is something very Platonic in Lessing's vie
and in her view of critics. Plato criticized art because
never match the significance of the Real; our everyc
was said to be but a pale imitation of that Reality, ar
imitating everyday reality, was thought literally to t
the wrong direction, to seduce us into turning our ba
the True. And, of course, in this scheme of things,
gets us still further from the Real by constructing
imitations out of the materials of artistic imitation.

It is true that something is lost in every stage of
To simplify in a way that in its details but not in
might appall Lessing, the reality of her life is si
richer, significantly more intricate, more complex,
than its fictionalization in the Martha Quest seri
Anna Wulf of *The Golden Notebook* is in some way
plete than Martha Quest, just as the Anna Wu
Women" is less—in some ways—than her titular

Lessing's new humanity descends from Oriental mysticism, not Western rationalism. The narrator of *Memoirs* has a kind of preternatural sense of the continuity of history; she sees visions, not hallucinations, of other times and other worlds behind the walls of her crumbling apartment. The worlds behind the walls become an Eden into which the narrator and her band escape from a society dying of its own inertia. *Briefing for a Descent into Hell* is a more fanciful but in some ways a more developed exploration of a variant of the theme of the new humanity. It is also a reminder that the new humanity is really the old humanity, that the mystic powers in which Lessing believes have always been among us. Charles Watson, being treated in a London psychiatric ward for what seems to be amnesia, is considered insane to the extent that he remembers the divinity within him. In his visions, he senses the continuity of history even more thoroughly than does the survivor in *Memoirs;* he remembers civilizations on earth destroying themselves because of the propensity of earth's inhabitants to selfishness, to isolation, to separation from what a medieval theologian would have called the harmony of the spheres. As an avatar of Mercury, the perpetual messenger, his task and that of his helpers is to recall to humankind that natural sense of communion with the universe that is essential for survival. At the end of this bleakly pessimistic novel, he is "cured"; he has forgotten his divinity, returned to his wife, broken contact with the small circle of individuals who seemed about to recall their own godliness. His cure, to quote Wordsworth, is "a sleep and a forgetting."

As yet, Lessing's most convincing picture of homo-superior—that is, the most developed, the one that shows most persuasively her vision of our next evolutionary step—occurs at the end of *The Four-Gated City.* Like Charles Watson, Lynda Coleridge has a history of oddness before her breakdown; both Charles and Lynda are unusually sensitive, and for both the psychiatric treatment is an imposition of limits upon their expanded awareness. As Martha Quest learns more of Lynda, she begins to understand that Lynda is a gifted telepath, a receiver, in a society in which such powers are considered impossible. Lynda, like the children in *Briefing* who are forced to sleep, to be quiet, in order to be "good," is forced to take tranquilizing drugs. But she does manage to awaken Martha's natural sensitivity, and she and Martha become a nucleus around which other persons with latent and developing powers group. After the holocaust, such groups begin to reorganize the world. It will, if it can survive long enough to get a good start, be a far better world than ours because telepathy makes isolation and selfishness impossible.

It is especially tempting for hard-headed Western critics to accept Lessing's visionary works as nothing more than highly literate science fiction—warnings of the kind written by Zamyatin, Huxley, Orwell, John Brunner, and a host of lesser writers who extrapolate our follies into future catastrophies. Although it is true that the warning is there, and that as speculative science fiction the novels are well worth reading, such an interpretation ignores both Lessing's sympathy with Sufism and its belief in spiritual powers and her own statement of purpose as a novelist:

> Yesterday, we split the atom. We assaulted that colossal citadel of power, the tiny unit of the substance of the universe. And because of this, the great dream and the great nightmare of centuries of human thought have taken flesh and walk beside us all, day and and night. Artists are traditional interpreters of dreams and nightmares, and this is no time to turn our backs on our chosen responsibilities, which is what we should be doing if we refused to share in the deep anxieties, terrors, and hopes of human beings everywhere.
>
> What is the choice before us? It is not merely a question of preventing evil, but of strengthening a vision of a good which may defeat the evil. (*Voice*, p. 7)

The fuller description of that more complete human being, with all its mental powers, is, I believe, Lessing's deliberate attempt to strengthen that "vision of good which may defeat the evil."

I have spent so much time describing Lessing's vision of humanity's next evolutionary step because that is the background against which her artists must be measured. In some major ways, Mark Coleridge, the novelist of *The Four-Gated City*, is symptomatic of the condition of the artist at present. A social visionary, he writes—with Martha's help—a description of a Utopian city, a "four-gated city," that first becomes a kind of cult book and then becomes, at least in a limited way, the plan upon which the emerging society will build. He does present, in other words, that "vision of good which may defeat the evil." But Mark is essentially unevolved; he can create the vision only with Martha's help, and it can become a reality only with the help of those who have taken the next evolutionary step. The result is a kind of agony—an agony of lost effort, wasted motion, doubts about the importance of the vision, doubts about the ability to and the value of expressing it. Although Mark, unlike Anna, does not suffer from a writer's block, he comes perilously close, even to the point of keeping notebooks in which he doubts both his purpose and his sanity. "All this is crazy," he writes.

> I know that.
>
> I don't see any point in writing any more—what point has there ever been? To whom? What for?
>
> I write every night when the camp is quiet and Rita has gone to bed but I don't know who or who to. Lynda, I suppose, or Martha. (*City*, p. 614).

Mark believes both to be dead, although his son, a clairvoyant, has told him that Lynda is not dead and that Martha is still alive (the distinction is important to a mystic). Although Mark is still too much the rationalist to believe, he will not "ask why or how or where. If they [his son and others who share the faith] find the thought of forgiving ghosts a help, then why not." But Mark himself remains a mere administrator, helping the new world to form but embittered because it is a new world and he is too much a part of the old. "Who," he asks, "can I talk to, who can share what I feel?"

(*City*, p. 613). He continues to write—not out of certainty, not even out of a desperate faith, but simply out of a need to write, to make order of his experience.

In *The Golden Notebook*, the need to write is almost pandemic. "Everyone was going to be a great writer, but everyone!"[3]—not only former party members, but also the capitalist Richard Portmain and the psychiatrist Mama Sugar. It is as if one frequent manifestation of the kind of social consciousness that leads to involvement is accompanied by a desire to make fictions of that commitment, to impose upon it a form and thereby give it a kind of specious reality. Although Lessing does believe in mute inglorious Miltons (she is much concerned, for example, with the fates of writers whose native language is spoken by only a small portion of the earth's population), she is far too unsentimental to tell us that the desire to write creates the ability to write. For most of her writers, in fact, the attempt to create art is a pitiful attempt to escape reality by manipulating it in ways that make it unreal. Richard ceases writing when he loses his liberal vision of the world and learns that he can manipulate money and people instead of words; those who have retained their faiths create work in which "the writing is bad, the story lifeless"; their work is "frightening" because "it is totally inside the current myth" (*Notebook*, p. 296). At an editorial meeting of the party press, Anna is asked to defend her judgment of a typical propaganda novel; she replies,

> "As far as I can see the author has lifted his memories from the 'thirties intact and made them true of Britain 1954, and apart from that he appears to be under the impression that the great British working-class owe some kind of allegiance to the Communist Party." (*Notebook*, p. 347)

The work is bad not because it is propaganda, but because it is not true, and because it is not true it can have neither life nor style. Elsewhere Lessing has written that she sees no reason why good writers should not, if they have a bent that way, write angry protest novels about economic injustice. Many good writers have. . . . But propagandist literature, religious or political, is as old as literature itself, and has sometimes been good and sometimes bad.

Recently it has been very bad; and that is why the idea of committedness is in disrepute. (*Voice*, pp. 3–4)

The novels are not bad because the party members have experienced too little, or because they are not committed to something valuable, or because they have not paid their dues as human beings—one of the recurring themes in Lessing's work is the genuine suffering of dedicated party members: they are bad because total commitment to an ideal, however heroic, is fragmentation of the individual, a fragmentation that destroys the will and the vision necessary to make a fictional world sufficiently complex even to suggest the richness of the real world.

Noncommunist writers are no less exempt. Jimmy Wood, Mark Coleridge's engineering partner, writes "space opera" and turns Mark's company into an experimental station testing a variety of abhorrent devices for the government. It is as if, we are told, he "had been born with one of the compartments of the human mind developed to its furthest possibility, but this was at the cost of everything else" (*City*, p. 488). Even among such serious writers as Camus, Sartre, Genet, and Beckett "the type of Western literature is the novel or play which one sees or reads with a shudder of horrified pity for all humanity" (*Voice*, p. 11). Both the communist and the Western oversimplifications are, Lessing feels, "aspects of cowardice, both fallings-away from a central vision . . . easy escapes of our time into false innocence" (*Voice*, pp. 11–12).

"Innocence" is, of course, a strange word to use of a writer like Genet, or even Beckett, unless by it one means a kind of tunnel-vision, an achievement of intensity by limitation rather than by the weight of the complexities reality has in store for

us. Lessing goes on to speak of the "responsible" writer's need
for

> a balance which must be continuously tested and reaffirmed
> . . . . The point of rest should be the writer's recognition of
> man, the responsible individual, voluntarily submitting his
> will to the collective, but never finally; and insisting on mak-
> ing his own personal and private judgements before every act
> of submission. (*Voice*, p. 12)

The strength required is not only the strength to stand against
external pressures (Lessing is almost contemptuous of those),
but the strength to stand against "the inner loyalty to something felt as something much greater than one's self. . . . the
inner censor is the enemy" (*Voice*, p. 12).

A large part of Anna Wulf's writer's block is that she insists,
in Lessing's terms, upon writing responsibly or not at all. As
the Yellow Notebooks show, she certainly has not lost the inspiration for fiction; the ideas come frequently and well, and
"The Shadow of the Third," which occupies a large part of the
Yellow Notebook, shows promise of being a more than pass-
able novel. One way of approaching Lessing's conception of
the artist as seen in Anna Wulf is to note that Anna suffers
from something very like Sartrean nausea: she is repelled
whenever she sees deeply. She speaks of her successful novel,
"Frontiers of War," with "disgust" (*Notebook*, p. 58), even
though she recognizes that, as novels go, it is not bad. She
had

> said nothing in it that wasn't true. But the emotion it came out
> of was something frightening, the unhealthy, feverish illicit ex-
> citement of wartime, a lying nostalgia, a longing for licence,
> for freedom, for the jungle, for formlessness. . . . Yet no one
> seems to see it. It is an immoral novel because that terrible
> lying nostalgia lights every sentence. And I know that in order
> to write another, to write those fifty reports on society which I
> have the material to write, I would have to deliberately whip
> up in myself that same emotion. And it would be that emotion

which would make those fifty books novels and not reportage. (*Notebook*, p. 61)

And so Anna refuses to write for publication because she will not accept the only emotion she feels can give form to her work. (It is interesting that Ella, the protagonist of "Shadow of the Third," is considering writing a novel much like *The Golden Notebook* and suffers a temporary block because in looking for the outlines of a story she finds "again and again, nothing but patterns of defeat, death, irony." Saner than Anna Wulf at this point, she "tries to force patterns of happiness or simple life. But she fails. . . . She waits, she waits patiently for the images to form, to take on life" (*Notebook*, pp. 399–400).

I am not sure what to call this quality that refuses the easy innocence of oversimplification—certainly intelligence, intellectual and moral integrity, even arrogance. Most of all, perhaps, it involves a stubborn refusal to settle for anything less than the most complete version of the truth that one can get. Perhaps that is why there are so few slogans in Lessing's work, why there is so seldom a phrase that one can use to describe her work without some major qualification. Perhaps that is why, although there are startling images and memorable phrases, nothing in Lessing's work seems to sum it up. Hence also her annoyance at those critics who simplified *The Golden Notebook* into a feminist novel.

Mary Ann Singleton, writing some time after the first wave of criticism of *The Golden Notebook*, found no less than "seven main dualities that Anna must resolve." The

first is the need for emotion set beside the difficulty of enduring it in a world that offers so much pain. Second is the problems of the traditional versus the modern woman. . . . The third duality is between "creative naivety" and cynicism. Closely related is the fourth, between idealism and a hopeless sense of fatality. Fifth is the dichotomy between the individual mind and, as Lessing says elsewhere, "the collective": humanity as a whole, the sum of individual lives. Sixth is the duality between form and chaos. Finally, there is the dichotomy between generosity or helpfulness and "joy-in-spite" or "joy-in-destruction."⁴

The listing is as good as any other and has the advantage of showing something of the marvelous complexity of Lessing's concerns; there is no level of human experience on which Anna does not feel tension. Not only can she not, like Beckett, simplify by accepting one side of a dilemma (say, the existential angst), she must be concerned with the day-to-day problems of feminism on both a political and an emotional level, of political commitments and individualism, free will and determinism, metaphysical anarchy versus metaphysical order, and so on. In her richest works, like *The Golden Notebook* and The Children of Violence series, Lessing never lets us forget that we are complex creatures torn among myriad forces. To do less, as both Lessing and Anna Wulf know, is to present only a version of the truth.

How does the responsible artist develop this awesome sense of integrity? Characteristically, Lessing says very little about the special equipment of the artist. Unlike James Joyce, Joyce Cary, and a host of others who (at least when writing of artists) seem to divide the world into those with genius and those without, Lessing divides the world into the committed and the uncommitted. Although it will be necessary to explore the idea of commitment further, it can be said for now that the only commitment worth having is a commitment to humanity, to the realization of the fullest human potential. Perhaps that is why—despite the many differences in detail and in thematic implications of the novels in which they appear—it is appropriate that Martha Quest and Anna Wulf be so similar. Each develops as a normally rebellious young girl who becomes a communist partly because it is the excitingly rebellious thing to do, partly because she is sensitive enough to notice the injustice that surrounds her. Each becomes disillusioned with the party for much the same basic reason: its discipline denies both their impulse for sympathetic treatment of other human beings and their intellectual sense of the world about them. If Anna were a good communist, she could cheerfully keep only one notebook; if Martha remained a communist, she would have to deny many of the lessons her experience has taught her. Each woman is acutely aware of the world disintegrating around her; each deliberately courts madness and achieves a sanity beyond madness. I do not want to make too much of the similarities between two characters who, in many important senses, are very different, but it is important to recognize that they are both developed through the consciousness of a writer who is exceptionally consistent in her understanding of the world and its people.

Perhaps the point can be made this way: Anna Wulf does not have the integrity that drives her through madness because she is an artist (like, for example, Cary's Gulley Jimeson); she is an artist simply because that is one of the things she does—just as Richard is a businessman or Cy Maitland a brain surgeon because those are the things they do. One way of pointing out Anna Wulf's responsibility as an artist is to note that she refuses to limit herself to being only an artist. Her ability to create is a talent, given in the mysterious and random way talents are given, different from but ultimately no more explicable than Richard's grasp of business affairs or Lynda's telepathy. For Lessing, the question of what makes an artist—or an engineer or a political leader—is far less interesting than the particular responsibilities of the role and, even more importantly, the way those responsibilities must be integrated into a whole human personality.

For Anna Wulf, and for Lessing herself, that integration is won painfully. It is difficult to discuss discursively because the integration must be an integration of every aspect of experience—political, sexual, artistic, moral; the concepts appropriate to analysis, as Lessing has often told us, are not appropriate for dealing with either the intricacies of human experience or with the harmonization of varied areas of experience. As the narrator of *Briefing for a Descent into Hell* says in a tone of exasperation, "*I gotta use words when I talk to you.*"[5] Then follows a stylistically very strange section describing the brief-

ing of the emissaries to Earth. The scene begins as if an ec-
umenical conference of pagan gods were being convened.
After several pages, the narrator interrupts:

> Ah yes, all very whimsical. Yes, indeed, the contemporary
> mode is much to be preferred, thus: that Earth is due to re-
> ceive a pattern of impulses from the planet nearest the Sun,
> that planet nearest on the arm of the spiral out from the
> Sun. . . . (*Briefing*, p. 136).

After a paragraph in that vein, the terminology becomes that
of a contemporary meeting of a corporation's board of direc-
tors: "Minna Erve was in the Chair. A forceful and animated
woman, with particularly arresting eyes, she was the obvious
choice, because of her position as Chief Deputy's oldest
daughter" (*Briefing*, p. 124).

The point Lessing makes is that one can speak of certain
things only in metaphors, and that no metaphor is completely
satisfactory. It is, in fact, tempting to read Lessing's involvement with communism, Jungian psychology, Laingian psychology, and Sufism as personal attempts to find prefabricated
metaphors for the wealth of her experience and her sympathies.

Whatever metaphor Lessing uses (mostly Sufi in *Briefing*,
Jungian in *The Golden Notebook*, and Laingian in *The Four-
Gated City*) she is, I think, trying to capture the same experience—a kind of birth trauma that the mature individual must
undergo in order to achieve integration. In Anna's case, it
involves, on the conscious level, a complete breakdown. As
Saul Green, another responsible artist going through rebirth,
says to her just after they reach the turning point in their
madness, "We can't either of us ever go lower than that"
(*Notebook*, p. 548). But the conscious level is only one level;
although it may be superficially and practically the most
important level, it is merely a symptom of what happens in
the unconscious.

In *The Golden Notebook*, the burden of the unconscious
seems to be the complete past of Anna Wulf, a past that the

"dream projectionist" makes her relive and relive with an accuracy and fullness impossible in her novel, in her notebooks, or in her conscious memories. In *Briefing*, it is almost a racial memory, a recalling of eons of experience; in *Memoirs of a Survivor*, it is a vision of past possibilities that open to a future certainty; in *The Four-Gated City*, it is an opening to communion with the thoughts of others; in *The Making of the Representative for Planet 8*, the fourth volume of Canopus in Argos: Archives, it is the development of a collective memory and sensibility. One of the things that makes Lessing's view of the artist so unique is that, among her major characters who transcend madness, her artists are the least evolved. I am not certain whether this is an accident of time (*The Golden Notebook* was written before *The Four-Gated City* and presumably before some of Lessing's more unorthodox ideas were fully developed) or whether it is simply a function of the peculiar tensions of the novel. Accidental or not, it is significant; it is part of the same mental set, for example, that permits Lessing to make Mark Coleridge, the writer-visionary in *The Four-Gated City*, less fully evolved than either Martha or Lynda.

If the content of Anna Wulf's dreams is the necessity of realizing the fullness of her experience, the informing principle is represented by a peculiar dwarflike figure whom she characterizes as "joy-in-destruction." Like all the figures in Anna's dreams, it has a waking counterpart, a Mr. de Silva, a man who delights in causing personal suffering merely to "see what will happen next" (*Notebook*, p. 427). Despite the waking counterpart of the dwarf, Anna is forced to redream the dream until:

> This time there was no disguise anywhere. I was the malicious male-female dwarf figure, the principle of joy-in-destruction; and Saul was my counter-part, male-female, my brother and my sister, and we were dancing in some open place. . . . But in the dream, he and I, or she and I, were friendly, we were not hostile, we were together in spiteful malice. There was a terrible yearning nostalgia in the dream, the longing for death.

We came together and kissed, in love. It was terrible, and even in the dream I knew it. Because I recognised in the dream those other dreams we all have, when the essence of love, of tenderness, is concentrated into a kiss or a caress, but now it was the caress of two half-human creatures, celebrating destruction.

There was a terrible joy in the dream. When I woke up the room was dark, the glow of the fire very red, the great white ceiling filled with restful shadow, and I was filled with joy and peace. I wondered how such a terrible dream could leave me rested, and then I remembered Mother Sugar, and thought that perhaps for the first time I had dreamed the dream "positively"—though what that means I don't know. (*Notebook*, p. 508)

It would be tempting to write a Jungian explication of this almost textbook anima-shadow dream, but the dream speaks quite well for itself. Curiously, Anna has previously hinted what dreaming the positive might mean. She has told Mother Sugar:

"I'm going to make the obvious point that perhaps the word neurotic means the condition of being highly conscious and developed. The essence of neurosis is conflict. But the essence of living now, fully, not blocking off to what goes on, is conflict. In fact I've reached the stage where I look at people and say— he or she, they are whole at all because they've chosen to block off at this stage or that. People stay sane by blocking off, by limiting themselves." (*Notebook*, p. 402)

Which is precisely what Anna's integrity prevents—up to a point. As Tommy and other characters remark, Anna wears her goodness arrogantly. The games she plays with those who want to buy the rights to her novel, her attitude toward Richard, her attitude toward her lovers—all express a kind of smugness, a kind of "I'm-too-good-for-all-this" that Anna recognizes intellectually but does not recognize emotionally. Her refusal to publish, as both Tommy and Mother Sugar point out, is an act of blatant arrogance—lesser souls, Anna fears, simply won't be able to cope with the difficulty and the honesty of her work. And it is more than probable that her disgust with "The Frontiers of War" is not merely that she dislikes the emotion on which it is based, but that she wishes to continue to block off the knowledge that that emotion is a part of herself. It is no wonder that the penultimate step in understanding her unconscious is the realization that the dwarf who personifies "joy-in-destruction" is a part of herself, that even that must be a part of what is integrated into her awareness of herself. Only after that can the repeated dreams of the Mashopi experience be shared properly, because only then does that experience make sense. In the final dream, Anna struggles toward a new understanding, a less arrogant acceptance of what she is capable of doing.

The final dream is a version of the "boulder pushing" metaphor which is first mentioned in "The Shadow of the Third" and then is repeated and expanded in the notebooks. It is the notion that there are a very few great individuals, individuals whose wisdom is far in advance of their times; the mass of decent, dedicated persons are condemned to making small improvements in their world, to pushing a boulder three inches up a mountain and watching it roll back two inches. One way of describing Anna's arrogance is to say that she lacks the peculiar kind of humility and courage required of the boulder pusher. Anna's last dream raises that issue:

> The projectionist now being silent, I called to him, It's enough, and he didn't answer, so I leaned out my hand to switch off the machine. Still asleep, I read the words off a page I had written: That was about courage, but not the sort of courage I have ever understood. It's a small painful sort of courage which is at the root of every life, because injustice and cruelty is at the root of life. And the reason why I have only given my attention to the heroic or the beautiful or the intelligent is because I won't accept that injustice and cruelty, and so won't accept the small endurance that is bigger than anything.

I looked at these words which I had written, and of which I felt critical; and then I took them to Mother Sugar. I said to her: "We're back at the blade of grass again, that will press up through the bits of rusted steel a thousand years after the bombs have exploded and after the world's crust has melted. Because the force of will in the blade of grass is the same as the small painful endurance. Is that it?" (I was smiling sardonically in my dream, wary of a trap.). . .

"But the point is, I don't think I'm prepared to give that much reverence to that damned blade of grass, even now."
(*Notebook*, pp. 543–44)

Someone once quipped that Hemingway's heroes had the courage to face anything except Monday morning—for the boulder pusher, every morning is Monday. (In a haunting short story, "The Sun between Their Feet," Lessing shows that, whatever Anna's feelings, Lessing herself does understand that "small painful endurance" as few writers have, as she describes with wonder the efforts of a pair of beetles to push a mudball in which their eggs are kept up an incline.)

But to admire that small endurance and to settle for it are quite different. If one were to try to specify one particular difference between Anna Wulf and Doris Lessing as writers, ignoring Lessing's obvious freedom from writer's block, it might be at precisely this point. Although still uncomfortable with the notion of the small endurance, Anna Wulf produces only "Free Women"; Lessing, refusing to settle, produces *The Golden Notebook*—which is both an acknowledgement of the necessity of boulder pushing and a presentation of a vision worthy of the gifted ones who sit at the top of the mountain.

Despite the incredible complexity of themes in *The Golden Notebook*, it is a novel about novels in a very precise way: one of its major subjects is in fact the transmutation of reality into fiction. Lessing describes one of her purposes in writing *The Golden Notebook:*

You know, the Free Women section in *The Golden Notebook*—the envelope—I was really trying to express my sense of despair about writing a conventional novel in that. Actually that is an absolutely whole conventional novel, and the rest of the book is the material that went into making it. One of the things I was saying was: Well, look, this is a conventional novel. God knows, I write them myself and doubtless will again. One has this feeling after writing a novel. There it is: 120,000 words; it's got a nice shape and the reviewers will say this and that. And the bloody complexity that went into it. And it's always a lie. And the terrible despair. So you've written a good novel or a moderate novel, but what does it actually say about what you've actually experienced? The truth is—absolutely nothing. Because you can't. I don't know what one does about novels. I shall write volume 5 [of Children of Violence] with my usual enthusiasm. I know perfectly well that when I've finished it I shall think, Christ, what a lie. Because you can't get life into it—that's all there is to it—no matter how hard you try. (*Voice*, pp. 81–82)

We've already seen this theme stated explicitly in Anna Wulf's reaction to "The Frontiers of War." And it must be said immediately that the problem is not exclusively a literary problem. Martha Quest and Kate Brown (the protagonist of *The Summer before the Dark*) are well aware of the insufficiency of words. Anna herself realizes that her diaries not only fragment experience, but that even when they cover the same content they interpret it differently. Looking at Saul Green's diary, she

remembered that when I read my notebooks I didn't recognise myself. Something strange happens when one writes about oneself. That is, one's self direct, not one's self projected. The result is cold, pitiless, judging. Or if not judging, then there's no life in it—yes, that's it, it's lifeless. . . . If Saul said, about his diaries, or, summing his younger self up from his later self: I was a swine, the way I treated women. Or: I'm right to treat women the way I do. Or: I'm simply writing a record of what happened, I'm not making moral judgements about myself—well, whatever he said, it would be irrelevant.

Because what is left out of his diaries is vitality, life, charm.
(*Notebook*, p. 488)

Early in the novel, Anna draws up two columns of words describing Willi; one column contains the words "ruthless,"
"cold," and "sentimental"; the other column, "kind," "warm,"
and "realistic" (*Notebook*, p. 67). The irony is that the words
in both columns apply equally; only when one tries to recapture the experience, and especially to recapture it in words,
must one choose column A or B. But to make such choices is,
as Anna later names it, "sterility." In a late dream of the filming of her first novel, Anna is startled because although all the
details are right, the filming is wrong; every choice of camera
angle, every inflection, suggests an experience different from
the one she remembers. Responding to her consternation,
the director tells her that the important thing is to film something, anything: it does not matter so long as the film is completed. Asked by Mother Sugar to name the dream, Anna
replies, "sterility" (*Notebook*, p. 450). The sterility in the
dream, I believe Lessing wants us to understand, is twofold.
It is not, first of all, merely that there are differing possible
interpretations of the experience. It is, on the one hand,
Anna's paralysis in the face of the limitations inherent in any
particular symbolic form and, on the other, the director's opposite attitude, his irresponsible willingness to settle cheerfully for the incomplete, for the version rather than for the
vision.

As Anna moves from dreams and diaries to fictions, isolated
ideas and events go through strange permutations. "Frontiers
of War" is given us in various guises—from a fairly straightfor-
ward synopsis, through a series of parodies (including a version set in England and a musical version), to mock reviews
Anna writes for the Soviet press to show the response to the
novel at different times. In the notebooks, Anna is approached by various agents who suggest outlandish remakes
of "Frontiers of War" to placate unenlightened audiences. In a
role reversal, Anna's alter ego Ella, the heroine of "The Shad-

ow of the Third," is sent to Paris as an agent to buy rights for a French story for an English magazine. To the disgust of the French author, she has to suggest changes in order to avoid shocking her proper English readers.

Anna's fictions not only reverse experiences, they also distort them. The noble young airman of "Frontiers of War" was Paul Blackenhurst, a rather shallow aristocratic airman of the Mashopi period; the affair with the Black girl that makes the story of "Frontiers" actually involved George Hounslow (the twin of Thomas Stern of Children of Violence). An idea for a story about a man's callous writing-off of a woman he once loved later occurs as an event in Saul's diary; the ideas for short stories in the Yellow Notebook, in fact, each have one or more close parallels elsewhere in the novel; the parallels are duly noted with numbers corresponding to the numbered story ideas.

Typically, in addition to the nineteen ideas for stories, Lessing gives us two rather extended fictional versions which Anna creates from her own experience and from the agony she is suffering. Anna meditates on Ella:

> I see Ella, walking slowly about a big empty room, thinking, waiting. I, Anna, see Ella. Who is, of course, Anna. But that is the point, for she is not. The moment I, Anna, write: Ella rings up Julia to announce, etc., then Ella floats away from me and becomes someone else. I don't understand what happens at the moment Ella separates herself from me and becomes Ella. No one does. It's enough to call her Ella, instead of Anna. Why did I choose the name Ella? Once I met a girl at a party called Ella. She reviewed books for some newspaper and read manuscripts for a publisher [very much like Anna herself]. She was small, thin, dark—the same physical type as myself. (Notebook, p. 343)

This is a very rich passage. The mere "naming," Anna's code word for defining a situation, creates its own universe of discourse, its automatic removal from the experiential reality. Yet, as "The Shadow of the Third" shows, Anna never gets completely away from Ella. Paul Tanner, the charming but shallow doctor with whom Ella has an affair, is in personality very much like the Paul who was the basis of the hero of "Frontiers of War"; Ella's marriage to George has too many parallels to Anna's marriage to Willi-Max to be ignored. More importantly, the theme of the novel is to be Jungian shadows, those contrary selves that make up our other half, who are wise where we are foolish, foolish where we are wise; selfish where we are generous, generous where we are selfish. To summarize rather quickly, one of the major developments in "The Shadow of the Third" is the growing awareness in the main characters (Ella, Paul, and Paul's wife) of the role the shadow plays in their lives, in their relationships with each other. As Anna's conception of the novel matures, she becomes fascinated first by the realization that Paul's wife must be everything Ella is not—that is, must be her shadow—and then by her realization of the importance of her own shadow-self. The realization is one of the most important steps Anna takes in her break through her disintegration.

Equally important, Ella is in many ways Anna's shadow. We have seen that Ella is planning a book with something of the emotional tone of *The Golden Notebook,* and that her experiences as sometime agent are opposite those of Anna as author; further, Ella has a son, Anna a daughter; Ella works for a slick commercial publisher, Anna for a party editorial outlet. Ella claims to be nonpolitical (although she shares with Tanner the typical Lessing vision of the ideal city); Anna has a period in which she is frantically political. Ella, although bothered by the complexities of her society and the difficulties of her female role, functions rather smoothly; Anna is driven to and through insanity. Quite important also are their very different attitudes toward men. In a moment of almost excessive self criticism, Anna remarks that she has been much too hard on men, that she has used "femaleness as a sort of standard or yardstick to measure and discard men," that she "invited defeat from men without even being conscious of it" (*Notebook,* p. 410). Ella has been too willing to accept what are usually considered the masculine traits of her lovers. To oversimplify somewhat, Ella loses because she tries too hard to please, Anna because she insists (at least to herself) too much on being pleased. Significantly, at this stage Anna has not yet realized that the sexually ambiguous dwarf of her dreams is a part of herself.

As Anna continues to contemplate "The Shadow of the Third," she becomes aware of the identity of Ella and her own shadow-self; the Anna who thinks herself worldly-wise enough to fictionalize her experiences under the title "Free Women" begins to understand Ella:

> It is as if this novel were already written and I were reading it. And now I see it whole I see another theme, of which I was not conscious when I began it. The theme is, naivety. From the moment Ella meets Paul and loves him, from the moment she uses the word love, there is the birth of naivety.
>
> And so now, looking back at my relationship with Michael (I used the name of my real lover for Ella's fictitious son. . .), I see above all my naivety. Any intelligent person could have foreseen the end of this affair from its beginning. And yet I, Anna, like Ella with Paul, refused to see it. Paul gave birth to Ella, the naive Ella. He destroyed in her the knowing, doubting, sophisticated Ella and again and again he put her intelligence to sleep, and with her willing connivance, so that she floated darkly on her love for him, on her naivety, which is another word for a spontaneous creative faith. And when his own distrust of himself destroyed this woman-in-love, so that she began thinking, she would fight to return to naivety. (*Notebook*, pp. 182–83)

In other words, Anna's creation of Ella has permitted her to realize that her love of Michael activated in her a part of her shadow-self, a part in strong contrast to the usual sophisticated, analytical, somewhat tough and unsentimental Anna Wulf.

If "The Shadow of the Third" may be read in part as Anna's

fictionalization of a part of her inner life, "Free Women" may be read as a fictionalization of Anna's external life. Except for Saul-Milt, the main characters in Anna's present keep their own names (Molly, Richard, Marion, Tommy). The Anna Wulf of "Free Women" (AW to distinguish her from the Anna of the Notebooks) seems a much less complete, much less intense, person than Anna; she is keeping notebooks, suffering from a writer's block, anxious about her sexuality and about the state of the world, but the concerns are comparatively low key; it is as if Lessing is deliberately understating AW in order to underline the comparative poverty of art and the richness of the reality from which it springs. Perhaps the difference can best be seen in the crises each woman undergoes. Anna's relationship with Saul Green, which precipitates her crisis, occupies almost a hundred pages. It includes some of the most intense dream sequences in *The Golden Notebook*, a series of ideas for stories, agonizing relivings of Anna's past, scenes of bitterly intense jealousy and loneliness, and—most decisively—the exchange of first lines that puts an end to Anna's and Saul's writers' blocks. The painful explication of the anguish within these pages makes them among the most harrowing in contemporary literature. The corresponding scenes with Milt occupy a scant ten pages; much of it is in pseudo-Hemingwayesque dialogue. Milt removes scraps of newspapers from AW's walls; they make love almost accidentally and fall into a discussion of their personal problems. AW, without much prompting, realizes that she is "only temporarily a nut" (*Notebook*, p. 546). By the sixth day, she asks him to stay; he perversely knows that he must move on. By the end of "Free Women," AW is cured of her writer's block: she no longer wants to write and will no longer try. The ex-party worker is planning to join the Labour Party, "teach a night class twice a week for delinquent kids," and assist a marriage counselor (*Notebook*, p. 568). If Anna's writing of the adequate but not completely accurate "Free Women" is boulder pushing, AW's future is pebble pushing.

Yet for all the slightness of "Free Women," it—like "Frontiers of War"—tells its portion of the truth. Statistically, the odds are that the "free women" will end up like AW rather than like Anna, will end up being "integrated with British life at its roots" (*Notebook*, p. 568), as Molly ironically describes it. What had begun apparently as an attempt to give a shape to Anna's experience has ended by describing the shape of experience of less gifted women. Just as the portrayal of Ella had led Anna to understand her own naive shadow by creating a fictional incarnation of it, the portrayal of AW quite possibly leads Anna to understand fully the self that does not want to write, by showing it as a less feeling, less intense, less alive aspect of her own character.

For the author, then, fiction is a realization of the possibilities inherent in personal experience, a realization of the potentialities of both the externals of the situations and of the internal development of the author. That is why, in order to fulfill its role, fiction must constantly touch base with the reality the writer has known, and why it must simultaneously grow away from that reality. It is not, as Anna wants to believe, an embodiment of either an event or a memory. It is, as Lessing knows, a way of organizing possibilities. I do not want to make the mistake of insisting upon autobiographical readings of the Children of Violence novels and of *The Golden Notebook*, of claiming that AW is Anna is Martha Quest is Doris Lessing—but even the casual reader of Lessing's biography and her novels and stories must be struck by the fact that the same experiences are lived and relived, situations repeated, characters renamed, as if Lessing, through her protagonists, were attempting to map varieties of development possible for a woman of her background and sensibilities. That is why, from the author's point of view, the novel fails if it falsifies. And that is also why the novel can disgust and terrify its creator: it presents the shadow, the other, the lesser self that one has just barely escaped falling into or, alternately, the better self that one cannot hope to rise to. Perhaps this is a part of what Lessing meant when, asked the traditional question about her advice to young writers, she replied:

You should write, first of all, to please yourself. You shouldn't
care a damn about anybody else at all. But writing can't be a way
of life; the important part of writing is living. You have to live in
such a way that your writing emerges from it. This is hard to
describe. (*Voice*, p. 49)

Yet, this would not be Lessing if the advice were so simply
one-sided. She also feels, equally strongly, the responsibility
of the artist to the audience. She describes the effects of reading felt by the young Martha Quest in *A Proper Marriage:*

Books. Words. There must surely be some pattern of words
which would neatly and safely cage what she felt—isolate her
emotions so that she could look at them from outside. . . . it is
a remarkable fact that she was left unmoved by criticisms of
the sort of person she was by parents, relations, preachers,
teachers, politicians and the people who write for newspapers;
whereas an unsympathetic description of a character similar to
her own in a novel would send her into a condition of anxious
soul-searching for days. Which suggests that it is of no use for
artists to insist, with such nervous disinclination for the responsibility, that their productions are only "a divine play" or
"a reflection from the creative fires of irony," etc., etc., while
the Marthas of this world read and search with the craving
thought, What does this say about my life? It will not do at
all.[6]

Even more dramatically, in "Free Women" the immediate
cause of Tommy's attempted suicide seems to be his discussion with AW after reading her notes on the artist's responsibility. With remarkable insight for one so young, he has accused AW of arrogance for refusing to write for publication,
for assuming that readers will not be ready for the bleakness
of her message (*Notebook*, pp. 243–45). In the Notebooks,
Mother Sugar challenges Anna on the same point, forcing
Anna to admit, despite her communist-based egalitarian sen-
timents, that if she were to create a novel whose form reflects

the chaos she sees in the world, people would reject it. Anna
tells Mother Sugar that

> "People don't mind immoral messages. They don't mind art
> which says that murder is good, cruelty is good, sex for sex's
> sake is good. They like it, provided the message is wrapped up
> a little. And they like messages saying that murder is bad,
> cruelty is bad, and love is love is love. What they can't stand is
> to be told that it all doesn't matter, they can't stand form-
> lessness." (*Notebook*, p. 406)

Curiously, although the argument continues with Anna denying that she holds an "aristocratic view of art," Lessing lets it
end inconclusively, perhaps in part because Anna is right in a
way that she is not yet sane enough to understand. Lessing
does know that the masses are not automatically moved by
great art, and in particular by art of great complexity. In a
rather interesting section of *A Ripple from the Storm*, the party faithful in Africa, true to their faith in the intellectual abilities of the proletariat, try to get Tommy, an only averagely
intelligent young soldier, to read Tolstoy. He tries mightily,
but the words and the ideas are too big.[7] Yet there is a more
important sense in which Anna's hesitancy to offer her vision
of chaos to the public is correct, or, at least, agrees with Lessing's view. We have seen earlier the high purpose Lessing
holds out for fiction; a novel whose formlessness reflects the
chaos of Anna's mind—and Anna in this respect is *not* Lessing—should not be accepted. There is, therefore, a kind of
perverse rightness in Anna's refusal to write for publication so
long as her vision of the world is chaotic.

For Lessing as a reader, the great novels are those of
Tolstoy, Stendhal, Dostoevsky, Balzac, Turgenev, Chekhov,
and Thomas Mann, precisely because they offer what Anna, in
her fragmented condition, cannot achieve. Lessing defines it
variously. It is a "realism which springs so vigorously and naturally from a strongly-held, though not necessarily intellectually defined, view of life that it absorbs symbolism. . . . [It]

is the highest form of prose writing," held together by a "climate of ethical judgement" (*Voice*, pp. 4–5). The nineteenth-century greats

> shared certain values; they were humanists. A nineteenth-century novel is recognizably a nineteenth-century novel because it is of this moral climate. (*Voice*, p. 5)

The common moral climate is not, definitely not, a community of beliefs, principles, intellectual formulations of any kind. Those are, Lessing seems to feel, mere crutches. Instructively, much of the early and middle sections of Children of Violence is spent in a harsh depiction of quarrels among true believers; toward the end of *The Four-Gated City*, when things are crumbling, the small groups that work together to save what can be saved have as their "chief characteristic no ideology, plan, constitution, or philosophy. We had grown as a community" (pp. 564–65). The successful community grows from shared sympathies, shared faith in humanity. And that is what Lessing as a reader looks for. Rereading for her own purposes, she says she would choose novels like *War and Peace* or *The Red and the Black*:

> I was looking for the warmth, the humanity, the love of people which illuminates the literature of the nineteenth century and which makes all these old novels a statement of faith in man himself.
>
> These are qualities which I believe are lacking from literature now.
>
> This is what I mean when I say that literature should be committed. It is these qualities which I demand, and which I believe spring from being committed; for one cannot be committed without belief. (*Voice*, p. 6)

What one believes in, it must be emphasized, must not be defined too precisely, must not be defined in terms of ideologies and philosophies. If we believe in a universal harmony, metaphors drawn from various theologies, science, and corporate meetings of the kind used in *Briefing for a Descent into Hell* are all equally valid and equally invalid; complete commitment to any metaphor, any ideology, removes from the individual the ability to choose for himself, to weigh accurately the complexity of his own experience. And that, as we have seen, is a step to fragmentation and dehumanization, to existential nausea or cheerful little tracts on economic development.

Although Lessing does not say it directly, her admiration for the novel and for humanism stems from the same source. There is a very real sense in which art, unlike other disciplines, and especially literature makes humanity the measure of all things. Literature does not prove ideas; it does not properly argue the truth of ideologies. It shows, rather, how it feels to live in a world in which this or that idea dominates; it shows the tensions among ideas and other areas of human experience. Anton Hesse of Children of Violence and Willi of the Notebooks may be ideologically correct in their doctrinaire assessment of the racial problem in Africa; their rational arguments for discipline, for restraint, for purity of purpose, for strategically organizing time and effort—their textbook approach to the injustice around them—miss what must be the main point, that their actions affect human beings. This is one of the reasons that Anna, despite her disgust when she remembers "Frontiers of War," feels that it deserves at least some respect: it attempts to show in its limited way that the inequalities caused by social and racial injustice are not mere problems in theory but tragedies of human suffering.

Unless the human concern dominates, nothing else suffices:

> Once a writer has a feeling of responsibility, as a human being, for the other human beings he influences, it seems to me he must become a humanist, and must feel himself as an instrument of change for good or for bad. That image of the pretty singer in the ivory tower has always seemed to me a dishonest one. Logically he should be content to sing to his

image in the mirror. The act of getting a story or a novel published is an act of communication, an attempt to impose one's
personality and beliefs on other people. If a writer accepts this
responsibility, he must see himself, to use the socialist phrase,
as an architect of the soul, and it is a phrase which none of the
old nineteenth-century novelists would have shied away from.
(*Voice*, pp. 6–7)

To be a writer is to accept an awesome responsibility.

Lessing feels that, unfortunately, we do not live in times
suitable for the production of great literature, however great
our need. The times are too chaotic; we can no longer

use Balzacian phrases like "sublime virtue" or "monster of
wickedness" without self-consciousness. Words, it seems, can
no longer be used simply and naturally. All the great words
like love, hate; life, death; loyalty, treachery; contain their opposite meanings and half a dozen shades of dubious implication. (*Voice*, p. 5)

Although I doubt that the world was ever so simple as Lessing
imagines it here—Tolstoy's agonizing doubts, his conversion
and repudiation of much of his youthful work are but one
symptom of the disharmony an earlier age found within itself—the fact remains that it is precisely the existence of such
gray areas for exploration that make for the best fiction. The
Blifils and Squares in Fielding's work, and their contrast with
the very different styles of virtue of a Tom Jones or a Parson
Adams, provide in outline much the same kind of challenge
for the great novelist as the Anton Hesses and the Mark Cole-
ridges for the modern novelist.

Lessing feels also that we are living in a "dull" literary period because,

What we need more than anything else, I am convinced, is
some serious criticism. The most exciting periods of literature
have always been those when the critics were great. (*Voice*,
p. 14)

She is quite frequently very hard on professional students of the arts, on reviewers, critics, academicians. In "A Man and Two Women," for example, Lessing tells us that

> A French critic had seen Jack's work, and suddenly he was successful. His show in Paris, then one in London, made money; and now he charged in the hundreds where a year or so ago he charged ten or twenty guineas. This had deepened his contempt for the value of the markets. . . .
>
> Of course Dorothy Bradford was not able to talk in quite the same way, since she had not yet been "discovered."[8]

Perhaps the theme that most runs through Lessing's attacks on professional interpreters of literature is that they are fragmented; a good reader requires something of the wholeness, the integrity of personality, of the responsible author. The communist editors in *The Golden Notebook* and the mock reviews of "Frontiers of War" (which sound all too accurate) judge what they read not as human beings but as party functionaries, as creatures who have surrendered their right to test literature against their personal experience. Academicians read with a doggedness unrelated to their human needs. Lessing advises students "who have to spend a year, two years, writing theses about one book" that

> "there is only one way to read, which is to browse in libraries and bookshops, picking up books that attract you, reading only those, dropping them when they bore you, skipping the parts that drag—and never, never reading anything because you feel you ought, or because it is part of a trend or a movement."
> (*Voice*, p. 39)

If, for Lessing as for Joyce and most other artists, the act of creation is an act of total involvement, a re-creation of the world that comes from the deepest and truest and most complete vision the artist is capable of, the moral Lessing draws is peculiarly her own and peculiarly liberating. Rather than expect the reader to surrender to the artist because he is an

artist, because he has painstakingly recreated his vision, Lessing asks for voluntary acceptance, given when it is ready. In
her wisdom, she knows that her vision will be accepted only
when the reader is ready, and that the only meaningful acceptance will be born of a sympathetic understanding that is complete because it is free.

In summary, it may be well to look at one of Lessing's remarkable short stories, "The Two Potters," from *A Man and
Two Women*. It is, in its quiet, almost understated way, a very
full revelation of Lessing's view of the relation of the artist and
society. The central character is a dreamer who has had a kind
of controlled recurring dream of an ancient potter forever
making his functional pots for a stagnating village. She tells
her dream to Mary, a ceramicist. After some time, Mary enters into the spirit of the dream and makes for the narrator a
rather strange ceramic rabbit or hare,

> but with ears like neither—narrower, sharp, short, like the
> pointed unfolding shoots of a plant. It had a muzzle more like a
> dog's than a rabbit's; it looked as if it did not eat grass—per-
> haps insects and beetles? (p. 156)

Mary has, of course, created an image of the ancient potter's
rabbit dreamed by her friend, rather than of the rabbits that
cavort in her garden. That night, Mary continues her dream,
taking the ceramic rabbit into the market place and giving it
to the old potter, who sprays it with water. It runs off to some
jagged brown rocks "where it raised its front paws and froze in
the posture Mary had created for it." The ancient potter returns to work. "A small boy crouched, watching, and the
water flung by the potter's right hand sprayed the bowl he
was making and the child's face, in a beautiful curving spray of
glittering light" (p. 160). The dreamer, the artist, the worker,
and the child—without the dreamer, there is no vision; without the artist, there is no communication of the vision; without the worker, there is no power to transform the village;
without the child, there is no future. The work of art, at the
right moment and in the right place, comes alive briefly for

whoever is ready to receive it and becomes the instrument by which stagnation is transformed into promise.

There is in Doris Lessing's view of art and artists no separation between the artist and the human being. Our human choices, Lessing believes, are clear: we either destroy ourselves individually and as a species, or we become whole individually and as a species. The achievement of personal wholeness is difficult, not because one happens to be an artist nor because of the artist's special sensitivity or vision, but because wholeness requires that the individual integrate within himself all the shattered fragments that make up both individual experience and social disintegration. Anna Wulf's hell is no less real than Martha Quest's, and each must be broken by an openness both to themselves and to the world. The achievement of wholeness as a society, of the four-gated city, requires the dreamer and the teller of the dream; it also requires the boulder pusher and the child who promises a future. It is much to expect of the artist, and it is much to expect of fiction, but—Lessing deserves the final word:

> True lovers of the novel must love it as the wise man in the fable did the crippled beauty whose complaint against fate was that she was beautiful—for what use was her beauty? She was always trying for humanity and failing. And he replied that it was because of the trying that he loved her. (*Voice*, pp. 99– 100)

Chapter 3

Patrick White

Art as Mandala

> *What do I believe? I am accused of not making it explicit. How to be explicit about a grandeur too overwhelming to express, a daily wrestling match with an opponent whose limbs never become material, a struggle from which the sweat and blood are scattered on the pages of anything the serious writer writes? . . .*
> *God is everywhere they told me.*[1]

The core of Patrick White's fictional universe is a reverence for the mystery of things. It is a reverence so intensely over-whelming that his exemplary characters who are not obsessed artists are generally tongue-tied before it, a reverence so great that the characters who experience any part of it sacrifice what most readers would consider normality. It is a reverence which White's villains— often choral characters speaking for the insensate mass of humanity—willfully lack.

In White's major fictions the saints—and *saints* is the proper word because White is concerned ultimately with the costs and consequences of reverence—are those with a special gift. The gifts range from Sir Basil's genius as an actor (*The Eye of the Storm*), through Voss's courage against the privations of inner Australia (*Voss*), to Arthur Brown's simple gift of love of persons (*The Solid Mandala*), or Mary Hare's oneness with things (*Riders in the Chariot*). But whatever the specific nature of the gift, it includes reverence for tables and chairs and stones and animals and trees and people.

The physical world in most of White's fictions has an almost but not quite mystical feel; perhaps it would be most appropriate to speak of a transferred mysticism. Holiness resides not in things, but rather in the saint's ability to perceive things with reverence. I suspect that, in a general way, White's discovery of one of his major fictional themes can be shown by the attitude toward physical reality in two early novels, *Happy Valley* and *The Tree of Man*, the first published in 1939, the second in 1955.

In *Happy Valley,* a promising but not especially successful novel, the major characters are uncomfortable with things—and by *things* I mean all the physical detail that makes up an environment: stones, trees, animals, furniture, persons. The Australian highlands are too cold, the scenery too harsh, the accommodations too spartan, the neighbors too ordinary for the protagonists of *Happy Valley.* The result is a whining bitchiness in all the major characters that grates upon the reader and that makes the protagonist's final acceptance of responsibility seem less a moral victory than a regrettable accident.

But by the time White has come to write *The Tree of Man* some sixteen years later, he has learned that without that reverence for the things that surround one his characters have little positive to say to the reader. Stan Parker, the central figure of *The Tree of Man*, is the kind of character Tolstoy might have created had his genius been formed in a democratic rather than an aristocratic society. Parker is almost totally uneducated; he leaves a fire-and-brimstone blacksmith of a father to become a dirt farmer on poor but arable land. Because of Stan's loving attention, the farm prospers moderately.

There is little poetry in his long life—a rescue of a beautiful damsel, an occasional memory of *Hamlet* (the only literary work he has read)—but there is poetry in his feel for the land and the things of the land:

> No one could sink a post hole like Stan Parker, or fell a tree, or shoe a horse. . . . If a poetry sometimes almost formed in his head, or a vision of God, nobody knew, because you did not talk about such things, or, rather, you were not aware of the practice of doing so.[2]

Stan is but one of a long line of White's saints for whom the complexity of the world is less impressive than its mystery, and for whom the complexity is irrelevant and the mystery ineffable.

Stan Parker is the spiritual brother of Theodora, the central figure of *The Aunt's Story*. Like several of White's other major characters (Voss, Duffield, Arthur), Theodora is interested in rocks, so interested that she would like to write a poem about them; but she is as artistically incapable as she is morally wise, and she doubts that she will "ever write a poem."[3] More fortunate economically than Stan Parker, Theodora is able to travel widely, but she remains the kind of person an insightful teacher told her she would remain:

> there is much that you will experience. You will see clearly, beyond the bone. You will probably grow up ugly and walk through life in sensible shoes. Because you are honest, and because you are barren, you will be both honoured and despised. You will never make a statue, nor write a poem. Although you will be torn by all the agonies of music, you are not creative. You have not the artist's vanity, which is moved finally to express itself in objects. (*Story*, p. 56)

And so Theodora lives, surrounded by those more brilliant than she, even sometimes meeting someone who can appreciate the depth of the mystery she sees in things. Near the end of the novel she is befriended by an American family who fear that she may be too simple-minded to survive on her own, but who recognize almost instinctively that she is one of those rare persons whose special perception of the world makes their survival imperative.

Perhaps the inarticulate but expressive reverence for things is most fully shown in Mary Hare and Arthur Brown. Mary Hare, a tiny and strange-looking elderly woman during the main action of *Riders,* moves through the ruins of her father's estate like a small animal finding its way easily along paths humans should not know; she experiences the tangled underbrush of the estate grounds as "an accompaniment to states of mind."[4] As a child, she

> found it impossible to like human beings, if only on account of their faces, to say nothing of their habit of relating things that had never happened and then believing that they had. . . . She liked animals, birds, and plants. On these she could expend her great but pitiable love, and because that was not expected it ceased to be pitiable. (*Riders,* p. 15)

Except for brief intervals, her distrust of human beings continues until she meets the other three *zaddikhim*—persons whose holiness, according to Jewish legend, withholds from the world the wrath of a justly irate God. She lives most of her adult life in the ruins of Xanadu, scurrying among the brambles, tending to injured animals, and communicating with plants and trees.

A scene between Mary and her father, when Mary is quite young, is typical of a number of scenes in White's work; Mr. Hare is educated beyond his wisdom, Mary inhumanly wise beyond her education:

> "All human beings are decadent," he said. "The moment we are born, we start to degenerate. Only the unborn soul is whole, pure. . . .
>
> "Tell me, Mary, do you consider yourself one of the unborn?"
>
> "I don't understand such things," she replied. "Not yet." And looked round at him.

"Liar!"

He would never forgive her eyes, and for refusing to be hurt enough.

"Oh yes, you can twist my arm if you like!" she blundered, through thickening lips, for his accusation was causing her actual physical pain. "But the truth is what I understand. Not in words. I have not the gift for words. But know."

The abstractions made her shiver. (*Riders*, p. 34)

Many years later, tormented by Mrs. Jolley, one of White's insensate chorus, Mary blurts out:

"I believe. I cannot tell you what I believe in, any more than what I am. It is too much. I have no proper gift. Of words, I mean. Oh yes, I believe! I believe in what I see, and what I cannot see. I believe in a thunderstorm, and wet grass, and patches of light and stillness. There is such a variety of good. On earth. And everywhere." (*Riders*, p. 57)

Mary's inability with abstractions, her inability to use words to do more than name the nature of her gift, is a part of the price she pays for her understanding of the real. And the cost is high. Less fortunate than Aunt Theodora, she is brutalized by her father and shamed by her mother's insensitivity; she is prey to the bitchery of her housekeeper-nurse, Mrs. Jolley, and, by implication, to all the Mrs. Jolleys who make up the society around her. The eagerness of her acceptance of human understanding from the other *zaddikhim* (and from one childhood friend who lives overseas) shows that she is not a recluse by choice; she would share her understanding with her fellow human beings if she were able. It is in the nature of White's universe that gifts, even the most precious gifts, are limited and costly.

The limitations and the cost are perhaps most extreme for Arthur Brown, another spiritual sibling of Parker, Theodora, and Mary. Arthur identifies with Tiresias, the sexually ambiguous seer whom Zeus cursed with blindness and blessed with understanding. (White's own sexual "ambivalence has given

. . . [him] insights into human nature denied . . . to those who are unequivocally male or female" [*Glass*, p. 154]). Arthur is difficult to describe; all of the obvious adjectives require explanation. He seems retarded, especially in contrast to his twin brother Waldo, a dapper librarian and frustrated litterateur (who also identifies with Tiresias, but with Tiresias the gadfly about town rather than the suffering seer); yet Arthur reads Shakespeare and Dostoevsky and the *Bhagavad-Ghita* with an intuitive understanding of their most profound meanings. He seems inarticulate, but when the occasion demands he can express himself with a simplicity and wisdom that astonish. (One of White's major strengths as a novelist is his ability to write convincingly the most difficult scenes, scenes that persuade readers of the profound depths of characters from whom only shallows are expected). Arthur seems isolated by his mental limitations and by his bumbling and ugliness, yet he forms deep and lasting attachments. It is tempting to sum up the difficulties of describing Arthur's character with a short scene from *Voss; Voss*, the intellectual and explorer, has been talking to Judd, the illiterate rancher:

> Judd excused himself, saying, "I am a simple man." Which can read, "Most complex," Voss suspected.[5]

The following exchange both shows White's power as a novelist and focuses on the themes at hand. Arthur and Waldo are twin brothers, Waldo the proper librarian and Arthur still only an errand boy. The scene occurs after a horrified young librarian has told Waldo that there is a shaggy old man in the reading room; his appearance in the library for the past several weeks has been disturbing the more timorous patrons, and his requests for books that seem so obviously far beyond his ability have aroused the suspicions of the staff. Waldo is horrified to find that the uncouth intruder is his brother. Later they talk:

> All the loathing in Waldo was centered on *The Brothers Karamazov* and the glass marble in Arthur's hands.

"And *you* understand!" he said to Arthur viciously.

Arthur was unhurt.

"Not a lot," he said. "And not the Grand Inquisitor. That's why I forgot Mrs. Allwright's glasses today. Because I had to get there to read the Grand Inquisitor again." . . .

"What will it do for you? To understand? The Grand Inquisitor?" . . .

"I could be able to help people," Arthur said, beginning to devour the words.

Arthur continues:

> "Everybody's got to concentrate on something. Whether it's a dog. Or," he babbled, "or a glass marble. Or a brother, for instance. Or Our Lord, like Mrs. Poulter says."[6]

Later, in a continuation of the same conversation, Arthur admits that "Love . . . is what I fail in worst," and concludes, "If . . . I was not so simple, I might have been able to help you, Waldo, not to be how you are" (p. 198).

Arthur, who on the surface seems to be one of the simplest of White's major characters, has come closest to formulating the importance of "things." Each of White's saints, from those who, in current psychological jargon, are the least cognitively complex to those who are the most—from a Mary Hare or Arthur to a Voss or a Sir Basil—are able to "concentrate on something," to give their complete attention to something beyond themselves, to accept or to create a mandala. And it is part of Arthur's message that it makes no difference what we do concentrate on. For Arthur, it is primarily his solid mandala, the marbles he carries around and occasionally gives to a kindred spirit; less often, it is the bread he makes; and once it is a marvelously evocative dance. Any thing, from Mary's trees to Basil Hunter's conception of *King Lear* to Himmelfarb's mortal obsession with his Jewishness, if approached with total concentration and reverence, may become a mandala.

As a boy, Arthur looks up that strange word in the encyclopedia and discovers:

> " 'The Mandala is a symbol of totality. It is believed to be the "dwelling of the god." Its protective circle is a pattern of order super—imposed on—psychic chaos. . . .' " (*Mandala*, p. 229)

The young Arthur turns to his father for help with the definition; the father, an intelligent, fairly kindly, but shallow man, can give no help.

> Then Arthur realized Dad would never know, any more than Waldo. It was himself who was, and would remain, the keeper of mandalas, who must guess their final secret through touch and light. (*Mandala*, p. 232)

Appropriately enough, it is to Arthur, the "keeper of mandalas," that White gives perhaps the most crucial insight: "To think," he said, "that the world is another mandala!" The Waldos, the Mrs. Jolleys, and the Mr. Hares never get beyond concentration on themselves and their own interests.

Arthur may also have explained inadvertently the mechanism that permits White's saints to appear so totally impressive despite their failures, so complete despite the cost they pay for their gifts, because to concentrate on some*thing* is to give oneself up to it totally. Mary Hare's father is one of those who cannot concentrate; he is "forever conceiving plans" that "were not always executed" (*Riders*, p. 10). He plans additions to Xanadu that never materialize, plans breeding *escargot de Bourgone*, printing his own poems "on sheets of coloured silk, woven for that purpose on his own property," of writing a treatise on Catullus (*Riders*, p. 10). And the irony is that, by all worldly standards, he is a remarkably successful man. Because he concentrates on nothing, nothing is sacrificed—nothing, that is, except the wisdom and the sometimes terrifying peace known only to keepers of the mandala. Unfortunately for Mr. Hare, he seems to be one of the few outsiders even vaguely aware of what he has missed.

The line between White's saints and his fools is as thin as it is definitive; White draws it very precisely in a scene between Aunt Theodora and Aloysha Sergei Sokolnikov. Sokolnikov is a braggart, a poseur, a phony; yet he claims to share the saint's reverence for things. He tells Aunt Theodora:

> "*I* am an artist. . . . Although I cannot produce any material evidence, and it is doubtful whether my sensibility will ever crystallize in just that way, I am the Artist. Very few people have the capacity for creating life, for being. . . . Take that gob of spittle, for instance. A moonstone, a jewel. There is no denying that I am an artist."
>
> "Or an old clown," said Theodora. (*Story*, pp. 162–63)

Later, White curiously reverses the scene; Theodora and Sokolnikov are dining:

> She took the glass and it trembled clearly in her hand. The little glass had a clear and innocent beauty, before which she could not humble herself enough.
>
> "How right it is," she said.
>
> "What is?"
>
> "Finally, almost everything," Theodora said. (*Story*, p. 195)

Although in each scene one of the characters responds to a bit of mundane reality with appreciation, what we know of Theodora lets us accept hers as genuine; what we know of Soloknikov suggests strongly the need for doubt. The chief difference is that in the second passage the narrator tells us that Theodora could not "humble herself enough"; in the first passage, the speaker seems to be trying to convince Theodora of his own self-importance. The one vice not permitted White's saints is egotism, for egotism not only prevents the egotist from reverencing "things," it prevents him from understanding himself.

The holy simpleton in *Voss* is especially interesting because he is one of White's few developing characters, one of the few for whom the gift comes late in life. The main movement of *Voss* is an exploration into the interior of Australia, an explora-

tion much like that in Conrad's *Heart of Darkness,* in which
the physical journey into the primitive wilderness is also a
journey of self-discovery; although inspired by Voss, a kind of
combination of Kurtz and Marlow, with the colossal drive and
willfulness of the former and the practicality and in-
sightfulness of the latter, the journey is a means by which
each of the explorers discovers his deepest nature, his ability
to, in the words of Brendan Boyle, a homesteader, "peel
down to the last layer" (*Voss,* p. 163).

The holy simpleton of the exploration group is Harry
Robards, a sort of more rugged outback version of Arthur
Brown. As the journey progresses, Harry grows "simpler . . .
with distance. His simplicity is such, he could well arrive at
that plane where great mysteries are revealed. Or else become an imbecile" (*Voss,* p. 212). Later, Harry tells Voss,

> "I could have learned to black your boots, if you had 'a'
> been there, sir. But you would not 'a' been. And it would not
> be worth it. Not since you learned me other things."
> "What things?" asked Voss quietly, whose mind shouted.
> The boy was quiet, then, and shy.
> "I do not know," he said at last, shyly, "I cannot say it. But
> know. Why, sir, to live, I suppose. . . . " (*Voss,* p. 355)

The irony of the last sentence, and the depth of its meaning,
come partly from the fact that even Harry knows that he and
Voss will soon die. Harry has, apparently, arrived "at that
plane where great mysteries are revealed." Put in other
terms, he has found his mandala—in this case not an object,
but the vision that Voss has led him to.

Although the natural world for White's saints is a mandala
and "almost everything" in it is "right," it is never an idyllic
world. The brambles make very real scratches on Mary Hare's
knees; in *The Tree of Man,* floods kill. In three novels, *A
Fringe of Leaves, Voss,* and *The Eye of the Storm,* the cruelty
of nature is one of the major factors in the development of the
protagonists: Mary Roxburg's maturity is not won until shipwreck and subsequent life among the Australian aborigines

has left her with nothing but a fringe of leaves; and, as we have seen, *Voss* is the story of the physical defeat and spiritual victory of the explorers who leave civilization behind. The natives who eventually kill Voss and those who remain with him are but the final deliverers of a natural blow.

Most often in White's work, even the cruelty of nature is part of the working of the world as mandala, as object for meditation. The title of *The Eye of the Storm* suggests both the mandala and the peace to be found in the center of natural violence. Mrs. Hunter, who if not a saint has her moments of insight, tells of her experience when an island she was visiting was struck by a cyclone:

> "After I had been deserted—and reduced to shreds—not that it mattered: I was prepared for my life to be taken from me. Instead the birds accepted to eat out of my hands. There was no sign of hatred or fear while we were—encircled. What saved me was noticing a bird impaled on a tree. It must have been blown against the sharp spike left by a branch which had snapped off. I think I was reminded that one can't escape suffering. Though it's only human to try to escape it. So I took refuge. Again, it was the dead bird reminding me the storm might not have passed."[7]

The impaled bird has taught Mrs. Hunter what Arthur Brown seems to have instinctively understood, and to have understood more fully. As Arthur puts it in one of his poems, a poem that drives Waldo to a frenzy,

> All Marys in the end bleed
> but do not complane because they know
> they cannot have it any other way. (*Mandala*, p. 202)

For those born saints, like Arthur or Mary Hare or Theodora, suffering is a fact of life and an occasion for love; for those on their way to achieving sainthood, suffering is one of nature's more effective attention-getters. The cyclone in *The Eye of the Storm*, the jungle in *A Fringe of Leaves*, and the sheer bleak inhuman distance in *Voss* force the characters to an awareness they could not otherwise know.

If nature is a sometimes cruel mandala, the social world is equally so. It should be said at the outset that, although White admits in *Flaws in the Glass* to becoming increasingly political late in life, as novelist he gives little attention to political, economic, or religious systems as such. Although the wars, the political upheavals, the contention of ideological systems affect the lives of White's characters, his concern is persistently with the individual. At worst, the various ideological and religious systems support the self-righteous, like Mrs. Jolley of *Riders in the Chariot*, but it is most often a support that they would normally enough find among their own kind without benefit of any institutionalized belief. At best, a system can become either a support or a kind of mandala; Arthur Brown's friend Mrs. Poulter is certainly more comfortable for her attendance at church services, and Himmelfarb's Jewishness gives a concentrated purpose to his life that makes it one of the most powerful of mandalas.

Society in its loosest sense—the individuals who make up the communities in which White's saints live—fares badly in the fictions. The chorus of the insensate is almost a trademark of White's works. Having no mandala, they are most often petty egotists—sometimes annoying in the way that an unpleasant smell is annoying, sometimes deliberately or inadvertently murderous. In several of the works there is a strong hint that a spouse volunteers for a fatal accident rather than endure a longer life with Mrs. Jolley's friend Mrs. Flack and their ilk.

Quite often the insensate function as bitter comic relief; Mrs. Gage's monologue is typical. A postmistress, she has spent most of her married life hating her husband because he chose to paint rather than to make "something of himself." She is talking to Amy Parker, Stan's wife, some time after her husband's death:

"Poor Mr. Gage himself would have been surprised as one thing, if he had been there. I was only sorry he had gone, as I could see we might have worked up quite a little business. Anyway, to cut the story short, I sold the paintings. I must tell you I did well. I sold all but one, which I would not part with, for sentimental reasons, and because it is a work of art, Mr. Goldberg says, unequalled. I have it above the fireplace in the lounge. The frame alone is worth fifteen pounds. It is the one of the woman, but you will not remember. She is standing there—well, she is naked, to be frank. But why not? I am broadminded now, since I know it is worth the while." (*Tree*, pp. 381–82)

Browning never did it better. The crassness, the self-serving, the willingness to alter one's moral position if it is "worth the while," the hypocrisy of White's insensate mass may not make of society a Sodom and Gomorrah, but the sometimes murderous effects of its pettiness may justify the wrath of White's problematic God and the need for the *zaddikhim*. It is thoroughly appropriate in White's world that Blue, the young man who leads the mock crucifixion of Himmelfarb that eventually causes his death, is the illegitimate son of Mrs. Flack, a woman whose self-righteousness is at once comic, pitiable, and terrifying in its ordinariness.

No matter how hateful White's insensate mass may be, its members are seldom justifiably hateable. Except in a very few instances, White portrays character as a given; although White never spends time showing how his villains got that way, it seems safe to assume that Mrs. Jolley has always been Mrs. Jolley in the same way that Mary Hare has always been Mary Hare. Repeatedly, White seems at pains to point out that one's gifts are given early in life; they can be neither rejected nor altered, only developed. The elderly Mary Hare who skitters about the underbrush and keeps a pet snake was once a girl who nursed a bird back to health; the artists who live only for their art—Hurtle Duffield, Alf Dubbo, and Basil Hunter—seem to have as their first memories an obsession with their art. The result is a lack of character change for both the villainous and the virtuous that in the hands of a lesser writer would be disastrous.

The characters who seem to be exceptions—most notably Voss and Himmelfarb—change less than one might initially suppose. I have called Voss's trek into the heart of Australia a journey of self-discovery, but that is in part misleading. What Voss discovers is not some mystery that leaves him forever changed, as Conrad's Marlow is changed; he discovers rather what he has always had—the courage, the will, the integrity to follow his dream through privation, pain, bone-killing weariness, and illness, to the inevitable death of himself and his remaining comrades at the hands of the aborigines. And he not only endures, he endures without significant change of character.

While still at the edge of civilization, Voss had been told that the poverty of Australia's frontier is attractive because it offers the chance

> "to explore the depths of one's own repulsive nature, [an exploration which] is more than irresistible—it is necessary." . . .
>
> [After a pause, Brendan Boyle continues], "To peel down to the last layer, . . . There is always another and yet another, of more exquisite subtlety." (*Voss*, p. 163)

Given White's view of the stability of character, the implied comparison with the onion is especially apropos, for each layer of an onion is shaped very much like the preceding. From the start of the novel, Voss is an exceptionally neat, meticulous person. Toward the end of it, he tends to the very ill Frank Mersault, cleaning the mud and slime and the "uncontrolled feces" and accepting "the bottomless stomach of nausea" which "are the true colours of hell. . . . when he was finished, and had sat down the iron dish, he said, 'But I am no saint, Frank, and am doing this for reasons of necessity and hygiene'" (*Voss*, p. 265). Voss meets his death with the same sense of imperturbable responsibility in the face of the inevitable; we feel that, to borrow a catch phrase from *The Tree of Man*—"it was intended" (p. 120). One feels quite certain that if, at the last moment, Voss were saved from the aborigines, he could calmly nurse the wounded, simply because it had to be done, would gather provisions from the bushmen just as diligently as he had gathered them from the businessmen and markets of Sydney, and would resolutely set out again.

Unlike Voss, who never swerves, Himmelfarb seems to make a major change of direction. The young Jewish intellectual of preholocaust Germany deliberately chooses to become an unskilled laborer in Sydney, putting behind him both his academic fame and the sense of community offered by his fellow religionists. But even despite this dramatic reversal in Himmelfarb's life, the change is a change only of externals. His earliest memories are of his father's growing denial of his Jewish heritage and his mother's consequent sadness. He learns early and never forgets that he must never deny his Jewishness, for that is the part of himself by which he is, in Doris Lessing's very deep sense, "named."

White's refusal to let his major characters change in fundamental ways accounts in part for the strange feel of his novels. Even those set in a very particular era seem almost timeless. Wars are fought, condominiums replace Xanadu and the picturesque environs of Sydney, floods and cyclones happen; White's saints endure it all, their attention fixed on their mandalas, and grow in their gifts. To be a saint in White's universe is to live in the eye of the storm, to remain fixed while all else rages.

Like his other saints, White's artists are born with a gift they can neither refuse nor abandon. They share the qualities of his other saints—White once remarked that "the state of simplicity and humility is the only desirable one for artist or for man."[8] But the artist's humility is qualified by, in the words of Miss Soppforth, Aunt Theodora's teacher, "the artist's vanity, which is moved finally to express itself in objects" (*Story*, p. 56). Although "vanity" may be a surprising word in this context, I suspect White chose it very deliberately; it draws attention to the peculiar nature of the artist's limitation and—a point that is generally similar but yet quite different—suggests that the artist is a superior person, not because of the ability to create, but because of the qualities the artist and the saint share.

Although White does write rhapsodically about music, painting, and dance, he persistently refuses to place art and artists on a pedestal. Repeatedly in White's work, the first requirement of the artist is also the first requirement of the saint: reverent attention to "things." Aunt Theodora would write a poem about rocks; Voss, almost an artist, becomes absorbed in his discovery "that each visible object has been created for the purposes of love, that the stones, even, are smoother for the dust" (*Voss*, p. 175); Hurtle Duffield, one of the few successful artists White depicts, "loved the feel of a smooth stone,"[9] and eventually does a series of rock paintings. The persistence of the stone as a motif in the work of White's artists is almost certainly his deliberate way of drawing attention to the need of the saint and the artist to concentrate on the most mundane of objects. Mary Hare crawling through the brambles and Alf Dubbo, the aboriginal artist of *Riders in the Chariot*, drunk on his knees observing the apparent reciprocity of the motion as he watches the water in a gutter run past a curb, are performing essentially the same act.

If White's ordinary saints—his Mary Hares and Arthur Browns—are humble to a fault, his artists are vain to a fault. As we have seen, his ordinary saints repeatedly admit that they are inarticulate, that they understand but have not the gift of expression. The artists are certain almost from birth that they have a gift of expression and that, despite the cost, they must use that gift. Although it is quite easy to laugh at Mrs. Gage (the wife of the artist in *The Tree of Man*), White seldom lets us forget that life with an artist is, at the very least, trying. As Mrs. Hunter remarks of her son, Sir Basil, "What good is an artist to those who want to love him?" (*Storm*, p. 103).

White's fullest exploration of what it means to be an artist is in *The Vivisector;* the discoveries White opens to us are those he opens in other works, but the emphasis here is on the cost that must eventually be paid for the gift—and upon the rewards of using it fully. Hurtle's talent manifests itself when he is quite young; the first description of him in the novel shows him as a toddler entranced by the reflections of light from bottles in his father's junkyard; his first activity seems to be to draw pictures in the road dust. The first hint of the price Hurtle will have to pay for his ability occurs when, not yet school age, he realizes that "Momma and Poppa" would not understand, that "they talked about what was 'right' and 'honest,' and the price of things, but people looked down at their plates if you said something was 'beautiful'" (*The Vivisector,* p. 12).

It is, of course, to be expected that the artist will be misunderstood; Mrs. Gage is but one of a small army of minor characters in White's fictions who wish that artists were more like themselves. Kathy Volkov, the talented young pianist with whom Hurtle has an affair, probably expresses White's less generous views about what the masses expect of their artists. Kathy writes to Hurtle:

> I promise them I'll come back someday and play them Chopin and Gershwin and the lot, and that their Little Kathy from Paddo will always love them. If I were a polio victim as well, I'd be seven times more their idol. (*Vivisector,* p. 493)

Even the educated Mr. and Mrs. Courteney, who adopt Hurtle because of his precocity, find his obsession with painting difficult to live with. Mrs. Courtney objects first to Hurtle's use of her walls as canvas, then to the independence and honesty which his vision forces upon him; Mr. Courteney, like White's own relatives, tries his best to interest Hurtle in ranching, a "man's" profession.

The portrait of Hurtle would not be so interesting if it were only another picture of the misunderstood artist. Although Hurtle grumbles and gruffs at the people around him, his major conflict is within himself, between aspects of character indispensable for the development of his art. As an artist, he must be both vivisector and lover. The conflict is expressed vividly in "Pythoness at the Bidet," a series of pictures Hurtle does of his adopted sister Rhoda. Rhoda is a hunchback. Despite the advantages provided by her wealthy parents, Rhoda knows the anguish of being a young girl growing up ugly in a society that worships beauty. Although she and Hurtle fight as children, they slowly grow to like each other and, after years of separation, to love. As an adolescent traveling with his foster family in France, he once opened a door and surprised Rhoda, who was nude, her deformity grotesquely visible, using the bidet. The sight shocks him and becomes a memory that occasionally flickers through his painting. Finally, after years of germination, the memory is ready to become a painting. The following passage shows Hurtle's curious duality of emotion, the cruel honesty of the vision and the reverence for the object:

> It was a curiously weightless relief: to draw his sister Rhoda Courtney standing beside the bidet on its iron tripod in the hotel bedroom at St. Yves de Trégor. If he had betrayed a timid, wizened tenderness by raucously breaking open the door protecting her nakedness, the drawing were at last a kind of formal expiation: Rhoda's hump sat for moments on his own shoulders. As his resistance of years collapsed, he knew how he should convey the iron in crippled bones; he saw the mesh of light, the drops of moisture in the Thermogene tuft. (*Vivisector*, p. 245)

Much later, after achieving fame as an artist, he returns to Sydney and meets Rhoda. He invites her to his home so that she might consider whether to move in with him. She is looking at some of the paintings he has kept:

> The painting at which Rhoda was now staring so painfully was an early "Pythoness": judging by the naturalistic treatment, probably one of the first. His own horror at their finding themselves in the present situation couldn't prevent him from experiencing a twinge of appreciation for his forgotten achievement:

the thin, transparent arm; the sponge as organic as the human claw clutching it; the delicate but indestructible architecture of the tripod-bidet, beside which the rosy figure was stood up for eternity.

This aesthetic orgasm lasted what seemed only a long second before the moral sponge was squeezed: its icy judgement was trickling in actual sweat down his petrified ribs.

He heard Rhoda's voice. "I was born vivisected. I couldn't bear to be strapped to the table again."

"I can't help it," he apologized, "if I turned out to be an artist." (*Vivisector*, pp. 406–7).

The anguish of being an artist, apart from the sense of isolation created by any obsessive interest and the occasional self doubt, is precisely the anguish of the vivisectionist who loves the animals on which he must operate. Without love, there is no reverent attention; with love, there is an honest seeing of the object, and the pain occasioned by that honesty. To put this another way, the saint must love what he sees too deeply to sentimentalize it, for to sentimentalize the object is to deny its uniqueness, to insist on prettifying it for his own benefit rather than experiencing it in its wholeness. The sentimentalists of the world are the Mrs. Jolleys and Mrs. Flacks, persons who cannot even pretend to love unless their imaginations have turned their families into sentimental clichés.

The artist, however, assumes a burden the saint does not share. The saint can love the object—the stone, the family member, the friend—for what it is and keep quiet about its imperfections; the artist is compelled to publicize the object, hunchback and all. And each of White's artists whom we get to know well—Hurtle, Alf, Sir Basil—are anguished by the cruelty such honesty entails. The ability to feel that anguish may well be the distinction between the mature and the immature artist. The precocious but in some ways still very immature Hurtle paints a horrifying picture of his tutor, Mr. Shewcroft, then learns from his irate Maman that Mr. Shewcroft has committed suicide. His reaction is totally cold:

"I could do another," he said, "in another few days—a better one." . . .

He listened to her swishing, crying, but angrily, down the
passage. He really didn't care whether Harry Courtney obeyed
her orders and came to beat him. For the moment at least, he
wasn't frightened. He was still too exhausted by what had
turned out to be, not a game of his own imagination, but a
wrestling match with someone stronger; so he lay drowsily
looking at the painting on the wall, particularly those places
where he could see he had gone wrong. He had been led astray
by the brilliance of the red; whereas "Jack" Shewcroft's suicide
should have been black black. (*Vivisector*, p. 87)

Appropriately, the immature artist thinks he has painted
badly simply because he has misjudged color, a technical
fault; in reality, he has misused color· because he has paid
more attention to the "brilliance of the live red" than to de-
picting faithfully his subject. Put another way, he has failed in
reverent attention. It is a mistake he does not make after his
maturity. Years later, he views his "Marriage of Light," a picture of Nancy Lightfoot, a former lover who was killed in a fall
outside his house. This time, he has to force himself to concentrate on technique in order to make himself "less conscious of the body of an actual woman fragmented in the cause
of art." The picture of the actual woman, "Nancy Lightfoot
lying broken on a rocky ledge," is

> another picture of course, unpainted, and in every way too
> *black:* black dress, wounds stitched with the jet of flies, al-
> ready the long caravans of ants. By comparison, the "Marriage
> of Light" was a declaration of love. (*Vivisector*, p. 254)

His later paintings of Mr. Cutbrush and Kathy Volkov are
also, each in different ways, declarations of love, in Kathy's
case obviously so, in Cutbrush's less obviously. The inspiration for the Cutbrush painting is Hurtle's chance meeting one
night with the local grocer. During their conversation, Hurtle
tells Cutbrush of the unrequited homosexual love Hurtle's

agent felt for him and which Hurtle rejected. As Hurtle walks away, he turns to see Cutbrush masturbating; the scene becomes the subject of a painting.

Of most interest here is the fact that one source of the painting, in many ways one of Hurtle's cruelest, is a moment of shared understanding. Hurtle later describes the meeting with Cutbrush to Olivia, a rather jaded collector of his works. Cutbrush, he says, has

> "something rotten about him, but only slightly, humanly rotten in the light of the Divine Destroyer. I mean the grocer's attempts at evil are childlike beside the waves of enlightened evil proliferating from above. (*Vivisector*, p. 306)

Olivia, misinterpreting as the public often does in White's works, is harsher in her judgment than is the artist-vivisectionist. She interprets Hurtle's intention as the depiction of "a damned soul in the body of a solitary masturbator." In a wonderful later scene, Cutbrush tells Hurtle that at first he was horrified by the painting

> "till suddenly I realized that, unbeknownst to myself, I had been consummated, so to speak!" . . .
> "It was more than that. It was like as if, after attending regular service for years in a not very eyesthetical church, the same surroundings was illuminated by a—*religion!*" (*Vivisector*, pp. 513–14)

Despite the comedy of Cutbrush's naive overreaction, White's point is quite serious. Cutbrush has been transformed from an almost suicidal homosexual into a reasonably well-adjusted human being because he recognizes that he has been seen with honesty, understanding, and reverence.

The same development from selfish to sympathetic art occurs as Alf Dubbo, the painter in *Riders in the Chariot*, matures. Alf's early attempts at a Christ, undertaken merely to fulfill a promise made to get permission to use oil paints, are failures; his last painting, undertaken in partial atonement for his denial of Himmelfarb, is, we are given to understand, magnificiently moving. Once again, as in the "Pythoness at the Bidet" and the Cutbrush painting, there is that link between betrayal and portrayal, and the anguish that the latter requires the former.

Although the ability to create art is, for White, a gift, it is a gift that requires not only the anguish of betrayal but also the pain of labor and the agony of doubt. None of White's successful artists succeeds easily; a part of their gift is a passion for work. Hurtle Duffield, Alf Dubbo, and Kathy Volkov are obsessed not only with the desire to become artists, but equally with the desire to practice their crafts almost beyond the limits of human endurance. They practice their crafts with a kind of frenzy: Hurtle repeats his studies, constantly experimenting with shape, with color; Alf, barely able to read, pours over art books and finally literally paints himself to death; little Kathy Volkov, convinced of her talent, spends much of her childhood learning the incredibly difficult Lizst piano concerto. Even Sir Basil Hunter, the actor in *The Eye of the Storm*, blessed from birth with all the advantages of talent, wealth, and social connections, is noted for *"doing his homework. . . . .* Given a part which interested him, yes, he would ferret out the last refinement" (p. 130).

But despite the pages White gives to showing his characters learning their crafts, he says very little about technique. He writes almost contemptuously of teachers who stress it, as if they were a necessary evil. Mr. Khrapovitsky, Kathy Volkov's piano teacher, has "put together" "several machines" (*Vivisector*, p. 494). But the young pianist has learned her most important lessons from Hurtle, the old painter; he has taught her "to see, to know instinctively" (*Vivisector*, p. 494). Hurtle's own Mr. Khrapovitsky was a drawing master named Tyndall whose drawings were as "correct and silvery as himself" (*Vivisector*, p. 82). But before too quickly dismissing what the Khrapovitskys and Tyndalls have to teach, we must remember what Sir Basil tells Sister DeSantis when she asks him if he allows himself to be carried away by his emotions. He explains that the actor certainly has "got to *feel* the situation. But he musn't drown in it. That's where his technique saves him—leaves him free to speak and breathe—to convey." (*Storm,* p. 343)

We must remember also that for all his genius, for all his efforts, the entirely self-taught Alf Dubbo is never successful as a painter. His work is wild and it is magnificient; but, except for one moment at a drunken party, it is never accepted, its promise never filled. The music of Kathy Volkov or the painting of Hurtle may achieve that final purpose of art—if not of the artist: they may become mandala for others. Dubbo's painting remains a mandala only for Dubbo.

In addition to the agony of hurting others and the sheer physical labor of art, White's artists, at least those who reach maturity, are afflicted with doubts. The least significant perhaps is the purely personal doubt, the fear that one is not good enough, that leads Sir Basil to consider the " 'need to reject . . . before you are rejected' " (*Storm,* p. 345) and Hurtle to suffer through a dry spell. More significant is what might be called the metaphysical doubt, the doubt that stems less from fear of personal failure than from awe before the mandala of the world, from the recognition of the profundity of things so deeply felt that the artist fears that any attempt at expression will ultimately remain as inarticulate as the insights of a Mary Hare or an Arthur Brown.

For Sir Basil, the doubt is about his ability to play Lear, that most demanding of all dramatic roles that "can probably never be played" except and only perhaps by a Blake or a Swift (*Storm,* p. 350). The role, which to Sir Basil seems to represent the ultimate truth about humanity, is simply too awesomely real. Its analogue for Hurtle is the painting he plans in order to "refute all controversies." His sister tells him,

"I think I'm beginning to understand your painting, Hurtle, after these last two exhibitions. The horrors are less horrible if you've created them yourself. Is that it?" . . .

"No," he said, and it cannoned off the coarse white kitchen

place. "I'm trying"—already he realized how stupid it would sound—"I'm *still* trying to arrive at the truth."

"Then perhaps I don't understand after all. The truth can look so dishonest."

"Exactly!" He ricocheted, when he should have shot her straight to the floor. "That's why we're at loggerheads. . . . it's not dishonest! It's not! If it were only a question of paint—but is it dishonest to pour out one's life-blood?" (*Vivisector*, pp. 472–73)

At the conclusion of the confrontation, Rhoda tells him:

"Your painting. And yourself. But those, too, are 'gods' which could fail you."

This, perhaps the worst truth of all, he had never been able to face except in theory. (p. 474)

Despite their doubts, Sir Basil will "have another go" at Lear (*Storm*, p. 350); and Hurtle, infirm, hampered by a stroke and by pain, will attempt his largest work.

Despite the intense, often painful and always heroic work the gift demands of artists like Hurtle, Sir Basil, Alf, and Kathy, White goes to great lengths to humble his artists, to remind them and us that their insights are not unique, and that even the incommunicative saint may make art. Perhaps the most direct reminder, and the most humbling, occurs in the conversation between Sir Basil and his mother's housekeeper, an elderly lady who had once been a music-hall entertainer. Sir Basil, who has been knighted for his talent as an actor and who takes his abilities so seriously that he is willing to participate in an act that will hasten his mother's death in order to gain enough income to continue his work, listens as the housekeeper describes her past performances:

"the life of theatre is necessary for us—for you and me, Sir Basil Hunter. This drunkenness! This is why—when my family is murdered—the man who is my *Lieb' und Leib* is lost—I still look to *Tingeltangel*—why, when I run out through the

drenching lights, I can bear their worst laughter, their whis-
key breath, afterwards the kisses, the praise and promises, the
dirty gestures of both men and women. Even though these are
only skulls, and false bosoms, and male vanity around the tables, I have to air my song—the little dance-step they expect—*ein zwei drei.* . . . I have no voice. Except that of
drunkenness. Which is what they have been longing for. It is
their need—and mine. They laugh. They wish to touch my
hat, my stick, my coat-tails of almond velvet. They aspire—to
what? to be translated out of themselves? to be destroyed?
Certainly, Sir Basil Hunter, there is nothing of this that you
will not have experienced."

He was too humiliated to reply. (*Storm,* p. 148)

Much later, Sir Basil is almost equally chagrined when Sister
De Santis reminds him that acting is much like nursing—both
require a delicate balance of technique and involvement.

Although White's artists are energetic creators, dedicated
to little but learning their crafts so that they can better express
their visions, he has a high respect for the occasional work of
art, the spontaneous creative overflow of powerful feelings
into an art form, the celebration of a moment of epiphany by
song or dance or poetry. Although the celebration is presumably forever beyond the reach of the Mrs. Jolleys and the Mrs.
Gages, it seems within the range of anyone who can experience completely and appropriately some aspect of external
reality. The celebration may be as fleeting and as surprising as
the dance of the unnamed demolition worker near the end of
Riders in the Chariot:

How the young labourer became inspired enough to describe
those great sweeping arcs with his moulted fan, nobody understood, nor did the artist himself realize that, for all its elasticity
of grimace and swivelling impudence of bum, his creation was
a creaking death dance. But the young man danced. For the
audience, his lithe thighs introduced an obscenity of life into
the dead house. The candid morning did not close down on his

most outrageous pantomime. The people hooted, but in approval. Until at the end, suddenly, the tattered fan seemed to fly apart in the dancer's hand, the tufts of feathers blew upward in puffs of greyish-pink smoke, and the young man was left looking at a few sticks of tortoiseshell.

At once he began to feel embarrassed, and went off stage, careful to close the door upon his exit. (*Riders*, p. 503)

The dance, including the final embarrassment and the exit, is as dramatically appropriate and effective as any scene Sir Basil could have staged. Like Arthur Brown's dance near the end of *The Solid Mandala,* and like the final paintings of Alf and Hurtle, it is an ecstatic yet painful summation, the creation of a memory, a mandala, for the spectators to carry away.

Arthur's dance, like his poetry, is the expression of deepest feeling; it is also an expression of his intuitive understanding of the persons who most touch his life. The dance itself is a moving mandala with Mrs. Poulter, a friendly neighbor, the only witness. The passage deserves lengthy quotation because it speaks so eloquently of White's faith in the ability of the inarticulate saint to express, on rare occasions, the love and understanding that are the reward of a lifetime of reverent attention:

In the first corner, as a prelude to all that he had to reveal, he danced the dance of himself. Half clumsy, half electric. He danced the gods dying on a field of crimson velvet, against the discords of human voices. Even in the absence of gods, his life, or dance, was always prayerful. . . .

In the second corner he declared his love for Dulcie Feinstein, and for her husband, by whom, through their love he was, equally, possessed, and their children still to be conceived. Into their corner of his mandala he wove their Star, on which their three-cornered relationship was partly based. . . .
In Mrs. Poulter's corner he danced the rite of ripening pears, and little rootling suckling pigs. Skeins of golden honey were swinging and glittering from his drunken mouth. Until he

reached the stillest moment. He was the child she had never carried in the dark of her body, under her heart, from the beat of which he was already learning what he could expect. . . .

Mrs. Poulter was at that point so obviously moved, she would have liked to throw the vision off, or stop him altogether, but he would not let her.

He had begun to stamp, but brittlely, rigid in his withering. In the fourth corner, which was his brother's, the reeds sawed at one another. There was a shuffling sound of dry mud, a clattering of dead flags, or papers. Of words and ideas skewered to paper. . . . Thus pinned and persecuted, what should have risen in pure flight, dropped into a dry twitter, a clipped twitching. He couldn't dance his brother out of him, not fully. They were too close for it to work, closest and farthest when, with both his arms, he held them together, his fingers running with candle-wax. He could not save. At most a little comfort gushed out guiltily, from out of their double image, their never quite united figure. In that corner of the dance his anguished feet had trampled the grass into a desert. . . .

Till in the centre of their mandala he danced the passion of all their lives, the blood running out of the backs of his hands, water out of the hole in his ribs. His mouth was a silent hole, because no sound was needed to explain.

And then, when he had been spewed up, spat out, . . . he added the little quivering footnote on forgiveness. (*Mandala*, pp. 256–58)

Despite the fact that the non-artist, and even the most inarticulate of saints, may occasionally create, the power of the creation is, it would seem, largely contextual. Arthur's dance, like the dance of the demolition worker, inspires the spectators precisely because they are already involved in the scene and precisely because the scene is one that requires an appropriate gesture. White seems to claim that they may speak with eloquence and passion only on those rare occasions when the circumstances are exactly right; the true creative genius literally lives to create, lives to hone talent to the sharpest possible edge in order to express intentionally what the saint expresses accidentally. White's saints may by chance create a mandala; his artists create their mandalas deliberately and repeatedly.

Perhaps because of the deliberation, the technique, and the power of the creative genius are effective publicly rather than privately. Arthur's dance affects Mrs. Poulter and the reader profoundly because we are privy to the meaning of Arthur's experience. His dance is an epiphany, a celebration of a series of events we have shared, and moves us because it incarnates in a single memorable vision much of the complexity and intensity we have vicariously shared with Arthur. In a sense, the dance is an embodiment of all that Arthur is. By contrast, Sir Basil's roles are, to an extent, an embodiment of all that he is not. Although his great ability as an actor does stem from his past, from all that he has seen and done and felt, there is an important sense in which he knows that great actors must be empty, lest their knowledge smother their roles. Rather than project self, as Arthur does, the genuine artist must achieve something very like what Keats called "negative capability"—the ability to become, selflessly and completely, the other. I suspect that is why Sir Basil knows that he is not yet ready for Lear; he has the technical ability to empty himself, but still lacks the courage to fill himself with the agony of the abandoned, half-mad king.

Perhaps White's greatest tribute to art is his willingness, wherever feasible, to use the creation of a work of art as a mandala to summarize the significance of his own works. To Arthur's dance and Sir Basil's possible Lear could be added White's descriptions of the final paintings of both Hurtle Duffield and Alf Dubbo. Hurtle's final days are spent laboring, despite a stroke and its ensuing weakness, over a gigantic painting that

> might grow eventually into what he saw as his compendium of life. Sometimes memory fed him; more often, intuition: in-

sights of such intensity he felt he should have been able to relate them to actual experience; but in this he failed mostly. (*Vivisector*, p. 556)

Yet the painting contains echoes of Kathy Volkov, of his rock series, of cats—of almost all that he has known and loved. But despite the work's admitted self-indulgence, Hurtle knows that he is "also this girl," and that he is "being painted with, and through, and on" (*Vivisector*, p. 556). The same inspired fury, the same rush of the past, impels the last work of Alf Dubbo as he paints furiously to record the meaning of Himmelfarb's death before he himself dies.

Although the final paintings of Hurtle and Alf are perhaps the most impressive of the mandala-art works in White's novels, they are so appropriate that they are expected; the only surprise is White's ability to carry off the obvious and, by the intensity of his style and the completeness of his vision of the mandala, to make it effective. The mandala at the end of *The Tree of Man* is, on the other hand, a complete surprise. The grandson of the protagonist, still a very young boy, is moved to begin contemplating what may very well be his first poem:

> So he would write a poem of life, of all life, of what he did not know, but knew. Of all people, even the closed ones, who do open on asphalt and in trains. He would make the trains run on silver lines, the people still dreaming. . . . Little bits of coloured thought, that he had suddenly, and would look at for a long time, would go into his poem. . . . His poem was growing. It would have the smell of bread, and the rather grey wisdom of youth, and his grandmother's kumquats, and girls with yellow plaits exchanging love-talk behind their hands, and the blood thumping like a drum, . . .
>
> As his poem mounted in him he could not bear it, or rather, what was still his impotence. And after a bit, not knowing what else to do but scribble on the already scribbled trees, he went back to the house in which his grandfather had died, taking with him his greatness, which was still a secret.

So that in the end there were the trees. The boy walking through them with his head drooping as he increased in stature. Putting out shoots of green thought. So that, in the end, there was no end. (P. 499)

Like the paintings of Hurtle and Alf, or the dances of Arthur and the demolition worker, the young boy's incipient creation is White's way of focusing for the reader the meaning and the emotion of what has happened.

Although at this stage the poem is still White's and not young Parker's, the art does for the boy and the reader what White feels art must do. Reality, without the interpretation of art, can, as Rhoda tells Hurtle, "look so dishonest." The truth, the reality, within the novels is the death of Himmelfarb and Tom Parker, Rhoda's hump and Mr. Cutbrush's lonely masturbation, Frank Mersault's torn anguish at the pain of life and Mary Roxburgh's reduction to nothing more than that strength she has within herself; it is the hurricane and the desert expanse of Australia. Truth is the suicide of Hurtle's tutor, Mr. Shewcroft, whom Rhoda had "always seen . . . as unkempt and repulsive, but as soon as he's killed himself I began to think of him as handsome and brave" (*Vivisector*, p. 473). Rhoda, the non-artist, can endure reality only by sentimentalizing it. Hurtle, years after the painting, realizes that he had to make the painting of Shewcroft, however imperfect it was, so that he could "find some formal order behind a moment of chaos and unreason. Otherwise it would have been too horrible and terrifying" (*Vivisector*, p. 473).

It is tempting, at this point, to say the usual things about art as a formal vehicle for the discovery of order, and most of those things would probably be appropriate. It is, after all, art—both White's art and White's description of Alf's art—that places Himmelfarb within a context that both intensifies Alf's tragedy and shows its place within the pattern of our culture, just as White's thrusting of young Parker into prominence at the end of *The Tree of Man* magnifies both the poignance and the significance of the life of Stan Parker. But within White's view of the role of art is another role perhaps most analogous to the sacrifice of the Last Supper.

White certainly invites the analogy with the Christ symbolism that so heavily surrounds the death of Himmelfarb and, to a lesser extent, Arthur's dance. The sacrifice, it must be remembered, is an act of love; we have seen that Hurtle's and Alf's early pictures are failures because they are without love, and we have seen the reverent attention that the artist and the saint must give to things. Alf's painting of Himmelfarb, Hurtle's paintings of Rhoda and Kathy and Cutbrush and stones and cats are acts of love, as is Arthur's dance and young Parker's poem. Like Christ, the artist is both priest and willing victim at the sacrifice. Hurtle, Alf, and Arthur each clearly assume the pain of those they portray; for each, the actual creation is a period of intensely triumphant pain—Hurtle and Alf, painting their final works, are acutely aware of the suffering their work causes them; Arthur, during his dance, develops a series of wounds that suggest the stigmata. Even young Parker, too youthful for his final passion, is aware of the personal hurt that will accompany creation.

I do not mean to suggest that the artist or the saint suffers deliberately in order to alleviate the suffering of the rest of us; Himmelfarb, the most thoroughly Christlike of all White's major characters, seems to be the only one (with the possible exception of Arthur) to have any sense of that possibility. They suffer because that is their nature, because Hurtle and Alf and Arthur and Mary Hare and Theodora and Frank Mersault and Voss and as many others understand unflinchingly the pain that is a part of life, and because they empathize with those who suffer it. Yet, regardless of the intention of the artist, White insists on the palliative power of art.

Most broadly, to continue the Last Supper analogy, art is communion, not only between the artist and his subject but between the subject and the viewer. Like the bread and wine, themselves a kind of mandala, a token of the supreme hidden forces of the universe—the work is a viaticum for the sharing of the full experience of the artist, for sharing the love, the understanding, the sacrifice. Those who are not in a state of grace will feel none of its power. Like Turner and Ralph Angus as they discuss Frank Mersault's poems, they are likely to be disturbed, finding only "mad things . . . to blow the world up, anyhow the world that you and me knows." Although Turner is "partial to a good read" of poetry, he suggests that Frank's poems are "like certain bits of the Bible. They are cut up, like, but to make trouble, not to make sense" (*Voss*, p. 256). The poems merely disquiet Turner. But Voss, who is surprisingly sensitive to poetry, music, stones—all the things that White reverences—finds Frank's poems too much to bear; he reads them with much the same despair and anger that Frank must have felt when he wrote them.

Reactions to art range in White's work from rapt involvement (usually when an artist or saint is admiring the work—Hurtle listening to Kathy Volkov play, for example, or Theodora living through and in the cello music of Moriatis), through a sharing of peace and understanding, to a simple improvement of mood. When Topp, the music master in *Voss*, plays his flute,

> Exquisite, pearly, translucent notes would flower on that unpromising wood, and fall from the windows as they faded, causing bullock teams to flick their tails, or some drunkard to invoke Jesus Christ. On days when Topp played his flute the dumpy house was garlanded with music, and it did sometimes happen that people passing in the street, through dust or mud, would grow gladder without thinking to discover why.
> (P. 27)

Most often, though, only those who are ready for it acquire peace and understanding. As Amy Parker looks at the paintings left by Mr. Gage, she learns that "also a bottle can express love. She had never before seen a bottle of adequate beauty. This one tempted her to love her neighbor" (*Tree*, p. 289). Many years later, watching a performance of *Hamlet*, Amy Parker reviews her life, a life of almost unrelieved plainness, and learns that she "was too humble then," that she "could have been loved in any disguise" (p. 417). Stan Parker reacts to the same performance by realizing that he is going to die; the realization is met with restraint and acceptance.

Although White frequently describes in great detail what gets into the paintings and plays and music that make up such a large part of his subject, he does not tell us overtly what they transmit. We never know precisely what in *Hamlet* leads Stan and Amy Parker to their meditations. We know, rather, with all the power and all the imprecision of deeply felt emotional knowledge. Like Arthur Brown fumbling through the *Bhavagad-Gita*, White believes that at the center of the work of art is a love that will somehow help us "not be how we are." Neither its nature nor its message can be specified further, for like Arthur's stones and Mary Hare's trees, the work of art is a mandala, a call to purification rather than thought, an aid to meditation upon the mystery of the universe rather than a symbol that demystifies the mysterious. To those in the state of grace it is, like the stones and the bread and the chairs that are such frequent motifs in White's work, neither more nor less than an object for reverent attention.

Chapter 4

John Fowles

The Artist as Aristos

> *He still clung to his inmost grain of conviction—that freedom, especially the freedom to know oneself, was the driving-force of human evolution; whatever else the sacrifice, it must not be of complexity of feeling, and its expression, since that was where, in social terms, the fundamental magic (or chink in the door) of mutation inside the nucleic-acid helix took place.*[1]

Near the end of *The French Lieutenant's Woman*, Sarah Woodruff attempts to explain her refusal to renew her relationship with Charles Smithson by telling him that she has seen "artists destroy work that might to the amateur seem perfectly good." Charles replies that he cannot be answered "with observations, however apposite, on art." Sarah replies that "they were intended to apply to life as well."[2] Sarah's comparison of life and art is both appropriate for her and revealingly typical of Fowles. From the living theater of Conchis's retreat in *The Magus* to a young woman's telling a detective that the key to a disappearance might best be discovered by conceiving of it as a fiction in "The Enigma," from the art student in Fowles's first published novel, *The Collector*, to Milt Green in *Mantissa*, art enters Fowles's world as a topic in itself, as a metaphor for life and for living, as a test of character, and as an analogue for all things created and their creation. Among Fowles's published fictions, only the translation of "Eliduc" in *The Ebony Tower* lacks a central character who is either an artist or in some way associated with artists. In his latest, *Mantissa*, Miles Green and his Muse, Erato, spend almost two hundred pages bickering, like lovers who have known each other so long that both the quarreling and the lovemaking have become rituals; Erato even tells Green, a thinly disguised Fowles, that all his major heroines have been representations of the Muse.

The high population of artists and near artists would seem obsessive, even narcissistic, were it not that Fowles's special understanding of the similarities between art and life are conducive both to fine fictionalizing and to a broad and balanced view of reality. With very little stretching, a definition drawn from Fowles's depiction of successful artists is almost a textbook definition of the fictional hero: the artist is the person who chooses, whose right choices reflect his deepest and best self, whose choices directly conflict with powerful and significant forces (sometimes internal, sometimes external, sometimes both). In Fowles's work, the drama of being an artist has little to do with the clichéd artistic temperament and crocheteness (Henry Breasley in "The Ebony Tower" is the only notable example of that) and almost everything to do with being an individual, a human being who elects to stand apart from others and from the pressures of his age. Miles Green's problem in *Mantissa* is precisely to learn to compromise with a muse whose notions about art have been formed by her past and to not compromise with an age that demands that he write novels that distort his understanding of the world, of himself, and of the nature of the novel. Whether one seems born with the quality, like Breasley; realizes it is unattainable, like David Williams in "The Ebony Tower"; or agonizes his

way toward it, like Daniel Martin—Fowles's conception of the
artist has a built-in tension that permits him to use the art-life
comparison both as a thematic metaphor and as an integral
element in the drama.

A commitment to art, Fowles feels, is a commitment to life;
a commitment to life is a prerequisite for art. Perhaps none of
Fowles's characters learns that so sadly and so emphatically as
David Williams. It is, in fact, one way of approaching the
dominating idea of "The Ebony Tower." Williams is a kind of
more unfortunate Daniel Martin—more unfortunate perhaps
because the short-story form allows him only one opportunity
to make a crucial decision. He apparently has everything: his
paintings sell, his wife and children seem to have no problem
more serious than measles, and even his reviews win him
friends. Like most of Fowles's major characters (the only exception appears in *The Collector*), he is given an opportunity
to make a free decision, specifically, to make love with a
young lady he much admires. There is no reason to believe
that there would be any unpleasant repercussions. But he
hesitates for the briefest of moments; the spell is broken, the
opportunity lost, and "he had failed both in the contemporary
and the medieval sense; as someone who wanted sex, and as
someone who renounced it."[3]

The failure to decide either way is for Fowles a consequence of the greatest sin; as David realizes, "his failure . . .
was merely the symbol, not the crux of the matter" (*Tower*,
p. 109). Some of the ramifications of this wonderfully rich story will have to wait for discussion; for now, the important issue
is that David's failure to decide is symptomatic of his limitation as an artist. For the first time, he is forced to realize that
he is chronically "crippled by common sense" (p. 112), that
"he was born, still was, and always would be: a decent man
and an eternal also-ran" (p. 113).

David's artistic career has been a series of compromises, a
halting, a withdrawal from any extreme; "always fond of being
liked, he developed a manner carefully blended of honesty

and tact" (p. 14). His criticism always finds something good to say about a show; although abstractions, his paintings are a comfortable size and pattern and color for hanging in a living room; his style hangs back just a bit from being extreme. The results are superficial success and profound failure—and, more terribly, a realization that, as Durrell puts it, he will be one of those who have died without having lived. His last words in the story, when his wife asks him about his experience, are, " 'I survived' " (p. 114).

David's failure may be stated in another way, one that leads more precisely—albeit more circuitously—to one of Fowles's major themes: given an opportunity, he refuses to exercise his freedom. Here it is appropriate to consider Fowles's view of the universe and our place in it before further defining the province of art. For Fowles, freedom is such a central concept that he admits of "only one good definition of God: the freedom that allows other freedoms to exist" (*Woman*, p. 106). Like Dostoevsky in The Grand Inquisitor scene from *The Brothers Karamazov,* he is realistic enough to know that the only meaningful freedom is the freedom to, in theological terms, sin or, in more practical language, err. Like Dostoevsky, he accepts the fact that mistakes entail unpleasant consequences, which is precisely why they are mistakes. An author's "deafness" during a robbery results in the destruction of his manuscript ("Poor Koko" in *The Ebony Tower*); a refusal to accept Alison's love leads to the reeducation of Nicholas on Phraxos (*The Magus*); Charles's uncertainty about his feelings permits Sarah to escape easily (*The French Lieutenant's Woman*). Again with *The Collector* as the only notable exception, each of Fowles's fictions examines the consequences of choosing or not choosing. Remembering the Kierkegaardian image of stepping into darkness, Daniel Martin realizes that "not stepping became the supreme folly and cowardice" (*Martin*, p. 561). What one chooses is infinitely less important than the act of choosing.

The essential trick is to avoid the choice of any ideology that locks one into a position—a trick which, for all practical purposes, means avoiding commitment to any ideology. Fowles sums up several possibilities:

> A Christian says: "If all were good, all would be happy." A socialist says: "If all were happy, all would be good." A fascist says: "If all obeyed the state, all would be both happy and good." A lama says: "If all were like me, happiness and goodness would not matter." A humanist says: "Happiness and goodness need more analysis." This last is the least deniable view.[4]

Much of Fowles's fiction is devoted to the destruction of illusions of "absolute knowledge and absolute power. The destruction of such illusions seems to me still an eminently humanist aim."[5] His scorn is persistently directed against characters who are, like Mitford (*Magus*) and Mrs. Poulteney (*Woman*), so bound by their moral positions that they judge others by them; his pity is reserved for those who, like Anthony Mallory (*Martin*), learn to live without the specious comfort of dogmatism or who, like David Williams and Charles Smithson, glimpse a freedom that they may or may not be able to attain.

Although Fowles does not do so overtly, it is fair to relate his detestation of moral inflexibility to his conception of evolution. Basically, he sees moral inflexibility as socially anti-evolutionary: it promotes stasis because of its obsessive acceptance of the rightness of a past formulation of a code of behavior and, consequently, denies others the freedom to develop the variety of traits necessary if natural selection is to have a sufficiently broad pool of human abilities from which to select. Perhaps the quickest way to work into Fowles's view of evolution is to state rather baldly the attributes he ascribes to it: evolution is impersonal, social as well as natural, and horizontal. Whatever telic or inertial force guides the development of our universe cares nothing for humanity either individually or generally; humanity may be "an aberration of evolution, a doomed sideline" (*Aristos*, p. 62). Individually, in Fowles's metaphor, no matter how important my flowers are to me, "I cannot assume that the purpose of evolution is to give them to me" (*Aristos*, p. 25). Our only importance is self-importance; our only worth, self-worth.

Social evolution implies both that societies evolve and that social evolution is as impersonal as natural evolution. The idea of social evolution permeates *The French Lieutenant's Woman* from its realization by Charles to its announcement as one of several possible chapter headings; from the development of Charles's character and the presentation of minor characters to frequent asides that require us to note social change. Early in the novel, Fowles begins reminding us that styles of dress change, that the fashion in discomfort has changed from Victorian boredom to contemporary neurosis, that the Victorian ideas of the creation of the world have changed, that sexual mores have changed. Whether the incident is as trivial as the comment upon the gaudiness of Ernestina's dress or as socially significant as Sam's rise from valet to entrepreneur, almost everything is in flux. Yet Fowles is equally persistent in forcing us to notice that despite the changes, the extent and quality of human happiness probably remain constant, that social evolution is neither a progressive vertical climb to perfection nor a downward slide to chaos but—from a human perspective—a kind of horizontal movement that may greatly affect individuals, but which neither benefits nor harms humanity as a whole.

A large part of the purpose of *The French Lieutenant's Woman* seems to be to force contemporary readers to understand that we are neither wiser nor more foolish, neither better nor worse, than our ancestors. Fowles lets us laugh briefly at Charles and Ernestina in their preposterous dress, then reminds us that ours is no more rationally conceived—that Charles hunting fossils in woolens is as comfortable as we would be in cut-offs. He sends Sarah to bed with a maid, only to remind us that the price we pay for sexual sophistication is an ignorance of innocence. In a wonderfully complex scene, Charles and Sarah make love with what seems to be a passion hardly conceivable for Victorians, until Fowles reminds us that the act took only ninety seconds. Just as it seems that our disdain of the stereotypical Victorian sexual performance is after all justified, we are forced to remember that for Sarah it was an artfully contrived seduction and that for Charles it was at least as passionate as anything a modern might experience. As Conchis tells Nicholas in a passage that could almost be a note to *The French Lieutenant's Woman:*

> You young people can lend your bodies now, play with them, give them as we could not. But remember that you have paid a price: that of a world rich in mystery and delicate emotion. It is not only species of animal that die out, but whole species of feeling. And if you are wise you will never pity the past for what it did not know, but pity yourself for what it did. (*Magus,* p. 149).

Not only do whole species of feeling die, but social classes rise and fall. Most of the characters in *The French Lieutenant's Woman* are shaped by the currents of their age and are, in part, exempla of the shaping power of those currents. Mrs. Poulteney and Ernestina are shaped by currents that are rapidly dying, and so are both comic and pathetic. Dr. Grogan is Victorian enough to threaten to horsewhip Charles for being a cad, but modern enough to be a Darwinian; Sam's predecessors accepted their lowly roles in a relatively stable society, but Sam himself becomes that typical figure of the late nineteenth and twentieth centuries, the self-made businessman. Charles is acutely uncomfortable with most of the Victorian values, and he is intellectually modern enough to be a Darwinian, but he is totally unaware of Karl Marx working nearby in the British Museum Library and too personally conservative to change his allegiance to the new aristocracy, the emerging merchant class. Ernestina, in many ways the ideal Victorian woman, is replaced by Sam's granddaughter, just as Charles's place in society is taken by Sam. Fowles wants us to understand that the changes are not an unmixed blessing; there is neither progress nor regress, but simply change.

Perhaps nothing so dramatizes Fowles's insistence upon the horizontality of social evolution as the endings of *The French Lieutenant's Woman*. If we include the false ending, Charles's dream, each of the three conclusions is built around a moral imperative, a social norm so generally accepted that—although it may be frequently violated—it is seldom questioned. The norm in the dream ending, in which Charles returns to Ernestina and enters her father's business, is properly Victorian, appropriate to a world in which duty and responsibility are the only socially acceptable bases for choice. But for Charles, that ending can be only a dream; Charles is too little a man of his century to let its imperatives dominate him. The ending that Charles would prefer is the second, in which he finds and holds Sarah; it assumes a world in which Love Conquers All, a world in which decisions are based on devotion rather than duty, romance rather than responsibility. It is a world whose aspirations and moral sense are embodied in the countless light operas written in the first quarter of this century and whose exemplary event is the abdication of King Edward "to marry the woman I love." It is a world in which, if Charles gets Sarah, we may assume that God's in his heaven and all's right with the world. Although many romantics still prefer such an ending, the third seems best to epitomize the contemporary moral imperative. Sarah rejects Charles for motives that to earlier ages would have seemed incredibly selfish, but which many moderns accept: the affair with Charles was an experience which she needed for her personal growth; she has benefited from the experience, and Charles is no longer necessary.

If we try to choose which ending is "right" either morally or in terms of consistent character development, we fall precisely into the same traps that Fowles has set consistently throughout *The French Lieutenant's Woman*—those of judging others' standards by our own and of assuming an inflexibility of character that denies freedom. It is typical of the precision with which Fowles works that each ending fulfills the hopes of one of its participants at the expense of the others: if the Victorian Ernestina wins, Charles and Sarah lose their preferred options; if the more modern Charles wins, Ernestina loses and Sarah is denied her freedom; if Sarah wins, Charles and Ernestina are left alone. Whichever moral imperative operates—duty, love, personal growth—the amount of human happiness seems to remain constant. It is a splendid example of what Fowles in *The Aristos* calls "relativity of recompense"—the notion that (a) in whatever stage of social or natural evolution, the quantity and quality of pleasure remains the same and (b) although the case may be different for humanity because we can, unlike other creatures, compare our experiences, the comparison is a "'mirage'" (p. 59). This notion of relativity of recompense or horizontal evolution is for Fowles probably the major intellectual basis for morality, for "comprehending the purpose (and ultimately, the justice) of existence in human form" (*Aristos*, p. 142).

Fowles is neither so naive as to believe that freedom is absolute nor so pessimistic as to believe that it is unattainable. He admits the obvious physical limitations to freedom, even to the point of admitting the "genetic injustice of life," the fact that not all men are born with "an equal dispensation of energy, talent and good luck" (*Martin*, p. 72). The hope for freedom, Fowles argues in almost everything he writes, lies in the kind of education that forces sufficient self-examination so that any crucial choice is an act of will rather than an act of inertia. Our greatest fear, Fowles writes, is of the "nemo"—literally the fear that we are a "nobody." The fear is so great that "all of our acts are partly devised to fill or to mask the emptiness we feel at the core" (*Aristos*, p. 49).

There are two principal ways to defeat the nemo: I can conform or I can conflict. If I conform to the society I live in, I will use the agreed symbols of success, the status symbols, to prove that I am somebody. Some uniforms prove I am a success; others hide that I am a failure. One of the attractions of the uniform is that it puts a man in a situation where part of the blame for failure can always be put on the group. A uniform equalizes all who wear it. They all fail together; if there is success, they all share it.

16 I can counter my nemo by conflicting; by adopting my own special style of life. I build up an elaborate unique *persona*, I defy the mass. I am the bohemian, the dandy, the outsider, the hippy. (*Aristos*, p. 50)

In *Mantissa*, Fowles explains the psychological mechanism by which the nemo takes over, and incidentally perhaps explains Breasley's power as an artist and David's superficiality. As *Mantissa* opens, with what we learn later is a short story in the process of being conceived and born within the novel, Miles Green is beginning treatment for amnesia, that most absolute loss of self. The muse Erato, in her persona as Dr. A. Delphi, explains the basis of the treatment, which consists of sexually arousing the repressed victim:

"Memory is strongly attached to ego. Your ego has lost in a conflict with your superego, which has decided to repress it— to censor it. All Nurse and I wish to do is to enlist the aid of the third component in your psyche, the id. Your id is that flaccid member pressed against my posterior. It is potentially your best friend. And mine as your doctor [and, as we learn later, muse].[6]

Although Fowles's comments about choice would indicate that conformity is a valid option if it is indeed freely chosen, his fictions persistently show a deep suspicion of that as a choice—partly, I suspect, because conformists are not especially interesting to write about since their uniform permits them to avoid conflict, but more importantly because ultimately the test of freedom is to knock against one's barriers, not to remain willingly within them.

The significant source of lack of freedom for Fowles's characters—both those who are unfree and those who are learning their freedom—is the inertial force of their accepted roles.

We have seen that inertia in David Williams, who spends a lifetime avoiding extremes and thereby avoiding choices; and of Charles Smithson, who hesitates between Ernestina and Sarah and may be left with neither. It also determines the fate of Daniel Martin, who complains at the beginning of his book that he feels as if he had "been taken over by someone else. Years ago" (*Martin*, p. 15). It is even true of "Poor Koko," who eventually recognizes that he has suffered his greatest loss because he persisted in his role of man of letters in a situation in which he should have listened rather than spoken; it is even true of Miranda, the victim in *The Collector*, who recognizes that she fails with her captor in part because she persists in her role of clever and somewhat vain art student. And, of course, Nicholas Urfe, Daniel Martin, and Miles Green sacrifice—at least temporarily—women (or, in Green's case, a muse) they love to the sexual roles they have grown into.

The problem of freedom for the individual is partly at least a problem of balancing the influence of the past and the "hazard"—probably best defined as an opportunity for choice—of the present. The problem is beautifully stated in the epigraph to the chapter in *Daniel Martin* entitled "The Umbrella" (p. 75):

> What can a flame remember? If it remembers a little less than is necessary, it goes out; if it remembers a little more than is necessary, it goes out. If only it could teach us, while it burns, to remember correctly.
>
> George Seferis, "Man"

If we are not the product of our past, we have no identity; if we are merely the product of our past, our identity is not our own.

Fowles's favorite word for the crucial event (or events) in human life—"hazard"—expresses both the randomness and the risk involved. Conchis describes it as

> "like a point of fulcrum. At that time you must accept yourself. It is not any more what you will become. It is what you are and

always will be. You are too young to know this. You are still
becoming. Not being."

"Perhaps."

"Not perhaps. For certain."

"What happens if one doesn't recognize the . . . point of
fulcrum? . . .

"You will be like the many. Only the few recognize this
moment. And act on it."

"The elect?"

"The elect. The chosen by hazard." (*Magus*, p. 109)

Perhaps the slightest story in *The Ebony Tower*, "The Enigma," is in part Fowles's attempt to give us an unusually simple
and charming example of the workings of hazard. A conservative member of parliament, with no reason to disappear,
has disappeared. The investigating officer, Michael Jennings,
is a young policeman; despite coming from three generations
of policemen, he is not typical. More generally, he remains
his own person even against the demands of his past and of his
profession. During the investigation he meets, questions,
learns to like, and finally beds Isobel Dodgson. It is a slight
story, but Fowles makes its point significant. Michael questions Isobel even though he has no reason to, simply because
"a pretty girl makes a change, even if she knows nothing"
(*Tower*, p. 223). They are, as Fowles tells us, "hazard-met" (p.
235); Michael, unlike David Williams, accepts the risk. The
story ends as Michael and Isobel become lovers; the final
paragraph points the moral:

> The tender pragmatisms of flesh have poetries no enigma,
> human or divine, can diminish or demean—indeed, it can
> only cause them and walk out. (P. 247)

God—and his analogue, the novelist—permit such freedoms
to exist so that the individual might have the opportunity to
hazard all.

To accept the hazard—that is, to accept whatever gifts and
limitations destiny has given and whatever risks it places in

our way—is to become one of the elect, to become an "aristos," a "magus," a "magician." Whatever the term, the central feature is attitudinal rather than situational; it is a feeling of self-determination, of "choosing oneself" (*Martin*, p. 551), rather than a sense of specific direction. (I should say immediately, by the way, that the aristoi are neither always spokespersons for Fowles nor are they intended to be infallible. For example, Fowles gives both Breasley and Conchis lines about the novel quite opposite opinions Fowles has expressed elsewhere, and he has Breasley attack one of his favorite modern painters, Picasso.)

One of the bases of being an aristos is a kind of timelessness, the strength to stand apart from the values of one's age and society. David Williams's success is a direct result of his being perfectly in step with his world (just as Sam's is). His failure is an equally direct result of his inability to be anything but a man of his time and class and profession. Old Breasley, on the other hand, is an anachronism; he seems proud of the fact that he has outlived his age, and even prouder of the fact that, when younger, he refused styles of painting the period would have forced on him. Like the "genius" described in *The Aristos*, he

> is largely indifferent to contemporary success; and his commitment to his ideals, both artistic and political, is profoundly, Byronically, indifferent to their contemporary popularity. (P. 201)

Fowles's aristoi do not so much ignore their pasts as control them. The aristos "accepts the necessity of his suffering, his isolation, and his absolute death. But he does not accept that isolation cannot be controlled and its dangers limited" (*Aristos*, p. 213). Even Fowles's least dramatic aristos, Daniel Martin, cannot gain control of himself until his dying friend, Anthony, gives him a kind of lay absolution for past offenses. From that point on, he is free to begin to make his bid for self-determination. More dramatically, both Conchis and Sarah Woodruff control their own pasts—and thereby their presents—by creating their own versions of the past. Although Conchis creates his pseudo-autobiography primarily to educate Nicholas, it also, despite being largely untrue, is precisely the kind of development most appropriate for someone like Conchis. What permits Erato to dominate Miles Green is that she can be whoever she wants to be in the present simply by changing the story of her past; Miles is limited to being either an amnesiac or what events have made him. Perhaps it is not too much to say that if one is to be free to choose one's present and future, one must also be free to create one's past.

The most telling selection of a past in Fowles's work is, of course, Sarah's. The role she has chosen for herself simply cannot be achieved by one who has been only a governness and a companion. With uncanny instinct and courage, Sarah realizes that she must create a past for herself which will bar her from the role society would force upon her. Her adopted guise as a "fallen woman" effectively places her outside the determining pressures of Victorian society. From her initial appearance in the novel, standing alone on the cliff, to her role as resident in one of England's most unconventional households, Sarah evokes only those elements in her past that will contribute to her freedom and reshapes those that would keep her bound.

To deny or to recreate one's past is both a personal and a social matter. It is to say, "I refuse to be a product of the society that formed me." As a result, the aristoi stand apart from evolution. They are not so much precursors of a new order—for any new order is merely a stage that will pass—as they are perennial exempla of the fullest potential of the free individual. That is why, for example, the third ending of *The French Lieutenant's Woman* feels right: it is the only ending that seems to result from a free choice on the part of one of the characters. But its rightness lies precisely in that freedom, not in the act that constitutes its expression, and certainly not in the suggestion that its content creates a kind of exemplum, a moral imperative for others. David Williams, Ernestina, Sam, Dr. Grogan, Mrs. Poulteney, Mrs. Trantor—all these are period-bound, all conditioned to function with efficiency and some degree of contentment in a particular time and on a particular level of society. On the other hand, like Sarah (the only character in *The French Lieutenant's Woman* repeatedly compared to persons from other eras), the aristoi are for all time and for no particular time—not because they have no identity of their own, but because they have the strength and the will to create their individual identities despite the pressures of the age.

It is no accident that each of Fowles's most notable aristoi is also an enigma. The reason is partly technical, as I suspect Fowles tries to tell us in the famous intrusions in chapters 13, 45, and 55 of *The French Lieutenant's Woman*. The novel as a form does not readily lend itself to showing freedom; we expect characters to be consistent; and if they are not consistent, we want them to be given sufficient cause for their changes. Traditionally, much of the art of fiction has consisted of making its conclusions—and therefore the choices of its main characters—seem inevitable, which is but a softer way of saying "determined." As Daniel Martin remarks, "The one principle the ordinary writer tries to abolish from his work, at least in the finished text, is precisely that of randomness" (p. 271). Fowles's problem with his aristoi is precisely that of creating characters whose actions can seem convincingly undetermined, convincingly random.

If a novel is not to feel chaotic to the reader, Fowles's solution may be among the best available. It consists of, in the case of *The French Lieutenant's Woman*, authorial intrusions arguing for the freedom of the characters, discussions of fight fixing and coin tossing, and—in both *The French Lieutenant's Woman* and other works—leaving the motivation of the aristoi ultimately inexplicable. We can speculate about why Sarah seduces Charles, why she determines to become pregnant, why—in short—she is so purposefully different from what we expect of a proper Victorian governess and lady's companion. And we can speculate about why Conchis plays the God-game, why he selects Nicholas. But in either case the spec-

ulation comes from our desire to make conventional sense of
the characters, to, in other words, wrap them neatly in a chain
of cause and effect. Fowles very carefully gives us no answers,
other than repeated uses of words like "freedom" and "hazard" and "enigma."

At a crucial point in *Daniel Martin*, Daniel contemplates
the novel he intends to write. Having spent his maturity writing movie scenarios that had no significant relation to his own
experience, he wants his novel to be an honest depiction of
himself, especially of the sense of failure he has experienced.
His problem, stated simply, is that the *Zeitgeist* requires an
unhappy ending and a story in which any display of contentment is somehow in bad taste. In *Mantissa* Fowles has Miles
Green sketch that *Zeitgeist* as he lectures his muse about the
modern conception of fiction. Erato has asked, very reasonably, why, if the novel is supposed to reflect life and if there is
humor in life, there is no humor in modern fiction. Green's
reply could come from any of a number of fashionable studies
of narratology:

> "Serious modern fiction has only one subject: the difficulty
> of writing serious modern fiction. First, it has fully accepted
> that it is only fiction, can only be fiction, will never be any-
> thing but fiction, and therefore has no business at all tamper-
> ing with real life or reality. . . .
>
> "Second. The natural consequence of this is that writing
> *about* fiction has become a far more important matter than
> writing fiction itself. It's one of the best ways you can tell the
> true novelist nowadays. He's not going to waste his time over
> the messy garage-mechanic drudge of assembling stories and
> characters on paper. . . .
>
> " . . . Obviously he has at some point to write something,
> just to show how irrelevant and unnecessary the actual writing
> part of it is. . . .
>
> "Third, and most important. At the creative level there is in
> any case no connection whatever between author and text.
> They are two entirely separate things. Nothing, but nothing,

is to be inferred or deduced from one to the other, and in either direction. The deconstructionists have proved that beyond a shadow of doubt. The author's role is purely fortuitous and agential. . . .

"If you want story, character, suspense, description, and all that antiquated nonsense from pre-modernist times, then go to the cinema. Or read comics. You do not come to a serious modern writer. Like me. . . .

"Our one priority now is mode of discourse, function of discourse, status of discourse. Its metaphoricality, its disconnectedness, its totally ateleological self-containedness." (*Mantissa*, pp. 118–20)

Finally, he tells Erato, whom he has accused of not being a very effective source of inspiration because she understands neither the modern world nor modern fiction,

"You still go on as if the world's a pleasant place to live in. There's no more flagrant giveaway of superficiality of approach to life in general. Every internationally admired and really successful modern artist of recent times has shown it's totally pointless, black and absurd. Complete hell." (*Mantissa*, p. 121)

To which Erato cunningly replies, "Even when you're internationally admired and really successful, Miles?" (*Mantissa*, p. 121).

Daniel Martin may be read as a dramatization of some of the implications of that *Zeitgeist*. Daniel, who has been used to accommodating his writing to the formulas of the cinema and knows well the critically acceptable formulas of modern fiction, also knows that life has been far better to him than it has to many. He knows that he has a profession most would envy, a beautiful and loving mistress, and reasonably good health. He contemplates giving his central character—Simon Wolfe (a partial anagram for "Fowles," by the way)—cancer in order to motivate the requisite suffering, but he realizes that to falsify would deny his own identity, and that forbidding himself a real self reduced him to being a psychic investigator who began his inquiry by requesting an exorcism that, if it worked, would leave no ghost to inquire about.

The least thinking reader will have noted a third solution, but it had not occurred to the writer-to-be until this moment. . . .

Free will. . . .

To hell with cultural fashion; to hell with elitist guilt; to hell with existentialist nausea; and above all, to hell with the imagined that does not say, not only in, but behind the images, the real. (*Martin,* p. 405)

"Free will" here has a double force. It applies to Daniel Martin, who at this point chooses the freedom to write as he wants; but it also applies to the fictional character Simon Wolfe. Given the fact of freedom, there is no reason why his fictional experiences need follow the cultural pattern that is currently dominant. In a sense, Daniel is making the same decision here, both for himself and for his protagonist, that Sarah Woodruff must have made sometime before the beginning of her story. It is, essentially, the decision to ignore expectations from whatever source, to break the stereotype, and to create the pattern that is most meaningful for one's personal direction. Later in *Daniel Martin,* Daniel calls it "Daimon: choosing oneself" (p. 551) and feels terror at the thought.

Fowles's penchant for leaving at least a hint of ambiguity at the end of his novels prevents us from knowing for certain whether Daniel completes his novel or not. Although we are told that Daniel's novel lies "entirely in the future" (p. 629), the frequent first-person narration suggests that it is in part also eternally in the present. The touch of ambiguity also closes both *The French Lieutenant's Woman* and *The Magus.* The former leaves Charles with "an atom of faith in himself, a true uniqueness, on which to build" as he is cast "out again, upon the unplumb'd, salt, estranging sea" (*Woman,* p. 480). In *The Magus,* Nicholas and Alison seem ready for each other, but the novel closes before they are definitively reunited. Such endings for emergent aristoi are, of course, the only appropriate endings, for to have achieved freedom is precisely to be no longer determined by one's past. To conclude with the certainty that Daniel must write, that Charles must—for example—become a serious paleontologist, or that Nicholas must find happiness with Alison is to deny them the freedom they have earned.

We have already seen Fowles's answer to the problem of evil—which in *The Aristos* he states as "in the whole, nothing is unjust. It may, to this or that individual, be unfortunate" (p. 15). It seems very much like the eighteenth century's "All partial evil, universal good," but with the loss of that century's anthropomorphism. The fall of one social class is balanced by the rise of another, the death of Victorian sensibility by contemporary honesty, the extinction of a species by the creation of a new. Fowles, like the true modern, would also probably object to the eighteenth century's notion of "good." For Fowles, the world is the way it is; the individual cannot control the game unless he acknowledges its rules. This implies an acceptance of the horror of Belsen (the example of the ultimate horror given in *The Magus*) or of Hitler (the example given in "The Ebony Tower").

Acceptance, it must be added emphatically, is not approval. It is that Dostoyevskian recognition that a world without sin is also a world without virtue. As Breasley tells David Williams, " 'Don't hate, can't love. Can't love, can't paint' " (*Tower*, p. 46). Breasley's formulation adds, of course, another element to the old notion of good and evil being two sides of the same coin. Both hate and love come from passion, which in this sense might be defined as the emotional impetus to realize one's own values. Fowles reminds us repeatedly of a lesson we do not like to remember—that Sarah's freedom destroys Ernestina's dream and Daniel's self-determination is purchased by pain to Jenny. As Breasley tells David as they argue about the place of passion in art,

"Good wines, know what they do? Piss in them. Piss in the
vat. . . . Not oil. Pigment. All shit. If it's any good. *Merde.*
Human excrement. *Excrementum.* That which grows out.
That's your fundamental. Not your goddamn prissy little bits
of abstract good taste." (*Tower,* pp. 43–44)

The possibility of evil is for Fowles proof that freedom exists; its personal effect, individual unhappiness, is the goad
toward freedom. Before beginning their various educations,
Charles Smithson, Nicholas Urfe, and Daniel Martin are
quite similar in one telling respect: in varying ways, each has
avoided any severe personal unhappiness. Charles's social
position has isolated him from personal suffering in much the
same way that Nicholas's emotional detachment and Daniel's
refusal to look at himself have isolated them. The education of
each begins when he is forced into despair—although that
word may be a bit too strong for Daniel's condition. In a few
short pages, Charles loses his prospects, his honor, and his
love; Nicholas is made to despise the woman he thinks he
loves and to believe he has lost the woman he does in fact
love; Daniel is described at that point in his life when he begins to realize that nothing he has done—his work or his personal life—has truly been his, that he had been "taken over
by someone else. Years ago" (*Martin,* p. 15). Even Sarah and
Conchis had their goad: Sarah's was the hopelessness of living
surrounded by things that were not hers, children she was to
tend but not have, and freedoms she was to observe but not
enjoy; Conchis's was, perhaps, the agonizing decision to con-
demn his fellow villagers to death because he would not club
to death a Greek resistance fighter.

Although Fowles does not belabor the point—to do so
would be to argue against freedom—he clearly prefers that
the freedom of the aristoi be exercised responsibly. If God is
the freedom that permits other freedoms to exist, the aristoi
are the freedom that permits the non-elect to choose freedom. Sarah's wilful seduction of Charles inadvertently forces
him to reexamine his past; although his realization of his free-

dom may begin after he is finally sent away by Sarah in the final ending, the freedom itself begins when, for the first time in his life, he makes a choice based on passion; immediately after he begins to try to control his own life. Conchis's God-game with Nicholas, as deliberate in its pedagogic purpose as Sarah's was incidental, forces Nicholas to choose the kind of person he may become. At a moment only slightly less dramatic than that of Conchis's terrible choice, Nicholas must decide whether or not to whip brutally the woman who has tormented him. It is clear that the choice is his alone; there will be no retribution from Conchis or from society if he does choose to beat her. The choice is completely free. Yet it is clear that we are to understand that Nicholas's final refusal to use the whip is a double victory: it is both his refusal to give in to his immediate conditioning, which has led him to detest Lily, and it is his acceptance of what he recognizes as perhaps the only commandment: *"Thou shalt not inflict unnecessary pain"* (*Magus*, p. 641).

Those who understand the responsibility of freedom understand both the proud sadness of the Rembrandt self-portrait that tells Daniel Martin that "it is not finally a matter of skill, of knowledge, of intellect; of good luck or bad; but of choosing and learning to feel" (*Martin*, p. 629) and the "implacable" (*Magus*, p. 147) smile of the bust Conchis shows Nicholas.

In a universe in which the continued existence of humanity is doubtful and in an evolving society in which the happiness of the individual is irrelevant, the surest hope—we have seen—is an escape from time. I have described the time-lessness of Sarah and Breasley and the control that Sarah and Conchis exercise over their pasts. In addition, both Conchis and Daniel Martin play time games: Conchis stages scenes that reenact possible pasts, from primal sexual fantasies and Edwardian idylls to the horror of Nazi reprisal killings during World War II; much of *Daniel Martin* is an attempt by Daniel to bring his past into the present, not only by recalling events from it, but also by literally marrying it. Our best hope against time, Fowles writes in *The Aristos*, is art (p. 184); it may even be art's chief function—it is certainly the one Fowles returns to most often and in most detail. A large part of the power of that "implacable" smile comes from the fact that its antiquity gives it authority; it is a kind of proof that through the ages at least a few have understood the world in which we live and have paid the price of freedom. Like the Rembrandt, it represents "a presentness beyond all time, fashion, language; . . . and a profound and unassuageable vision" (*Martin*, p. 628).

This "presentness beyond all time" comes both from the nature of the artist and from the nature of art. The artist is the magus with a special talent, a birthright that is one of those inequities of nature that Fowles accepts as a condition of being human. The ability of Breasley to stand outside contemporary fashions in art and life and Daniel Martin's decision to reject the thematic demands made upon the contemporary novelist are strengths that David Williams will never know, unless in some story yet to be published he is offered another hazard—and, in the worlds Fowles creates, choice and chance are always possible. But before considering the problems and rewards of being an artist, it will be well to consider what Fowles has to say about the nature of art itself.

Fowles repeatedly compares art and science. Each is an attempt to "escape from time"; each is "symbolization," and

> all symbols summarize; evoke what is absent; serve as tools; permit us to control our movements in the river of time, and are thus attempts to control time. But science tries to be true of an event for all time; while art tries to be an event for all time. (*Aristos*, pp. 153–54)

Despite Fowles's occasional acknowledgement of the equality of science and art, including the claim that "neither the scientifically nor the artificially expressed reality is the most real reality" (*Aristos*, p. 154), Fowles's recognition of the claims of science is usually grudging, as if he has both a very firm intellectual realization of the ability of science to open the world imaginatively for us and a profound doubt about the ultimate value of science.

The doubt takes two forms, one general and one specific. Since the latter is the simpler, I shall consider it first. We are living, Fowles feels, in "a phase of history where the scientific pole is dominant" and where, presumably, the "counterpole" of art has lost its authority. The result is an imbalance, for

> The scientific mind, in being totally scientific, is being unscientific. . . . The scientist atomizes, someone must synthesize; the scientist withdraws, someone must draw together. The scientist particularizes, someone must universalize. The scientist dehumanizes, someone must humanize. The scientist turns his back on the as yet, and perhaps eternally, unverifiable, and someone must face it.
>
> 37 Art, even the simplest, is the expression of truths too complex for science to express, or to conveniently express. This is not to say that science is in some way inferior to art, but that they have different purposes and different uses. (*Aristos*, p. 151)

As Anthony, the philosopher, tells Daniel, the playwright: "'You're locked up in the untenable dream, we're condemned to the tenable proposition. The word as game. The word as tool. Just as long as one doesn't pretend to be the other'" (*Martin*, p. 182).

Even art itself is now threatened by science in the world of Fowles. Although *The Collector* is perhaps too slight a novel to bear such a heavy burden, it can be read in part as an allegory in which science captures and kills art. In this reading, the collector, Ferdinand Clegg, becomes a duller version of those numerous Hawthorne villains who murder to dissect. After a stroke of luck in the lottery gives him the opportunity, he moves from collecting butterflies to collecting women; the novel details his first experiment. Perhaps what is most despicable about Clegg is that—despite his lack of any formal scientific training—he seems to embody two of the traits most conventionally valued in a scientist: he treats all things as objects because he is driven by the desire merely to possess, to control; and his desire is, except perhaps on the deepest level, totally impersonal. His possessing is entirely a thing of the mind, a need to show complete dominance over the object by knowing only those aspects of it he chooses to know. Miranda, his victim, is for him an assemblage of parts, some of which interest and some of which do not; he is less interested in pictures in which her face appears than in pictures in which it does not. Yet, despite the pornographic pictures he forces Miranda to pose for, he is a puritan. He is shocked by her attitude toward men and repelled by her life as an artist. He judges things in terms of " 'good or bad,' " she in terms of " 'beautiful or ugly.' "[7] His instrument, the camera, creates images; and in *Daniel Martin* Fowles tells us that "images are inherently fascistic because they overstamp the truth, however dim and blurred, of the real past experience" (p. 87).

If Clegg is an undeveloped scientist, Miranda is a developing artist, an art student of some promise but as yet no major accomplishment. Her drawings of Clegg show his "inner character," much to his annoyance—not because she has portrayed the evil in him but because she has distorted the surface features (pp. 73–74). She tells him that photographs are " 'dead, . . . Not these particularly. All photos. When you draw something it lives and when you photograph it it dies' " (p. 55)—as, of course, Miranda herself will die at the end of the novel.

In the same scene, she makes clear her charge against Ferdinand Clegg in a way that is both precise dramatically and thematically general:

> "I hate scientists," she said. "I hate people who collect things, and classify things and give them names and then forget all about them. That's what people are always doing in art. They call a painter an impressionist or a cubist or something and then they put him in a drawer and don't see him as a living individual painter any more." (P. 55)

The scene is precise dramatically because the accusation is a perfectly logical one for Miranda to make at that moment and because it foreshadows so accurately the way Clegg will treat

her. But it also expresses Fowles's concern that science kills
the arts not only with neglect, but with attention:

> all our modern technology-biased systems of education con-
> centrate far too much on the science of art, that is, art history
> and art categorization and art appreciation, and far too little on
> the personal creation of artefacts; as if diagrams, discussions,
> photographs and films of games and physical exercise were an
> adequate substitute for the real thing. *It is useless to provide
> endless facilities for the enjoyment of other people's art unless
> there are corresponding facilities for creating one's own.*
> (*Aristos*, p. 157)

When science does turn to art, it can, like Clegg, do nothing
more than photograph, and record, and kill the personal life
that makes art, art.

Apart from our own "technology-biased" age, Fowles has a
more general reservation about science. Science, as he puts
it, "tries to be true of an event for all time; while art tries to be
an event for all time." Science, therefore, is constantly at the
mercy of "truth," or, more precisely, our momentary conception of truth. What Fowles calls the "scientifact" in distinction
to the "artefact" can, therefore, be proved wrong, can lose its
"utility now," so that scientifacts become

> mere items of interest in the history of science and the devel-
> opment of the human mind, items that we tend to judge by
> increasingly aesthetic standards; for their neatness of exposi-
> tion, style, form and so forth. They become, in fact, disguised
> artefacts, though far less free of time and therefore less imme-
> diate and important to us than true artefacts. (*Aristos*, p. 185)

Thirteen years after making this distinction, Fowles provides
a variation of it in *Daniel Martin*. As Daniel admires some
ancient Egyptian artefacts, a wise old Egyptologist tells him
that "'conscious art did not exist for them. They wanted only
control'" (p. 514). And, ultimately, despite the passing bows
Fowles gives to the claims of science, the only final escape
from time is art.

When Fowles describes the work of art as an "event for all time," he seems to use "event" in a very precise sense. More than merely a lasting object, it is a symbol of a deeply felt understanding of the nature of things. As with the endings of *The French Lieutenant's Woman*, the content of the understanding is less important than the fact of it. To make the content important, to make its truth value primary, is to make of it a scientifact. Perhaps that is a part of what Fowles means when he describes *The Magus* as a "Rorschach test. . . . Its meaning is whatever reaction it provokes in the reader, and so far as I am concerned there is no given 'right' reaction" (p. 9). The implication is certainly not that the book is meaningless, but that the meaning is less important than the event: it is to be experienced, to be lived through. We are to read *The Magus*, and, I believe, Fowles's other work, in much the same manner as Conchis lives with the smile of the statuette. The historical truth it expresses—whether it is the bust of a goddess, a cult figure, a statue of a historical person—is so comparatively unimportant that Conchis becomes impatient when Nicholas asks him for the historical details. The smile is, for Conchis, emblematic of both the knowledge and the acceptance of the impersonal cruelty of nature, both human and nonhuman, and of the ability to live with that knowledge with neither defeat nor shame. Like the Rembrandt, it is "timeless, it spoke very directly, said all he had never managed to say and would never manage to say" (*Martin*, p. 628). It is a concrete universal, an individual embodiment of a universal experience. The experience, like Jung's description of the archetype, can be realized in any number of individuations; but any individuation of it, any description or definition, remains only that particular instance. Fowles re-presents this idea playfully in *Mantissa* with his portrait of Erato—sometime Greek nymph, Dark Lady of the Sonnets, modern psychologist, rock performer, succubus; tease, inspiration, nag, lover, goad; the spirit behind Sarah, Mouse, Jane, Lily and those other creations of Green-Fowles. We can no more duplicate each other's experience of art than we can lead each other's lives; in a very real sense, the ability to do one would be the ability to do the other. But, though experiences differ, it is the power of the archetype to bring us together for a moment of shared humanity.

Putting together a great number of things Fowles has said about art we can, I think, come very close to his conception of the kind of thing it is and the reasons it works as it does. But first, a negative—it is not style, at least not style in the sense of acquired technique. Style in that sense is a limitation, a handicap, a rut that keeps one forever mucking about the same ground (*Aristos*, pp. 115–56) or a flourish that "tends to produce a devaluation of the thought" (*Aristos*, p. 197). Much of what Fowles does say about the development of technique or style is said indirectly, in portraits of artists like Breasley, who are at their easels incessantly, or developing artists like Mouse and Miranda, who simply keep working until they get a glimmer of feeling in their work; or it is said directly in *The Aristos*. The aim for the artist should not be style, but what Fowles calls "polystylism," a quality he finds most notably in the works of Picasso and Stravinsky. It is

> skill in expressing one's meaning with *styles*, not just in one style carefully selected and developed to signal one's individuality rather than to satisfy the requirements of the subject-matter. This is not to remove the individual from art or to turn artistic creation into a morass of pastiche; if the artist has any genuine originality it will pierce through all its disguises. The whole meaning and commitment of the person who creates will permeate his creations, however varied their outward form. (*Aristos*, p. 203)

Most significantly, even polystylism is not an end in itself; it is merely a means, a set of tools necessary to create the event, whatever its nature and whatever its requirements, "for all time."

Equally significant, the artist—despite Fowles's assertion that "being an artist is first discovering the self and then stating the self in self-chosen terms" (*Aristos*, p. 156)—does not

impose his vision on the subject matter. He does not so much
react to his subject as interact with it. That is one of the reasons why "art is always a complex beyond science" (*Aristos*, p.
152); at its best, it expresses its subject matter in a way that
does justice both to external and to internal reality, to the
world the artist experiences and to his experience of that
world. The self-portrait of Rembrandt is not moving only because it is an accurate picture of Rembrandt's physiognomy,
nor is it moving only because it expresses Rembrandt's emotion. It is moving because it is both a record of and an occasion
for a very complex event—a human being looking at an aspect
of the world and responding to it with the fullest extent of his
humanity. If the work can be such a powerful double event, it
can be so only because it was first an "experience" in John
Dewey's sense of that word—a self-contained, total interaction of self and reality.

   This interaction of self and world that art captures and stim-
ulates is, I believe, the only description of art that points to
the content Fowles finds in its inclusiveness. If art is, as
Fowles has variously described it, "inclusion at all cost"
(*Aristos*, p. 206), humanizing, free, honest both to self and
subject, an "event for all time," it is so because it is so profoundly, so inexorably, human.

   Although up to this point we have been considering art only
as the product of genius, Fowles himself is quite impatient
with that limitation; much of the meretriciousness of contemporary art he sees as a result of the "obsession" of contemporary artists with being geniuses, of being willing to enter no
race if it is not "the Grand Genius Stakes" (*Aristos*, p. 202).
This need for ego-fulfillment results in the search for a style,
for a recognizable signature, that is the cause of much of the
obscurity of contemporary art. Genius, for Fowles, is merely
something that one does or does not have. It is not essential
for the production of art, which

> is not an activity inscrutably forbidden to the majority of man-
> kind. Even the clumsiest, ugliest and most ignorant lovers

make love; and what is important is the oneness of man in
making artefacts, not the abyss said to exist between a Leonardo and the average of mankind. We are not all to be Leonar-
dos; but of the same kind as Leonardo, for genius is only one
end of the scale. (*Aristos*, pp. 156–57)

In another sense, Fowles tells us in *The French Lieutenant's
Woman*, we are all novelists; when we think of our past we
"dress it up, . . . gild it or blacken it, censor it, tinker with
it . . . fictionalize it, in a word, and put it away on a shelf" (p.
106). Yet Fowles means something still more in his plea that
all persons be artists. When aristoi like Conchis or Sarah (who
are also, in their own ways, artists) create their pasts, they
create not the haphazard, flattering sketches that most of us
imagine for ourselves, but pasts that are works of art, that are
records of an experience of the world that has been fully imagined. It is that ability that is necessary for all of us non-ge-
niuses because we so desperately need the gifts of art.

All artefacts please and teach the artist first, and other people later. The pleasing and teaching come from the explanation of self by the expression of self; by seeing the self, and all
the selves of the whole self, in the mirror of what the self has
created. (*Aristos*, p. 154)

For the artist and for the enjoyer of art, the artefact is an
occasion for self-discovery; it is, therefore, much like the first
step in Conchis's Godgame, which is to see through the role
that one normally plays.

At one point, Fowles defines the artist "as we understand
the word today" as "someone who does by nature what we
should all do by education" (*Aristos*, p. 157). After lamenting
that contemporary art-education fails because it concentrates
"far too much on the science of art," he concludes that "*it is
useless to provide endless facilities for the enjoyment of other
people's art unless there are corresponding facilities for creating one's own*" (*Aristos*, p. 157). To fail to be an artist—which
does not mean to fail to paint, or write, or sculpt, or dance—is

to fail to be fully human. A successful painter like David Williams is, in this sense, not an artist; he is what Fowles contemptuously calls in various places a draftsman, a technician. His paintings are safe; they reveal nothing, discover nothing. Even the lesson he learns from his experience at Coët, Breasley's retreat, will not be a lasting discovery:

> he would go on painting as before, he would forget this day, he would find reasons to interpret everything differently, . . . A scar would grow over it, then fall away, and the skin would be as if there had never been a wound. (*Tower*, p. 112)

And that is the real tragedy of David Williams. He will, like the kind of painter he is, preserve his safety at the cost of forgetting his experience; and so, unlike Daniel Martin, he will never realize that other alternative for his life and for his work—freedom.

To return to another favorite word of Fowles, the artist, even the poor artist, accepts the "hazard." As Daniel Martin looks back over his professional career as a scene writer, he realizes that

> the distinction between the craftsman and the true artist is precisely between knowing what one can do and not knowing—which is why one occupation is safe, and the other always incipiently dangerous. I had only to glance back over my work to know which category I belonged to in the overwhelming bulk of it: it reeked of safety. . . . (*Martin*, p. 276)

Typically for Fowles, Daniel Martin's emerging decision to accept the dangers of art, the dangers of working in a form in which he has no experience and which he fears because it lacks the distancing power of the movie camera, coincides point by point with his ability to determine his fate in the other aspects of his life. Fowles is not so naive as to suggest that the ability to produce art is the cause of freedom, but he does believe that the ability to think and to feel with the imaginative freedom of an artist is necessary if one is to be fully human. And that, given the risks of "hazard," must be in the power of all persons.

Although all true art humanizes, Fowles makes two very strong cases for the supremacy of literature or "poetry," by which he means "whatever is memorably expressed in words" (*Aristos*, p. 204). The first case, which is primarily a philosophical argument based on the nature of the arts and of language, is made overtly in *The Aristos;* the second is made largely by example in his fictions. The overt argument, to summarize a great deal, is based on the fact that "the 'languages' of the other arts are all languages of the mind minus words" (*Aristos*, p. 204). This gives literature two great advantages, the least significant of which may be that

> the word is inherent in every artistic situation, if for no other reason than that we can analyse our feelings about the other arts only in words. (*Aristos*, p. 206)

Note that Fowles is being very careful here: he does not say that words are necessary for an adequate response to art, but rather that they are necessary for the analysis of our responses to art, that we cannot fully understand the effect of any work without the intervention of words. In the remainder of the passage, he gives the second philosophical argument for the supremacy of literature, in particular for the supremacy of words over other media:

> the word is man's most precise and inclusive tool; and poetry is the using of this most precise and inclusive tool memorably.
>
> 79 Some scientists say that man's most precise tool is the mathematical symbol; semantically some equations and theorems appear to have a very austere and genuine poetry. But their precision is a precision in a special domain abstracted, for perfectly good practical reasons, from the complexity of reality. Poetry does not make this abstraction of a special domain in order to be more precise. Science is, legitimately, precision at all cost; and poetry, legitimately, inclusion at all cost. (Pp. 206–7)

As Daniel Martin says, "The word is the most imprecise of signs. Only a science-obsessed age could fail to comprehend that this is its great virtue, not its defect" (*Martin*, p. 87).

This very imprecision (I must admit that I am uncomfortable with Fowles's word, although the context of his argument makes it relatively harmless) permits the inclusion, permits that "balance between particularization and generalization that the artist struggles to achieve" (*Aristos*, p. 188). Although music and painting can achieve that balance—Fowles gives the examples of a Holbein portrait and a passage by Webern—they do not seem to do it as naturally as literature. (Here I must admit that I am going somewhat beyond Fowles's argument in an attempt to reconcile various aspects of his position.) The tendency of painting is toward the particular, toward the literal, the representational; the tendency of music is toward the general, the nonrepresentational, the ineffable state of feeling. Both arts have developed extreme strategies to reverse their natural tendencies—abstract painting and program music, for example—but many observers (including, I suspect, Fowles, because his examples of successful paintings never include pure abstractions and the examples of successful music never include program music) find the cost prohibitive. Despite Fowles's obviously great admiration for certain individual paintings and musical works, he emphatically does "not believe, as it is fashionable in this democratic age to believe, that the great arts are equal; though, like human beings, they have every claim to equal rights in society" (*Aristos*, p. 204).

Literature, unlike the other arts, seems to thrive in that space just between the particular and the general precisely because it uses words. In fact, that realm between the general and the particular is the proper domain of the word; words are counters for concepts. They are never as individual as the reality behind the concept, nor, in combination with each other, as general as the concept. As analogues for things, they are able to combine in many of the ways the things they name may combine and thereby reflect something of the nature of reality; but because they are analogues and not things, they can be manipulated with a freedom that permits experiment and discovery. Their imprecision, their overtones, their nuances, lead the writer beyond his intention and even beyond his initial comprehension of the world.

Fowles explores this tension between the general and the particular, the idea and the reality, in a rather complex passage in *The French Lieutenant's Woman*. I shall quote it at length because it makes several significant points:

> This story I am telling is all imagination. These characters I create never existed outside my own mind. If I have pretended until now to know my characters' minds and innermost thoughts, it is because I am writing in . . . a convention universally accepted at the time of my story: that the novelist stands next to God. He may not know all, yet he tries to pretend that he does. But I live in the age of Alain Robbe-Grillet and Roland Barthes; if this is a novel, it cannot be a novel in the modern sense of the word.
>
> So perhaps I am writing a transposed autobiography; perhaps I now live in one of the houses I have brought into the fiction; perhaps Charles is myself disguised. Perhaps it is only a game. Modern women like Sarah exist, and I have never understood them. Or perhaps I am trying to pass off a concealed book of essays on you. Instead of chapter headings, perhaps I should have written "On the Horizontality of Existence," "The Illusions of Progress," "The History of the Novel Form," "The Aetiology of Freedom," "Some Forgotten Aspects of the Victorian Age" . . . what you will.
>
> Perhaps you suppose that a novelist has only to pull the right strings and his puppets will behave in a lifelike manner; and produce on request a thorough analysis of their motives and intentions. Certainly I intended at this stage (*Chap. Thirteen—unfolding of Sarah's true state of mind*) to tell all—or all that matters. But I find myself suddenly like a man in the sharp spring night, watching from the lawn beneath that dim upper window in Marlborough House; I know in the context of my book's reality that Sarah would never have brushed away

her tears and leaned down and delivered a chapter of revelation. She would instantly have turned, had she seen me there
just as the old moon rose, and disappeared into the interior
shadows.

But I am a novelist, not a man in a garden—I can follow her
where I like? But possibility is not permissibility. . . .

You may think novelists always have fixed plans to which
they work, . . . Only one same reason [for writing] is shared
by all of us: *we wish to create worlds as real as, but other than
the world that is.* Or was. This is why we cannot plan. We
know a world is an organism, not a machine. We also know
that a genuinely created world must be independent of its
creator; a planned world (a world that fully reveals its planning) is a dead world. It is only when our characters and
events begin to disobey us that they begin to live. (Pp. 104–5)

What we have here, among much else, is a demonstration of
the argument about literature made in *The Aristos;* it is a remarkable demonstration of the ability to be inclusive because
words are imprecise. For example, is Fowles writing a novel
or not? If it is not a modern novel in the modern sense of the
word, in what sense is it a novel? It is certainly not a novel in
the Victorian sense, because as Fowles tells us, he is not the
Victorian godlike creator. In other words, Fowles is reminding us that the phrase "modern novel" should refer both to a
particular and to a general, but that there is a tension between
its dual referents. Yet it is obviously the best phrase we have.
So we are led, one hopes, to an exploration. What kind of
thing is *The French Lieutenant's Woman?* In what ways is it
like and unlike both modern and conventional novels? If it is
not a novel, what is it?

Fowles answers the last question in the next paragraph. It is
an "autobiography," a "game," "a concealed book of essays."
Each description is both accurate and inaccurate, which is a
way of saying that there is still an unresolved tension between
the general ideas denoted by the words and the particular to

which they refer, a tension which forces us—if we are docile readers—to try to understand the peculiar relationship between the descriptive terms Fowles uses and the thing they describe.

Fowles plays essentially the same games with his description of Sarah. On the one hand he tells us that he does not understand her, that women like her have always been a mystery. On the other hand, his realization that she "would never have brushed away her tears and leaned down and delivered a chapter of revelation" does show a profound understanding of her character, or at minimum, a much greater understanding of it than would be shown by a reader who would tolerate the revelation. Our understanding of Sarah exists somewhere in that gap between the generalization that she is one of those women whom Fowles—and presumably we—have never understood and his particular presentation of her as capable of some acts and incapable of others. Because words are analogues to reality—to objects, to states of mind and feeling, to ideas—they direct our attention to reality. But because they are analogues and not reality, they also, when used artfully rather than scientifically, direct our attention to that space between thing and concept. And that space, I think Fowles would agree, is the ground of our human freedom. It is the only space we have in which we are freed both from the tyranny of brute reality and from the tyranny of our preconceptions.

I think we can now see how Fowles can make the apparently contradictory claims he makes in that long passage— that his "characters have never existed outside my own head" and that the "genuinely created world must be free of its creator." Hence the ambiguous status of character and scene in *Mantissa*. Is Erato a figment of Green's imagination, an imaginative projection that has become at least partly real, or a muse who from time to time enters Green's imagination? Does the action take place within Green's mind or within Fowles? Whatever our answers, Fowles's point is that the creatures who inhabit our imaginations, whatever their status, have value only when they have the freedom to talk back to us—when, like Sarah or Charles, they can refuse our demands.

The process of exploring that space between the general and the particular is an entirely verbal and therefore an entirely mental process. Yet the exploration can be undertaken only by balancing the particular real and the vicarious experiences Fowles may have had with persons like Sarah and his preconceptions about general human nature, social responsibility, freedom, evolution, and the whole mix of ideas that lie behind *The French Lieutenant's Woman*.

What effect is literature—and art in general—to have on the nonprofessional, the spectator? *The Magus* is in part a dramatization of an answer. If we concentrate on the hints Fowles provides in the preface to the revised edition, Nicholas is an Everyman and Conchis a "series of masks representing human notions of God, from the supernatural to the jargon-ridden scientific" (p. 10). Like Fowles's definitions of God elsewhere, Conchis is both the "freedom that allows other freedoms to exist" (*Woman*, p. 82) and the creator who has the tact to disappear (*Aristos*, p. 19). Significantly, Conchis chooses to educate Nicholas, and other initiates, by means of an art form, metatheater, a kind of drama with two unusual features. Least significantly, the audience disappears—which is merely another way of saying something more important: the audience becomes personally involved in the art. But more to our purpose, the other chief characteristic of the metatheater is that it gives the participants a relatively free hand. Conchis creating his metadrama is very little different from the narrator of *The French Lieutenant's Woman*. Each sets the scene, selects the participants, starts the acts in motion, brings to the production a certain philosophy and set of feelings; but neither has complete control over the characters— an obedient Sarah is not Sarah, a Nicholas who can be controlled (manipulated yes, controlled no) would not be the

Nicholas whom Conchis wishes to educate. It is no more permissible for Conchis to force the conversion of Mitford or the marriage of Nicholas and Alison than for the narrator of *The French Lieutenant's Woman* to follow Sarah or to impose upon her a revelation that would not be hers. The narrator who describes himself as having become merely an impressario has much in common with the impressario of the metatheater.

Like Everyman, at the start of *The Magus*, Nicholas has apparently learned nothing of value from his education; he has certainly not learned to be fully human, and he has not earned the freedom that would justify his ego. He is an educated drifter, a victim of inertia, moving rather purposelessly from job to job and from affair to affair, driven apparently only by a sense of boredom and an inability to imagine alternatives. His vices are as petty as his accomplishments. He seems to make some decisions, but—as with most of us—his decisions are reactions rather than free choices.

Although the notion may surprise at first, from his initial meeting with Conchis Nicholas is given the power to choose and is encouraged to choose; Conchis creates situations, he does not determine responses. From the tantalizing discovery of a book of T. S. Eliot's poems through his final decision about Alison, at each stage Nicholas is forced by Conchis to be aware that he—not Conchis—determines the outcome. The point is driven home quite early in the relationship between the two men when Conchis creates the situation in which Nicholas agrees to play a version of Russian roulette. Freedom is also the point of the stories, some of them perhaps true and some untrue, that Conchis tells Nicholas. In each of the stories Conchis tells about his past, the younger Conchis is placed in a situation that he did not create and in each case makes a crucial decision that turns his real or imagined life in one direction or another. The parallels between Conchis's decision not to beat to death the Greek freedom fighter and Nicholas's decision not to beat Lily is Fowles's most dramatic and obvious way of showing us that Nicholas must be taught what Conchis has already learned. One of Lily's epigrams describes, perhaps a bit too severely, the responsibility of the artist to the mass of humanity:

THE CHOICE
Spare him till he dies.
Torment him till he lives. (*Magus*, p. 549)

Like the narrator of Coleridge's "Rime of the Ancient Mariner," when we experience a work of art as we should experience it—whether it be the Rembrandt self-portrait that so moves Daniel or the metatheater in which Nicholas sees through his role—we become both sadder and wiser.

In most of his works, but especially in *The Magus*, Fowles makes it clear that the sadness that comes with wisdom is better than any of its alternatives. Conchis tells Nicholas:

"There is no place for limits in the meta-theater."

"Then you shouldn't involve ordinary human beings in it."

That seemed to register. He looked down at the table between us, and for a few moments I felt that I had won. But then his eyes were on me again, and I knew I hadn't.

Conchis continues, suggesting that Nicholas go back to the ordinary life of marriage and suburbia; Nicholas replies: "'I'd rather die'" (pp. 406–7). Nicholas, it must be remembered, has lived without risk, and he found it cheerless and valueless. And he speaks not only for himself, but for Sarah, for Charles, for Breasley, for Eliduc, for Daniel Martin. A Nicholas who would refuse his role in the metadrama, a David Williams too timorous to accept a new role, an Ernestina so vacuous that she will never know that she plays a role—such lives never experience the dignity of being fully human. As Daniel Martin learns from the Rembrandt self-portrait, there is "no true compassion without will, no true will without compassion" (*Martin*, p. 629). Whoever is unable to experience passionately will never be able to give strength to others—Nicholas inflicts most pain when he has least will; only when he has developed sufficient strength is he able to avoid inflict-

ing unnecessary pain. For those of us who must be educated
into freedom but who have no Conchis, there is Fowles—
sometimes wearing that implacable smile of the statuette,
sometimes the sad, proud face of the Rembrandt—always reminding us that the only escape from nothingness is our willingness to accept hazard.

Chapter 5

John Barth

The Comic View of the Tragic Vision

> *Stories last longer than men, stones*
> *than stories, stars than stones. But even*
> *our stars' nights are numbered, and with*
> *them will pass this patterned tale to a*
> *long-deceased earth.*[1]

Barth's artists, whether crafters of literature or of history, are incessant builders of funhouses. At their best they know, like Barth, that the principal purpose of a funhouse is to be fun, is to amuse and entertain, to stretch our credulity and our imaginations and nerves with a jumble of comedy that never quite passes into silliness and dread that never quite passes into terror. For Barth, the work of the literary artist (Barth's references to other kinds of artist are quite limited) must be judged not as an accurate picture of reality or as a final philosophical statement, but as a provider of pleasure. Yet, like the funhouse maker, Barth knows that human beings take most delight from that which is most human: the tortuous passageways that bend back upon themselves like a writer indulging in self-quotation please and thrill and frustrate because they play upon our contradictory desires to experience as much as possible and to end the experience as quickly as possible, and the artificial beasties and things that go bump in the dark draw their momentary life from our fear of the real beasties that live outside.

To work the metaphor in a slightly different way, a funhouse is a place apart from the so-called real world and yet constructed from its elements. It has its own traditions: several basic forms dictated by the necessities of travel and space allotment on the midway, sets of permissible motifs derived from the lore of the local folk culture, and even patterns into which those motifs may be grouped. For funhouse lovers, a part of the fun comes from the ability of the designer to surprise—to create what seems an endless maze in what our minds tell us is a moderately sized room, to alter the motifs sufficiently to startle and amaze, yet not so much that they are unrecognizable, and to give us what we expect when we do not expect it, and what we do not expect but would if we were more alert.

In Barth's work the funhouse is not only a metaphor for art, it is a metaphor for life. Although "in a perfect funhouse you'd be able to go only one way, . . . getting lost would be impossible,"[2] real funhouses are labyrinths. The central fact of life in a funhouse is that one must somehow escape, and that escape depends upon a series of choices that cannot but be arbitrarily chosen. The funhouse visitor has no map, no guide, only a constant succession of alternatives. And more often than not, even though the alternative chosen determines what will or will not be experienced in the funhouse, there is no way of knowing either that one blind choice is better than another, or that—in any absolute sense—the experience of one path is better than the experience of another. As Jacob Horner's doctor tells him, *The world is everything that is the case,* and what is the case is not a matter of logic."[3]

If the enigmatic nature of the world is one aspect of the problem Barth's heroes face repeatedly, the other is a persistent refusal to settle for less than heroism. As Giles puts it, "'How can a person stand it, not to be . . . marvelous?'"[4] Giles's question is, in one form or another, the question that motivates Todd Andrews, Jacob Horner, Ambrose Mensch, Ebenezer Cooke, Perseus, Bellerophon—even quite often, when he appears in his fictions, "the Author." It is also, in its way, the motivation of Barth's shape-changers—Polyeidus, Bray, and the Burlingames. Unfortunately, there are no models of the marvelous, at least none that work.

The world in which Barth's young heroes find themselves offers only false promises or none. Because Giles Goat-Boy is Barth's deliberately created archetypal hero, drawn straight from the pages of Lord Raglan and Joseph Campbell, it is appropriate to begin with his struggles to be "wonderful." He faces the usual difficulties: his father is a deity and therefore of not much help; his mother is a virgin and thereby in Barth's terms innocent and ignorant; he is almost slain, then exiled; he has a revelation of his true identity and a call to a mission. So much is prelude. In more certain times, perhaps, the path of the hero could be more certain (or at least, biographers could pretend to more certainty). When the Will of God is known or the Rule of Nature absolute, the hero's task is, although difficult, clear. But in our age and Barth's, we are too conscious that the way of the world is to delude us into accepting the untenable. And so Giles, the modern version of the archetype, must be deluded.

After Giles's realization that he is indeed a Grand Tutor, or at least that Grand Tutorship is his destiny, he initially behaves like a true, albeit rather lusty, inheritor of the Graeco-Christian tradition; he accepts, in other words, a set of moral and philosophical models. Like the most worthy of Christian heroes, he will bring peace and love to the world; he will avert the impending war between East and West, restore the Sears to conjugal bliss, convert the evil Stoker, and drive out the satanic Bray. And he will do it in a way that would be ap-

proved of by the most fanatic disciple of Aristotle: he will
make clear and proper distinctions. He will draw the line between East and West campus, disentangle the Rexford-Stoker
relationship, and even separate tick from tock. And if along
the way he should slip, like any good pre-Kantian realist, he
will argue that essence precedes existence, that if he is indeed
the Grand Tutor a slip is not a slip, for whatever path the
Grand Tutor stumbles onto is by definition the Grand Tutor's
path. Giles's attempt to live by the precepts of the past end, of
course, in disaster. The personal lives of those who have fol-
lowed his advice are ruined, the West Campus is in shambles,
and Bray reigns supreme. To distinguish passage from failure
is to enthrone failure. Like other of Barth's heroes, Giles must
redo his adventures but change his method. He tries to encourage what before he would alter, to join that which he had
separated, and to see himself rather than merely accept himself, with the result that the world gets back to normal. East
and West Campuses are again on the brink of conflict, Stoker
radiates evil, and Bray still reigns. Only after his double
failure does he finally realize that

> Passage *was* Failure, and Failure Passage; yet Passage was Pas-
> sage, Failure Failure! Equally true, none was the Answer; the
> two were not different, neither were they the same; and *true*
> and *false*, and *same* and *different*—Unspeakable! Unnamable!
> Unimaginable! (*Giles*, p. 650)

Giles's final vision is, of course, a variant of the mystic's traditional intuitive understanding of the paradox of the individuality and the unity of all things, that ineffable wisdom
about which so much as been written. It is no wonder that as
the twice-failed Tutor calmly awaits his eventual death, his
few disciples quarrel over the meaning of his life and the
model they would impose upon others.

The need to repeat (Barth's word is "recycle") adventures
is, in part, Barth's strategy for dramatizing the lack of absolutes. How can we imitate Perseus, for example, after he tells
us that in his repetition of his adventures

my mode of operation . . . must be contrary to my first's: on the one hand, direct instead of indirect—no circuities, circumlocutions, reflections, or ruses—on the other, rather passive than active: beyond a certain point I must permit things to come to me instead of adventuring to them. (*Chimera*, pp. 93–94)

And even supposing that we do imitate Perseus perfectly in both the cycling and the recycling or Giles in the doing and the undoing, Barth has Zeus, king of the immortals, remind us that if one perfectly imitates the life of a hero, one becomes only an imitation hero (*Chimera*, p. 296).

Although it is a bit too facile, there is truth in the observation that Barth's heroes are comic when they imitate a heroic pattern and pathetic when they have no pattern to imitate. Some of the funniest moments in Barth's work come when Bellerophon is attempting his imitation of Perseus and Giles is attempting to undo his doings—perhaps because the attempt to impose a pattern where it does not fit provides for dramatic incongruities, those mainstays of humor. But the tone is radically different when the hero has no model.

Like Barth's other heroes and pseudo-heroes, the young Ambrose Mensch wants to be wonderful. (He also wants to be ordinary, to be like other people in the funhouse and like his brother and his brother's friends, and for a time confusedly thinks that it would be wonderful to be ordinary, to be the kind of normal boy who would be accepted by the Sphinx gang and the kind of normal adolescent who might boldly squeeze a girl in the funhouse or look up a blowing skirt.) He wants to be a hero so badly that when he eventually does become a writer, he abandons his family name ("Mensch" or "man" in German) and publishes under the more heroic name "King."

In "Water-Message" Ambrose both recognizes his apartness from others and senses a hope that he might not be alone. Much of the story tells of Ambrose's depression because his age and his temperament—factors whose full effect he does not yet understand—isolate him from what contemporary jargon would call his role-models. At the end of the story he discovers a bottle floating in from the sea, and

> for the moment Scylla and Charybdis, the Occult Order, his brother Peter—all were forgotten. Peggy Robbins, too, . . . was caught up in the greater visions, vague and splendorous, whereof the sea-wreathed bottle was an emblem. (*Funhouse*, p. 55)

Breaking open the bottle, Ambrose discovers the message:

TO WHOM IT MAY CONCERN

and

YOURS TRULY

> The lines between were blank, as was the space beneath the complimentary close. . . .
>
> Ambrose's spirit bore new and subtle burdens. . . . (*Funhouse*, p. 56).

More will have to be said about the message, but for the present the important factor is Ambrose's elation, which is more than a boy's joy at finding a messageless note within a bottle. Within the limits of "Water-Message," Ambrose's reaction is plausible (the outsider now has his own secret) but not fully comprehensible; comprehension comes later, when we learn of the flasks sent out by the author of the "Anonymiad" and of the artist's desperate need to feel that there is someone, perhaps even only a past self—with whom he can communicate. In *Letters* we learn from Ambrose that the Author of the funhouse stories has kept much of Ambrose's own original story of the message, but missed the meaning of Ambrose's elation:

> *A message, a message—the heart of such a child longs for some message from the larger world, the lost true home whereof it vaguely dreams, whereto it yearns from its felt exile.* "You are not the child of your alleged parents," *is what he*

craves to hear, however much he may care for them. "Your
mother is a royal virgin, your father a god in mortal guise. Your
kingdom lies to west of here. . . ."

And mirabile, mirabile, mirabile dictu: one arrives![5]

As the older Ambrose knows from experience and as we know
from "Lost in the Funhouse" and *Letters*, the elation is to be
short-lived. The water-message is not the promise of the specialness Ambrose longed for but, as he tells Lady Amherst, "a
blank I've been trying now for 29 years to fill! All my fictions,
all my facts, Germaine, are replies to that carte blanche" (p.
38). Until his winning of Lady Amherst, Ambrose has not
filled the blank happily.

Even parents, in Barth's fictions, are not guides for young
heroes. Ambrose regrets that his father (his biological parent,
like that of most mythical heroes, is uncertain) had not

> taken him aside and said: "There is a simple secret to getting
> through the funhouse, . . . Here it is. Peter does not know it;
> neither does your Uncle Karl. You and I are different. Not
> surprisingly, you've often wished you weren't. . . . But you'll
> understand, when I tell you, why it had to be kept secret until
> now. And you won't regret not being like your brother and
> your uncle." (*Funhouse*, p. 91)

Todd Andrews, the narrator of *The Floating Opera*, spends
much of the deepest emotion of his long life hurt and be-
wildered by the fact of his father's suicide and—the even
deeper hurt—the fact that his father did not explain it, did
not tell him what there was about life that was so precious that
its lack made life valueless. Even when fathers do attempt to
be models, they fail. Few literary parents have attempted as
indefatigably as the Burlingame-Cooke succession to explain
their lives to their children so that their work would be continued, yet

> every firstborn son in the line has defined himself against what
> he takes to have been his absent father's objectives, and in so
> doing has allied himself, knowingly or otherwise, with his
> grandfather, whose name he also shares! (*Letters*, p. 407)

I have emphasized the ineffectiveness of any kind of guide for the young hero because it is such a crucial feature in Barth's work. Most fiction concerned with the ethical development of a person almost inevitably presents someone who leads, advises, provides an example—from Fielding's Old Man of the Hill to Fowles's Conchis, the pattern seems to require some figure that represents both the possibility of the attainment of the ethical ideal and exemplifies its value. The lack of such guides is in part a symptom of what is unique to Barth's vision. In very general terms, even in contemporary fiction there is usually a sense that, if we are observant enough and caring enough, if we are courageous enough, or if we are open enough, something or someone will eventually help us to get it right. Fowles's Conchis or Sarah will educate us, Lessing's Mother Sugar will help us interpret our inner selves, White's Himmelfarb or Arthur will bless us with their examples, or—like Durrell's Darley—the whole universe will give us a nudge. In Barth's world, there is no one to see that we get it right. We have seen that the Burlingame-Cookes, the hardest-working of the guides, produce revolt rather than acceptance. Even Max, the wisest of guides, can win Billy's love but not his understanding—at least not until Billy is older: it is a part of the sad paradox in Barth's world, and in ours, that wisdom can be understood only by the wise.

Not only is there no one to help us get it right; there is, as we have seen, no right. The Perseus who achieved heroism by subtlety must reachieve it by directness; what Giles did he must undo; Dunyazade's husband wins happiness by choosing "equal fidelity," yet is fully aware that his brother has attained equal happiness by choosing "equal promiscuity" (*Chimera*, p. 53); Todd Andrews learns that to recognize that nothing has intrinsic value is to recognize, even late, that "everything has intrinsic value" (*Letters*, p. 96); Barth himself reminds us that although Socrates teaches "that the unexamined life isn't worth living," Oedipus teaches us "that the well-examined life may turn out to be unliveable."[6]

If this simple cancellation of deeds and truths by their opposites were all that Barth had to reveal, there would be little profit in looking or not looking. It would be but another of those shocked and despairing reactions to our post-Einsteinian awareness of the unfathomable complexity of the world that echoed from the Lost Generation through the Age of Anxiety in the later 1940s and 1950s. Barth has described his own development as a move from Nihilism to Absurdism in his first novels to acceptance of what he calls "the Tragic View."[7] I suspect that Barth's terms do not mean quite the same to him as they do to most readers. Even the early novels show little of the pessimism and bitterness one associates with either nihilism or absurdity. The mature Todd Andrews never suffers from the nausea of the Sartrean existentialist heroes nor the emptiness of Beckett's; there is a good humour and affection about Andrews that makes him too likeable to be "absurd." And, although Morgan tells us in *The End of the Road* that "ultimately" nothing may be important, he insists that things do matter "immediately" (p. 39). The emotional involvement Barth wants us to feel at Rennie Morgan's death and Joe's anger is compatible with neither the absurd nor the nihilistic. The connotations of both terms are simply too negative, too disparaging of human feeling, to apply adequately to any of Barth's published works.

Nor does "tragic view"—despite Barth's fixation on the phrase—do justice to his vision. In an interview with Glaser-Wöhrer, he feels compelled to add that he does not regard it as "necessarily pessimistic"; it is simply the view "that there are finally just different ways to live, but those differences are very important" (*Barth*, p. 220). Todd Andrews's description of the stock liberal, his term for himself, elaborates on some aspects of the tragic view if the stock liberal

is in addition (as I have been since 1937) inclined to the Tragic View of history and human institutions, he is even easier to scoff at, for he has no final faith that all the problems he addresses admit of political solutions—in some cases, of any solution whatever—any more than the problems of evil and death; yet he sets about them as if they did. He sees the attendant virtues of every vice, and vice versa. He is impressed by the fallibility of people and programs: it surprises him when anything works, merely disappoints him when it fails. He is in short a perfect skeptic in his opinions, an incorrigible optimist in his actions, for he believes that many injustices which can't be remedied may yet be mitigated, and that many things famously fragile—Reason, Tolerance, Law, Democracy, Humanism—are nonetheless precious and infinitely preferable to their contraries. (*Letters*, p. 88)

Perhaps Barth's best description of the kind of emotional balance that is at the basis of the tragic view is given by that prototypical author of the "Anonymiad"; it is especially pertinent because of its explicit balance of tragedy and comedy:

For when I reviewed in my imagination the goings-on in Mycenae, Lacedemon, Troy, the circumstances of my life and what they had disclosed to me of capacity and defect, I saw too much of pity and terror merely to laugh; yet about the largest hero, gravest catastrophe, sordidest deed there was too much comic, one way or another, to sustain the epical strut or tragic frown. . . . time had taught me too much respect for men's intelligence and resourcefulness, not least my own, and too much doubt of things transcendent, to make a mystic hymnast of me. (*Funhouse*, p. 198)

Whenever Barth's other characters discuss their tragic views—whether of marriage, parenthood, sex, history, politics—the implication is always the same: the recommendation is always for perfect scepticism in opinions, incorrigible optimism in actions.

Barth's version of the tragic view accounts not only for much of the recycling his characters must undergo, it also provides an especially effective intellectual framework for fiction. Barth himself has noted that "to the extent that . . . [my novels] are novels of ideas—and that's a very limited extent—they are that because they dramatize alternatives to philo-

sophical positions" (*Introduction*, p. 16). Each of the first four
novels pits a protagonist representing a very particular set of
values against an antagonist—or alter ego—representing a
contradictory set: the nihilistic Todd Andrews versus the pur-
poseful Harrison Mack; Jacob Horner, victim of Cosmopsis,
"the cosmic view" (*Road*, p. 69), so detached from reality that
he cannot choose, even to move, versus the decisive Joe Morgan; the ignorant and innocent Giles and Ebenezer versus the
crafty and experienced Bray and Burlingame. A part of what
makes Barth's novels special is that such conflicts are so emphatically not simply retellings of stories of good versus bad
guys. The conflicts are between opposing visions of life, each
of which has merits and demerits. Andrews's unquestionable
decency is made less appealing by his inability to value his
own life; Harrison Mack's drive is made less appealing by his
fickleness. Although Horner's Cosmopsis (the closest Barth
comes to portraying the dourer versions of Continental existentialism) is based upon an absolutely, in Barth's view, correct view of the world, it renders him ineffective; Morgan,
who shares Horner's view that nothing is ultimately important, chooses but becomes simply arbitrary in his demands.
Ebenezer Cooke defines himself as a virgin and a poet, and
throughout most of *The Sot-Weed Factor* defends both his innocence and his identity against odds that would overwhelm a
lesser man; Burlingame defines himself as a lover of all, as a
Cosmophilist, and delights in having no fixed identity. And
both play havoc with the world about them.

The Giles-Bray contrast is, on the surface at least, the most
complicated, mostly because of the almost irresistible temptation to see Bray as evil and Giles as good. Our sympathies are
certainly all with Giles, even when he is most mistaken, for
the same reason that our sympathies are with Tom Jones—
there is about both an irrepressible good will that excuses
faults because it promises their amendment. That he is an
underdog—or undergoat—exiled and with the world against
him, also lends him our love. Bray, on the other hand, seems a
principle of chaos; he is foul and is described foully; he sub-

verts what Giles does through overt power and covert dishonesty. When we meet the Bray of *Letters*, our worst suspicions are confirmed. The avatar is a rapist, liar, kidnaper, megalomaniac, dolt, and madman. Although we will have to look at both Brays more fully later, for now we might note the Bray of *Letters* is the heir of Polyeidus, of the gadfly that brings the hero down to earth and which has lived on as voice and bee in the Dorset marshes. He has been stung by the same bee that stung our Author and led him to dream that Burlingame and Bray are aspects of himself. It would be interesting to describe the two Brays as Jungian shadows to both Giles and the author, as that figure that Jung sees in all of us that is most contrary to our self-image. Bray is certainly a parody of Barth as author. Barth has him claim to be the author of works that Barth abandoned and of debased versions of works that Barth published; his concern with a contentless novel mimics Barth's annoyance with the overcleverness he recognizes as his own chief vice; the Bray that wants to write, by computer, a novel of nothing but numbers is but an extension of the Barth who is fascinated by the logarithmic progression of the spiral and writes stories for performance by live voice and tape recorder. The Bray who is Giles's shadow exchanges masks with Giles. Dramatically, Bray is simply the mirror-foil of Giles: where Giles would make distinctions, Bray would join; where Giles would join, Bray would make distinctions. Again, it is tempting to read Giles as good and Bray as evil, but we must remember Giles's final insight—that passage and failure are both the same and different.

To the extent that the concept is translatable, it is not so in traditional Graeco-Christian terms. In Western culture, evil is precisely that which must be shunned at all costs and destroyed if at all possible. But in Eastern culture—and here it is helpful to recall the Shakyan, the mysterious tutor from the Orient who seems to remain above the hectic happenings of the West Campus—evil is the complement of the good. A Burlingame here would make a list of twins, beginning perhaps with Kali and Shiva, yin and yang, opposites defined by

each other and incomplete without each other. Even more to
the point, it is the "evil" aspect that creates the momentum
for good to be achieved. As many early Christian philosophers
still under the influence of Eastern thought understood, without sin there is no salvation. Without a Bray or a Stoker and all
that they represent, the Grand Tutor has no motive, no
ground on which to act, no message of import, no foe against
which to measure his heroism. Perhaps more clearly, without
Burlingame, the incarnation of the world's duplicity, Ebenezer is doomed to preserve his innocence and his ignorance.

It is the significance of that last that raises the next peculiar
point about Barth's thought. Traditionally, we associate innocence with virtue. We assume axiomatically that innocence
means "without guilt." Yet for Giles and for Ebenezer, innocence is disaster. Until Giles becomes wise enough to understand the compassionate cynicism of Max, his advice ruins
lives and even threatens the peace of the two campuses. As
Ebenezer tells his sister when she tries to console him for his
blunders by calling him "the very spirit of innocence,"

"That is the crime I stand indicted for, . . . the crime of
innocence, whereof the Knowledged must bear the burthen.
There's the true Original Sin our souls are born in: not that
Adam *learned*, but that he *had* to learn—in short, that he was
innocent."[8]

That is to say, the Brays and the Burlingames—those descendants of Polyeidus the gadfly—bear the burden of the world.

If innocence is the original sin, the demon who shrives us
of it and imposes penance is certainly not all villain. Although
the case is clearer with Burlingame, we should not forget that
Bray several times has Giles at his mercy—sufficiently so that
he could eliminate the threat imposed by his opposite if he
were pure evil. At Commencement Gate, in the belly of
WESCAC, and facing the mob, Bray presides not only over
Giles's suffering, but also over his continuation to the next

stage of the quest. Similarly, Burlingame repeatedly both endangers and saves Ebenezer's life.

Despite the rebellion of each generation of Burlingame-Cookes against its parents, the dominant motivation persistently seems to be to keep things astir. They are, as Andre Casteen himself describes them, creators of " 'action historiography': the *making* of history as if it were an avant-garde species of narrative" (*Letters*, pp. 72–73). And yet, with the possible exception of Henry Burlingame III (whose role is at least ambiguous), they are more. Just as Bray in *Letters* is the artist in Barth gone wild, the Burlingame-Cookes may be his politician gone wild. Like Barth, they have no faith in parties or policies: they will support the French, the English, the Colonists; Cook VI is suspected of being a Communist posing as an arch-conservative but is, like Barth at one stage of his career, something of an anarchist. A. B. Cooke's description of "the family dream" is, I suspect, a dream that Barth shares— "harmony not only between man & man, but between man & Nature" (*Letters*, p. 306). The dream is sufficiently general to permit casual involvement with all political parties and sufficiently utopian to permit allegiance to none. It is certainly not far from Max's definition of "graduation" as

> "learning not to kill students in the name of studentdom. And the only Examination that matters isn't any Final; it's a plain question that you got to answer every minute: *Am I subtracting from the total misery, or adding to it?*" (*Giles*, p. 92)

Burlingame III coins a name for the Burlingame-Cooke aspect of Barth's ethic—Cosmophilism, love of the cosmos. As Burlingame III puts it when he is explaining to Ebenezer his desire for a menage à trois including the two of them and Ebenezer's sister:

> "There are two facts you've yet to swallow, Eben. The first is that I love no part of the world, as you might have guessed, but the entire parti-colored whole, with all her poles and contradictories." (*Factor*, p. 490)

At the end of his disquisition on the duality of the universe as reflected in stories of twins, Burlingame expands on his plan and his philosophy:

> "Yet whether their bond be love or hate or death, . . . almost always their union is brilliance, totality, apocalypse—a thing to yearn and tremble for! . . . I am Suitor of Totality, Embracer of Contradictories, Husband to all Creation, the Cosmic Lover!" (P. 496)

Burlingame's confession of his philosophy deserves comparison with a description of salvation Barth worked out in preparation for writing *Giles Goat-Boy:*

> "*Salvation* in the individual . . . consists of the realization (brought about usually after a period of suffering, anxiety, and despair) of a transcendent reality beyond the particular visible world; union with it, release from conflicts of reason vs. passion; good vs. evil. Affirmation of wholeness of psyche and body; loving affirmation of unreason, passions, appetite, corporeity; freedom from vanity and selfishness; spiritual energy and 'lyric enchantment' with reality; a *joie de vivre* that accepts and exults in its suffering or whatever else comes; that discharges the force of its personality in love (compassion and charity; which may include lustful appetite out of joy but will involve no cruelty or destructiveness)." (*Introduction*, p. 77)

I certainly do not wish to claim that Burlingame qualifies on all counts for Barth's version of salvation. But he has anguished through a dark night of the soul in the absence of his parents, and has felt the unfathomable chaos of the universe sufficiently to tell Ebenezer that "'If you saw it clear enough 'twould not dizzy you: 'Twould drive you mad. . . . Blind Nature howls without'" (*Factor*, p. 345). He may not be a Passed Grand Tutor (even Giles, at the end of his career, does not fulfill perfectly Barth's definition of salvation—his work is in shambles and he has lost his zest for life), but he is certainly much more than a representative of chaos. And he may be right about the menage à trois: if into the gene pool he could throw a splash of his own vigor to add to Anne's ability to love and to Ebenezer's compassion, the result might be as close to perfection as humanity is likely to come. Without Ebenezer's contribution, the descendants of Anne and Burlingame play history with infinite zest and limitless because abstract love, but with no compassion.

In Barth's world, the alternatives to Cosmophilism are universally bleak. The Brays of both *Giles Goat-Boy* and *Letters* retain Burlingame's energy and some of his cunning, but by *Letters* their bitterness consumes themselves and others. Todd Andrews maintains a kind of decorous affection for everything—taking real pleasure in his relationship with Jean, his sailing and boat-building, his skill as an attorney—but the pleasure is merely pleasure, never joy. Poor Jacob Horner, like Ebenezer early in *The Sot-Weed Factor,* so loves the world that he cannot make choices; both suffer from Cosmopsis, an ailment Barth has noted in himself (*Introduction,* p. 18). Horner's case is so extreme that it completely immobilizes him.

Not even contentment, for Barth, is an adequate substitute for Cosmophilism. At the end of the "Dunyazadiad" he comments upon the wisdom of Arab story tellers, who

> ended their stories not "happily ever after," but specifically "until there took them the Destroyer of Delights and Desolator of Dwelling-places, and they were translated to the ruth of Almighty Allah, and their houses fell waste and their palaces lay in ruins, and the Kings inherited their riches." And no man knows it better than Shah Zaman, to whom therefore the second half of his life will be sweeter than the first. (*Chimera,* pp. 55–56)

Barth has repeatedly been interested in what happens beyond the "happily ever after." In some cases, such contentment is almost a curse. Both Perseus and Bellerophon have completed their heroic labors; by the logic of most storytellers, having survived the period of heroism, married well, and set their kingdoms in order, they should live out their days in glory and peace. Both refuse to do so. As Philonoë tells her husband,

> "Now, it may very well be that your most spectacular work is behind you—I've yet to read the *Perseid*, but what mythic hero isn't over the hill, as it were, by the time he's forty? However, it strikes me as at least likely that your *best* work may not be your most spectacular, and that it may lie ahead, if not be actually in progress. I mean the orderly administration of your country, your family, and yourself over the long haul; the patient cultivation of understanding into wisdom; the accumulation of rich experience and its recycling in the form of enlightened policy, foreign, domestic, and personal—all those things, in brief, which make a man not merely celebrated, but great; not merely admired, but loved; et cetera." (*Chimera*, pp. 139–40)

But, as Giles has asked, how can a person stand not to be wonderful? That urge drives both Perseus and Bellerophon through the recycling of their adventures. Barth's rejection of the conventional rewards due the surviving hero are so contrary to tradition and seem so whimsical that it is tempting to assume that, at the simplest, he is merely releading us through the funhouse or, on a slightly more complex level, dramatizing his theme that there is no right way to be a hero. But it is significant that the Author himself repeatedly finds contentment insufficient. I do not want to commit the fallacy of identifying the Author who appears in the fictions with the biographical Barth, but there is considerable overlap between the Author in the fictions and the author of the fictions. There are obvious similarities of ages in several works; there are also the trick of having Bellerophon deliver a lecture actually delivered by Barth, Barth's admission that Bellerophon's problems with Pegasus parallel his problems in writing the story, his self-caricature in "Dunyazadiad," humorously overstated complaints of middle age in "Life Story," and so on and on. But even as early as the *Funhouse* stories, the Author seems discontent when things are going well. The writer of the "Anonymiad" seems to speak for Barth, or at least for the Author, when he says that "the trouble with us minstrels is, when all's said and done we love our work more than our women. More, indeed, than we love ourselves" (p. 183). For Barth, the hero and the artist strive not to win rest, but to win what for them is the most important of all prizes—the opportunity to continue their labors.

This unswerving devotion to one's calling is both the sine qua non of his heroes and their most universal flaw. Without it, one is a Todd Andrews or Jacob Horner. Obsessed by it—as Giles, Bray, Bellerophon, and others are—one is blinded to the results of his actions. As Max explains to Giles, there are two kinds of heroes, the kind who determines to be a hero at all costs and who "slays peaceful dragons who never did anybody any harm" (*Giles*, p. 90), and the kind, like Moses, who does what he has to do simply because it has to be done. As Max makes quite clear, the problem with the first is that they hurt others, however inadvertently, and therefore fail what Max considers to be the only important final examination. The line in Barth between enthusiastic control of one's life and excessive manipulation of others is quite thin; even his best heroes stray back and forth across it. Burlingame III's Cosomophilism does not prevent him from making Ebenezer miserable and repeatedly threatening the safety of Maryland.

If Burlingamish zest is what spins the world around, love keeps it from shattering. Love ranges in Barth's works from Giles's simple good-hearted acceptance of whatever delights the world has to offer to Ebenezer's virginal love for the whore Joan Toast, through Todd Andrews's romantic involvement with Jean Mack and—to a lesser or at least different extent—her (possibly their) daughter, through the sexual rompings and the regimen that Ambrose puts Lady Amherst through, to the trust of Shah Zaman for Dunyazade. Barth does, of course, exploit the complications of sexual love for various novelistic purposes. The tumblings of Ambrose and Lady Amherst, the examinations of Anastasia, the good-humored sexual cynicism of Joan Toast keep the novels going by catering to that prurient interest we deep readers prefer not to admit. And, as Barth points out in the "Dunyazadiad," the comparisons between sex and art are numerous and inevitable; to talk of one is to slip into the language of the other. Dunyazade reports the Author and Scheherazade discussing the matter:

> "This last comparison [between a story the Author has in mind and the 'chains of orgasms that Shahryar could sometimes set my sister catenating']—a favorite of theirs—would lead them to a dozen others between narrative and sexual art, whether in spirited disagreement or equally spirited concord. The Genie declared that in his time and place there were scientists of the passions who maintained that language itself, on the one hand, originated in 'infantile pregenital erotic exuberance, polymorphously perverse,' and that conscious attention, on the other hand, was a 'libidinal hypercathexis'—by which magic phrases they seemed to mean that writing and reading, or telling and listening, were literally ways of making love. Whether this was in fact the case, neither he nor Sherry cared at all; yet they liked to speak *as if it were* (their favorite words), and accounted thereby for the similarity between conventional dramatic structure . . . and the rhythm of sexual intercourse from foreplay through coitus to orgasm and release. (*Chimera*, pp. 24–25)

Even romantic love, as Barth tells us, provides a neat dramatic frame for his fictions. What neater way of dramatizing the conflict of alternative sets of ideas than by embodying them in two males fighting for the love of the same woman? (*Introduction*, p. 20). Yet for all the playfulness and artfulness of Barth's depiction of love, it remains one of his most serious themes. Barth's conception of salvation, we have seen, is built around "affirmation of wholeness of psyche and body" and "may include lustful appetite out of joy." This conception of the relation of love and sanctity permits Barth to depict the possibly incestuous coupling of Todd Andrews and Jeanine Mack with what seems a tone of almost sacramental reverence. Todd's affirmation may be somewhat muted by his intellectual stance, and his *joie de vivre* lost in his sense of general valuelessness, but he becomes perhaps the most persistently compassionate, the most persistently caring, of Barth's major characters.

Perhaps Barth's view of love can better be understood through a closer look at Todd Andrews. For a variety of reasons, throughout *The Floating Opera* Todd avoids considering that he just might love his lover, Jean Mack. Over thirty years later, in one of his final letters to his deceased father in which he attempts to explain his life, he claims that he was not capable of love, but only of "affection, loyalty, goodwill, benignity, forbearance" (*Letters*, p. 261); but as the letter lengthens and his self-awareness grows, he finally admits that "as best we wretched Andrewses can love, Todd Andrews loves Jane Mack; has never ceased loving her since 1932, has never loved anyone else. How stupid my life has been, . . . empty, insignificant, unmentionable" (p. 270). The long-delayed admission that he can love and has loved comes during that prerequisite for salvation, "a long period of suffering, anxiety and despair." Only after recognizing the consequences of that admission can Todd finally realize that "everything has value." (And, paradoxically, only then is he ready for his suicide, which he has delayed some thirty years. His suicide at age thirty-seven would have seemed an act of pessimism, if not despair—the act of a man who has not made his peace with the world. At seventy, after his admission of love and the value of all things, his death, calmly and carefully prepared for, is an act of acceptance.)

Perhaps Barth's most poignant evocation of love, though, occurs in the wonderfully intricate "Menelaiad." It is the story of Menelaus told by a disembodied voice that was once Proteus; the tale is an involuted retelling of a retelling of a retelling that—technically at least—might have delighted the Faulkner of *Absalom, Absalom!* It is a story of an age before time has wasted away the remains of heroes and of gods. Helen, the fairest of all mortals, has been wooed by the strongest, the cleverest, the handsomest, the most eligible of men. But she chooses Menelaus. In Barth's version, the Trojan War begins not because Helen fled with Paris, but because she eventually had to flee from Menelaus's constant questioning of his good fortune, and her absence permitted (she tells Menelaus) the gods to shape from mist a substitute for Paris to love. Menelaus, convinced of his own unworthiness of Helen's love, importunes her with "Why?" He seems to ask the question a thousand times, in a thousand forms—Why me, less crafty than Diomedes, less artful than Teucer, less. . . . And Helen's only answer is "Love" (*Funhouse*, p. 155). During the Trojan War he even asks Paris if, when the wraith all take to be Helen lay with Paris, Paris ever asked why she chose Menelaus, and Paris replies, "Love."

> " "" "" 'If only she'd declared, "Menelaus, I wed you because, of all the gilt clowns of my acquaintance, I judged you least likely to distract me from my lovers, of whom I've maintained a continuous and overlapping series since before we met.". . . Or had she said: "I am truly fond of you, Menelaus; would've wed no other. What one seeks in the husband way is a good provider, gentle companion, fit father for one's children, whoever their sire—a blend in brief of brother, daddy, pal. . . ." Wouldn't that have stoked and drafted him! But "Love!" What was a man to do?' (*Funhouse*, pp. 156–57)

Like all of what Barth sees as best in this inexplicable world—the compassion, the caring, the kindness, even the choice to live rather than to die—there is no cause for love that we mortals can understand. Even Perseus and Medusa, estellated together for an eternity, can only wonder at the experience. When Menelaus is "lost on the beach at Pharos," and "is no longer,"

> he'll turn tale, story of his life, to which he clings yet, whenever, how-, by whom-, recounted. Then when as must at last every tale, all tellers, all told, Menelaus's story itself in ten or ten thousand years expires, yet I'll survive it, I, in Proteus's

terrifying last disguise, Beauty's spouse's odd Elysium: the absurd, unending possibility of love. (*Funhouse*, p. 167)

That "terrifying last disguise" of Proteus lives; the "unending
possibility of love" survives. And on another beach, halfway
around the world, survives another disguise of old Proteus,
Polyeidus turned gadfly turned bee turned transmitter and
inseminator of tales.

The possibility of love may be unending, but like all things
in Barth's world, its duration is for mortals at best uncertain.
As Shah Zaman tells Dunyazade, it is all "right to think love
ephemeral. But that life itself was scarcely less so, and both
were sweet for just that reason—sweeter yet when enjoyed as
if they might endure" (*Chimera*, p. 39). That "as if" and its
need is what gives the most moving of Barth's tales their poignance. For Scheherazade and the Author, the favorite words
are "*as if it were*" (*Chimera*, p. 24); the "as if" permits them
not only to dream their fictions and to talk their craft, but to
craft their lives. In other fictions also, the "as if," whether
present by name or not, permits not only metaphors, but life
itself. The mythotherapy designed to cure Jacob Horner of his
Cosmopsis is an extreme version, almost a parody, of it. Like a
Burlingame conceiving of history as art, Horner's doctor tells
him to give his life meaning by living as he were the hero of
his choice, for

> "In life . . . there are no essentially major or minor charac-
> ters. To that extent, all fiction and biography, and most histo-
> riography, are a lie. Everyone is necessarily a hero of his own
> life story. . . .
>
> Now, not only are we the heroes of our own life stories—
> we're the ones who conceive the story, ... (*Road*, p. 83)

The trick is not only to find the proper roles for shifting conditions and even for shifting moods, but to live them fully.
Horner fails partly because he cannot live his role adequately,
he cannot accept an "as if" with the wholeheartedness that
might effect a cure. His doctor assigns him the role of teacher

of prescriptive grammar—a role calculated certainly to get one in the habit of making arbitrary decisions. But his relapse begins when he accepts an alternate role of temporary lover of Rennie Morgan, a role imposed on him by Joe Morgan, and a scenario in which he is expected to be, once again, a minor character. Even in that role he is confused: he is unable to act consistently as if any of the possible interpretations of his relationships with the Morgans were valid; the result is that instead of dominating his circumstances, circumstances once again dominate him. The result is a clumsy tragedy that leaves Rennie dead from a botched abortion, Joe on the verge of insanity, and Jacob more mentally incompetent than before. Ironically, Joe, who has steadily proclaimed the importance of living for the immediate value rather than for the uncertain ultimate value—of living "as if" immediate values were absolute, with all the fervor one puts into the absolutes in which one believes—suffers his breakdown because of a confusion as deep as Horner's, perhaps deeper because he will not admit that he is confused. He will not live as if he had been a complacent husband, nor will he live as if he had been a jealous husband; after Rennie's death, he cannot live as if Jacob were at fault, or as if Jacob were not at fault. His eventual suicide in *Letters* is the act of a person who cannot accept reality as it is, dream of it as it might be, or play with it as it provides him opportunity.

Of all Barth's major characters, Todd Andrews seems most completely to have accepted a world in which choices must be made "as if." Although intellectually certain that nothing has value, he is Barth's most persistent do-gooder. He prepares his attire and his sailboat with the same meticulous care he prepares his legal cases; until shortly before his death, he doubts his ability to love, yet lives a long adult life as if he loved Jean Mack; unconvinced of the efficacy of social and political programs, he remains a life-long liberal; when life is threatened during a political protest, he is the only person who acts as if human life is valuable. As we have seen, his reward for living as if everything has value is, at the end of his life, intellectual acceptance of what he has always seemed to accept emotionally.

It is one of the paradoxes of Barth's view that the erstwhile nihilist and constant sceptic seems at bottom to have a quite simple faith that betrays itself repeatedly in characters like Todd Andrews, Giles, Ebenezer, Menelaus, Max, and others. "The only way out of the mirror-maze," the narrator of "Title" tells us, "is to close your eyes and hold out your hands. And be carried away by a valiant metaphor, I suppose, like a simile" (*Funhouse*, p. 111). Like all such faiths, it is by definition irrational, and Barth is honest enough intellectually to admit its irrationality, wise enough aesthetically to present it sceptically, and passionate enough emotionally to make us scorn those characters who do not share it. It is a faith that, for whatever reason, human life is as precious as it is fragile, that loneliness is the greatest of all miseries, and that love is the only antidote to loneliness.

Despite Barth's commitment to this faith—a commitment that informs all his major fictions—he refuses to see the artist as primarily a moralist. His profound scepticism about the beneficial effects of institutions—a scepticism repeatedly stated in interviews, developed throughout the history of the Burlingame-Cookes with a persistence that would be tedious were it either merely playful or merely serious, and dramatized by the fate of Giles's teachings—precludes any attempt in his works at direct propagandizing. Rather than being "responsible for" his times, he prefers to be "responsive to" them (*Introduction*, p. 98). Although Barth does not clarify the distinction, the nature of his work shows his meaning. Even though *Giles Goat-Boy* is, on one level, a *roman à clef* with many of the figures of the cold-war period easily identifiable, the novel's major premise (the mutual convertibility of "passage" and "failure" and its implications) permits no easy distinction between heroes and villains and no moral not immediately deducible from Max's declaration that "the only Examination that matters isn't any Final," it is the question, "*Am I subtracting from the total misery, or adding to it?*" Yet along the way the novel does manage to take a stand on a large number of its period's major events and intellectual currents—ranging from the Holocaust and the creation of the computer through racism to various forms of capitalism, cult following, environmentalism, existentialism, nuclear energy, and the cold war. A part of the triumph of *Giles Goat-Boy,* like the lesser triumphs of *The Floating Opera, The End of the Road,* and even *Sabbatical,* comes from Barth's ability to dramatize the topical so thoroughly. The historical personages behind the Stokers, Max, Eierkopf, and the rest are a momentary interest; their recognition provides a pleasure not unlike that of the momentary thrill of recognizing the familiar Wolf Man in the funhouse. But their more significant identities are, first, as generally well-realized characters (in the peculiar way that satiric characters can be well realized despite their necessary flatness) within a narrative action and, second, as representatives of quite specific human types. In this respect, *Giles Goat-Boy* is much like Dryden's *Absalom and Achitophel,* which is still a joy to read not because of Dryden's sense of responsibility for his times, but because his responsiveness to his times was sufficiently passionate to enable him to view its events not merely as clashes between particular parties or ideologies but as clashes of human beings, clashes significant not because this party or that ideology influenced events, but because the human beings involved embodied perennial human traits. Although Barth seems less likely to be carried away by transient enthusiasms than many of us who are likely to read him—among intellectuals is there not more than a little embarrassment as we remember our enthusiastic propagation of existential angst and, say, the utopian promise some felt at the possibility of the development of nuclear power for peaceful purposes?—in general, he responds to his times with a kind of enviable and quite innocent sophistication. He refuses to be taken in by fads, however consequential they might seem at the moment; his typical response in his fictions is that of a sceptical observer, at times confused by the rival claims of this or that ideology and inevitably wary of any

solution that is offered, but stubbornly convinced that the
only thing that counts is the addition or subtraction to the
"total misery."

Two other aspects of Barth's general scepticism affect both
his theory of art and his practice of it: his notion that our sense
of reality, including history, is ultimately a human creation
rather than a reflection of what in fact has been or is the case,
and his awareness of the limitations of language. In a wonderfully amusing but quite serious exchange, Ebnezer wrestles
with an ancient philosophical question: how do we recognize
the identity of something if its appearance changes? Specifically, he is concerned with how Burlingame, perfectly disguised, has managed to establish his identity as Burlingame.
He thinks he has the answer:

> "Nay, this very flux and change you make so much of: how can
> we speak of it at all, be it ne'er so swift or slow, were't not that
> we remember how things were before? Thy *memory* served as
> thy credentials, did it not? 'Tis the house of Identity, the Soul's
> dwelling place! Thy memory, my memory, the memory of the
> race: 'tis the constant from which we measure change; the sun.
> Without it, all were Chaos right enough."

Burlingame then asks, "In sum, then, thou'rt thy memory?"
(*Factor*, p. 126). By the conclusion of a long argument, Burlingame has established "that all assertions of *thee* and *me,*
e'en to oneself, are acts of faith, impossible to verify" (p. 128).
This is but the most extreme statement of a theme that runs
throughout *The Sot-Weed Factor:* if one's very self-identity
depends upon memory, and memory is imperfect, our knowledge of our world must be even more uncertain. In preparation for the conclusion of *The Sot-Weed Factor,* our Author
dramatically breaks point of view to rephrase the discussion
and to point the lesson from it:

> We all invent our pasts, more or less, as we go along, at the
> dictates of Whim and Interest; the happenings of former times
> are a clay in the present moment that will-we, nill-we, the lot

of us must sculpt. Thus Being does make Positivists of us all. Moreover, this Clio was already a scarred and crafty trollop when the Author found her; it wants a nice-honed casuist, with her sort, to separate seducer from seduced. But if, despite all, he is convicted at the Public Bar of having forced what slender virtue the strumpet may make claim to, then the Author joins with pleasure the most engaging company imaginable, his fellow fornicators, whose ranks include the noblest in poetry, prose, and politics; . . . . (*Factor*, p. 743)

In the particular case of the history behind *The Sot-Weed Factor*, Clio's honor has been sullied by the ambiguities surrounding the merely probable historical Ebenezer Cooke who, his biographer tells us, may not have actually existed. Much of *The Sot-Weed Factor* is, in fact, an alternate view of history that seems less plausible than the standard versions only because they have become a part of our mythology, and, as Anteia, a militant feminist, tells Bellerophon, "mythology is the propaganda of winners" (*Chimera*, p. 277). Later, as Barth continues the chronicle of the Burlingames and the Cookes in *Letters*, he will write an alternate version of many of the crucial events in the history of the United States that is as plausible as the accepted version. The amount of space Barth gives to his pseudo-history in just these two works— sections that many readers find the most tedious in Barth— suggests the importance of the theme, a theme that recurs in other forms in Barth's versions of mythological stories.

Barth eschews realism, then, for the best of all possible reasons: the materials of realism—our history, our knowledge of ourselves, our knowledge of the everyday world around us, our knowledge of myth and history—are dependent on memory, that servant of "Whim and Interest." Barth's epistemological reasons for rejecting realism are in keeping with his personal inclinations and his sense of history. His obvious delight in artifice—despite occasional pulls the other way recorded by the grumblings about artificiality in such tales as "Life-Story" and "Title"—suggests that the writer of the "Anonymiad" speaks for Barth when he tells us that "I could never . . . take seriously enough the pretensions of reality" (*Funhouse*, p. 171); or, as Barth expressed it in an interview with Prince, "Reality is a nice place to visit, but you wouldn't want to live there, and literature never did, very long" (*Introduction*, pp. 29–30). Historically, Barth is convinced that "contemporary writers can't go beyond what's been done, and done better. . . . We can't write nineteenth-century novels" (*Introduction*, pp. xvii–xviii). But to avoid realism is not necessarily to be unfaithful to human experience, and to be artificial is not to be merely artificial.

Barth also shares his century's profound scepticism about the ability of language to mirror the world. Perhaps the best summation of Barth's views about the difficulties of language is given to Lady Amherst, who casually observes that "the world is richer in associations than in meanings, and that it is the part of wisdom to distinguish between the two" (*Letters*, p. 385). The passage is interesting because Lady Amherst has just described a series of coincidences that, it seems, ought somehow make sense. There seems to be a pattern, but the pattern can only be imposed by an interpreter. She is in very much the same position as the Narrator of the "Anonymiad," who recognizes quite clearly that to consider life either tragic or comic—to give it a name, to sum it up in a phrase of a treatise—is to force a meeting. But even more basically, the very fact that Lady Amherst is writing forces an organization upon her experience; the fact that she is writing to a particular person for a particular purpose furnishes the organizing principle. Despite the event-filled appearance of the letter, the description of coincidences is actually a description of only a minute part of her knowledge of the total situation. The act of telling, of using words, has by its very nature forced her to create at least apparent significance from what may be accidental associations of events. In this small scene Lady Amherst is very like a large number of other Barth characters who find that they cannot trust language, no matter how faithfully they try to use it. The labors of Giles are couched as

riddles, as is the "Pass All / Fail All" motto on his matricula-
tion card; on one very significant level, his sequence of blunders results from his acceptance of the naive notion that language is precise and unambiguous, that a phrase like "fix the
tower clock" is definitively interpretable. Barth even reminds
us that none of us will read the same New Syllabus. Not only
do the editors disagree among themselves, but Giles's disciples cannot agree on a meaning. Todd Andrews builds his life
around what seems to be a clear proposition, that "nothing
has value." He works it out with impeccable logic, buttressing
it with the appropriate associations of events from his past life,
only finally to come to the realization that to ascribe value to
nothing is to ascribe value to everything, that failure is indeed
passage, that they are the same yet different, and that that
difference is powerful enough that the acceptance of one
rather than the other changes not what one does but how one
feels about what one does.

Jacob Horner's problem with language is quite interesting,
not merely because he teaches prescriptive grammar or because it is a symptom of his Cosmopism, but because he recognizes that even using language, that seemingly most inac-
tive and contemplative of all acts, requires a complex series of
decisions, that "to turn experience into speech . . . to classify,
to categorize, to conceptualize, to grammarize, to syntactify
it—is always a betrayal of experience, a falsification of it"
(*Road*, p. 112). To speak of something means that we must first
decide what to name it; to call something an oak tree, for
example, rather than a shade tree, is to affirm certain aspects
of the reality and mute or ignore others; as we build the sentence, our choice of each word rests on similar distortions of
the reality; each conscious or unconscious decision about
grammatical structure takes us further from that wonderful
fullness of reality so beloved by the cosmophilist.

If I were a disciple of the deconstructionists, I would at this
point shriek a lament on the impossibility of meaning, and
perhaps cite the fate of the shape-changer Polyeidus, whose
destiny, Barth tells us, was to become a succession of tales and

voices and memories, forever the same Polyeidus yet forever changing into tales of Bellerophon and Bray and Napoleon and, indeed, by infection of Barth from the Celestial bee or gadfly, all of Barth's characters. Barth's Polyeidus is the mythological embodiment of the instability of the text. But as a devoutly practicing fictionalist, Barth proclaims not the impossibility of literature but the immense difficulty of it.

It is, to move the metaphor from the funhouse to the sideshow, an intricate juggling act. Language riddles and puns, as Giles learns; it is, according to Barth, "a compound code, and . . . the discovery of an enormous complexity beneath a simple surface may well be more dismaying than delightful."[9] "The world," puts "tempting symbols squarely in . . . [our] path" so that we are "baited into saying things . . . [we] don't really mean."[10] As if that weren't enough, forms themselves are recalcitrant, and stories develop such an intense life of their own that they fight back—as in "Title" and "Life-Story," so that the putative author who would like to write a simple story about decent ordinary people finds himself overwhelmed by the traditions of his genre and the prejudices of his era. Or the stories contain their own critics—like "Bellerophoniad," which not only includes Bellerophon's wife criticizing the story rather harshly but also includes critical lectures on everything from Freitag's triangle to mythic implications and a scholarly description of sources. A fledgling writer like Ambrose must contend, we learn from his narrative, with remembering such petty conventions as the use of italics and must worry about his readers' acceptance of the age-maturity levels of his adolescent characters. If the writer is as eccentric as Barth—or better, as professionally playful— he complicates the act still further by, for example, insisting upon a specific number of characters, preplanning the point at which the climax of a story will occur by a mathematical formula, imposing a visual form such as the spiral, or writing a story of seven paragraphs, each in the rhythm of "The Lord's Prayer." If he is as professionally responsible as Barth, he adds still another factor, "the desire to explore sounds, rhythms and ideas more thoroughly, and to develop more rigorously disciplined eyes, ears and attitudes" (*Introduction*, p. 81). Yet despite the impossibility of juggling all this and more, stories do get written, and they "last longer than men."

"Despite the impossibility" is, of course, precisely the wrong expression. Stories last longer than men *because* of the seeming impossibility of juggling it all. Nor do they last because they are mere technical displays of verbal sleight of hand. Perhaps more than any single other idea, Barth's interviews repeat his annoyance at his reputation for being a virtuoso without passion, a maker of imaginary funhouses with no real toads. In his May 1, 1967, address to the audience at the Library of Congress, Barth objected strenuously to a *Time* magazine review of *Lost in the Funhouse:*

> If my writing was no more than the intellectual fun-and-games that *Time* magazine makes it out, I'd take up some other line of work. That's why one objects to the word *experiment*, I suppose: it suggests cold technique, and technique in art, as we all know, has the same sort of value that it has in love: heartless skill has its appeal, as does heartfelt ineptitude; but passionate virtuosity's what we all wish for, and aspire to. If these pieces aren't moving, then the experiment is unsuccessful. (*Introduction*, p. 96)

Barth's special talent, and it seems deliberately cultivated, is his ability to play off the passionate and the virtuoso against each other. The virtuoso aspects of the work, which include the formal, the technical, Barth's idiosyncratic numbers games, and so on, foredoom any possibility of a naive presentation of the passionate. On the other hand, the passion (and here it is useful to remember Burlingame and his passion for all reality) and the desire to invoke genuine human emotion based upon an intelligent and caring concern for reality, forces ever greater virtuosity.

Earlier, I spoke of the "impossibility of literature" and then reversed myself. Like Giles, I shall have to reverse myself again, at least half way, to include both possibilities, for in an absolute sense, the artist never achieves total reality. In a beautiful exchange, Shah Zaman and Dunyazade are discussing the war between the sexes as they attempt to find a way to conclude one of its skirmishes. We have been told earlier that sex and art are by nature metaphors for each other.

> "Let's end the dark night! All that passion and hate between men and women; all that confusion and inequality and difference! Let's take the truly tragic view of love! Maybe it *is* a fiction, but it's the profoundest and best of all!"

Dunyazade fears it will not work; the Shah replies, " 'Nothing *works*! But the enterprise is noble; it's full of joy and life, and the other ways are deathy' " (*Chimera*, p. 53). Ultimately, perhaps, literature doesn't work, for "stones live longer than stories." But, like love, "the enterprise is noble; it's full of joy and life, and the other ways are deathy."

That desire for nobility and joy and life—as Giles would have it, the desire to be "wonderful"—is for Barth part of the origin of literature. In Barth's wonderfully comic allegory of the origins of literature, the beginnings are not the invention of story telling but the need of mythical beings like Perseus and Bellerophon to be wonderful. Literature's pre-origins are the deeds of the heroes whom Barth recreates not as young men eager to take on the world's Medusas and Chimeras, but as middle-aged men who have already succeeded, who have been wonderful but who fear they are no longer so. In his retelling of the Perseus story Barth creates a myth that in its outlines returns to what may be the earliest type of narrative—the explanatory myth, in particular an explanatory myth accounting for the configuration of the stars in the Andromeda constellation.

Whatever the psychological or social needs myth fulfills, the narrative that fleshes out the myth needs to be a good yarn, a tale of wonder involving beings whose exploits were so superhuman that they must be lifted from the earth and given life on Olympus or in the stars. But Barth's structuring of the Perseus story makes it clear that Perseus wins estellation not so much because of his deeds as because of his desires. We have seen that, like Giles, he must redo all that he has done. In the story of Perseus, Barth adds the motivation that what has been done is less important than the desire that leads to the doing. This is why both Bellerophon and Perseus are so profoundly dissatisfied: to *have been* a hero, to *have been* wonderful, is precisely *to be* no longer wonderful. The final cause of Perseus's estellation is neither that he has slain the Medusa nor that he has loved her, but the ever-present desire to be and to remain heroic.

If the estellation of Perseus is a triumph of desire, the fall of Bellerophon is a failure of desire. It is not that Bellerophon fails to want desperately enough, but rather that his desire is impure. The surviving twin who has somehow assumed his dead brother's name, the character we know as Bellerophon is driven not only by a simple desire to be wonderful, but by a desire to be as wonderful as Perseus. In a perfectly appropriate fate, this almost-hero, who has taken his brother's identity and yearns after another's fame, merges with Polyeidus, the eternal shape-changer and, in Barth's allegory of the history of humane letters, the spirit of literature.

Barth's allegory of the development of literature is charming—adventurous, profound, comic, poetically told—exactly the kind of tale calculated to win our suspension of disbelief. But I suspect that Barth is after something more than suspension of disbelief, that like all good allegories it is intended to win actual belief for a particular interpretation of reality. I should perhaps be Germanic here, and write literature with a capital *L* to signify that I am considering not specific literatures but what might, still in the Germanic mode, be called the Spirit of Literature.

I shall begin retelling the allegory by looking in some detail at a scene from *Letters*, a scene quite late in Barth's story of literature. The Author, in one of only two letters not addressed to one of the fictional characters (the other letter is the final letter, which is addressed to the "Reader") retells a dream; the letter is essentially a dream vision in the medieval

sense, describing a revelation. Its position in the first section
of the novel suggests that it is part of the exposition, part of
the background that we must have in order to understand the
work.

> I woke half tranced, understanding where I was but not at
> once who, or why I was there, or for how long I'd slept. . . .
> The only other sign of life, besides the silent files of spartina
> grass, was the hum of millions upon millions of insects—as-
> sassin flies, arthropods, bees above all, and beetles, drag-
> onflies, mosquitoes—going about their business, which, in
> the case of one *Aedes sollicitans*, involved drawing blood from
> the back of my right hand until I killed her. (p. 46)

At this point we must remember that Jerome Bray, who is
suing the Author for having stolen and bastardized his works,
is not only obsessed with bees—claiming to have written a
number of works in which they figure prominently—and the
letter *B*, but is writing an "autobiographical" series (his only
work to be written under the name "Bray"). The work, his
"magnum opus," is to be

> told from the viewpoint of celestial Aedes Sollicitans, a fresh-
> marsh native with total recall of all her earlier hatches, who
> each year bites 1 visitor in the Refuge and acquires, with her
> victim's blood, an awareness of his/her history. The 1st is the
> Tayac Kekataughassapooekskunoughmass, or "90 Fish," King of
> the Ahatchwhoop Indians. The 9th is Captain John Smith of
> Virginia; the 10th Henry Burlingame I, my own foster father's
> great-great-great-great-great-great-grandfather. The 360th
> (and the 1st to give himself to her unreservedly) is the Author
> [Bray], whom in return she gratefully "infects" with her nar-
> rative accumulation. (p. 29)

Given not only Bray's obsession with creatures with stingers
but also some of his own peculiarities (his apparent ability to
fly and his unique manner of impregnating females, shared
with his namesake in *Giles Goat-Boy*) and his ravings at the
end of *Letters*, it seems reasonable to assume that he is here

giving an accurate account—accurate within the allegory—of
his inspiration. We have to assume that our Author shares the
"infection" from the same insect, since Bray claims that the
bite inspired not only versions of most of Barth's published
work but even versions of his unpublished.

To continue the dream-vision:

> The movement woke me further: I recognized that before
> consulting my wristwatch I'd felt for a pocketwatch—a silver
> Breguet with "barleycorn" engine-turning on the case, steel
> moon hands, . . . and my father's monogram, HB, similarly
> scribed before the appropriate Roman numeral IV—a watch
> which I did not possess, had never possessed, which could not
> with that monogram be my father's, which did not so far as I
> know exist! . . .
>
> . . . When I looked away. . . from my mind's eye-corner I
> could just perceive, not one, but several "youths," all lead-
> ing . . . to this point of high ground between two creeklets
> where I lay, stiff as if I'd slept for twenty decades or centuries
> instead of minutes.

He sees a youth, a version of himself, asleep.

> But beside it, like a still-sleeping leg that its wakened twin
> can recognize, was another history, a prior youth, to whom
> that pocketwatch and vest and a brave biography belonged.
> They shared one name's initial: bee-beta-beth, the Kabbalist's
> letter of Creation, whence derived, like life itself from the
> marsh primordial, both the alphabet and the universe it de-
> scribed by its recombinations. Beyond that, and their conflu-
> ence in the onstreaming Now, they had little in common, for
> this youth's youth was all bravura, intrigue and derring-do,
> sophistication and disguise.

The second youth, an avatar of the Author, is Henry Burlingame III.

> Then what was this third, faint-bumbling B, most shadowy
> of all, but obscured more by mythic leagues of time than by
> self-effacement or disguise? And not *retreated* to the midday

marsh, but fallen into it as though from heaven, become a blind, lame, vatic figure afloat on the tepid tide, reciting a suspect version of his history, dozing off in midexposition? (Pp. 46–47).

The third is, of course, a version of Bellerophon-Polyeidus-Bray, as we learn when Barth attempts to rationalize his dream by assuming that he fell asleep with his recent concerns—his just-completed *Sot-Weed Factor,* his notes for "Bellerophon," his invitation to accept an honorary doctorate from the University of Maryland, his plans for *Letters.* The explanation of the dream is sufficient until we remember that in the fictional world surrounding the dream Barth's artists are all mysteriously linked. Bray claims to be—and the claim seems substantiated later in *Letters*—a foster child of those artists of history, the Burlingame-Cookes. Ambrose bears a birthmark in the shape of a *B;* his name connects him with honey; and an episode with bees was one of the significant events of his childhood. The water-message Ambrose receives reappears in the "Menelaiad," the "Anonymiad," and the "Bellerophoniad," and so links him with the past of art, just as the queen of the Aedes Sollicitans links Bray and the Author. And, of course, all are neatly linked through the connection of the mosquito with Polyeidus-Bellerophon. Perhaps most significantly, we learn in the rationalization of the dream that in the author's notes the "Bellerophoniad" was to have been ("is" may be the correct verb) Bray's.

The last is especially curious, because we must remember that the "Bellerophoniad" is told by a disembodied voice, by the text that was once Bellerophon and Polyeidus. It is remotely possible that in telling us that he once intended to attribute the "Bellerophoniad" to Bray our Author is merely being playful; it is almost possible that he is merely recording a change in intention. But Barth seldom does anything *merely.* If we remember that Polyeidus's final form before falling to earth was the insect that stung Pegasus, and that Polyeidus and Bellerophon fell into the Maryland marshes, it seems reasonable to assume that Bray might acquire the story as pure text from his infestation by Aedes Sollicitans.

Several other pieces of information complete this part of the picture. Bellerophon-Polyeidus becomes not only the text of the "Bellerophoniad" but of other texts, including even letters from Napoleon Bonaparte and a speech Barth himself will deliver. (The connection with Napoleon comes partly from the use of the British warship *Bellerophon* to transport Napoleon, partly because of the initial *B*, and partly because Napoleon's fate is tied up with that of the Burlingame-Cookes.) More generally, Bellerophon-Polyeidus has become not *a* text, but textuality itself, the abstract archetypology of myth and narrative. If we add this to Barth's reminder that Polyeidus is but one of the aspects of Polyphemus, the primal shape-changer and one of the voices through whom the "Menelaiad" is told, we have here an allegory of the origins and transmission of Literature—not literature as separate stories, but as an almost Hegelian spirit of Literature. The archetype of the story, as distinct from its particular tellings—its *langue* rather than its *parole*—is an enduring possibility for realization.

(I suspect that this ontology of literature either accounts for or is a result of Barth's interest in restructuring myth—from the relatively pure retellings of classical stories to the fabulations of *Giles Goat-Boy* and *The Sot-Weed Factor* and the recyclings of his own stories in *Letters*. The characters of Giles or Jacob Horner, for example, are individual incarnations of a principle and as such may be recycled indefinitely in their own or other names—just as the story of Menelaus can and has been recycled countless times. In fairness to Barth, we must remember that recycling is not repetition; the artist tuning into this *langue* of literature is not a literal plagiarist for at least two reasons. On the one hand, conditions always change; Barth's telling of his hero's recyclings stresses repetition and undoing equally. On the other, which is more purely literary, every story is an incarnation; the archetype, the *langue*—whichever terminology is more comfortable—exists only as potentiality; the story, the *parole*, is the actuality.)

Before leaving the implications of the Bellerophon-Polyeidus fall from Olympus to literature, we need to consider still
more ramifications of this wonderfully rich myth. We have
seen that this spirit of literature begins in the days before
history, even in the days before writing, with the desire to be
wonderful. Those who achieve the desire do not create literature; they rather become the subject of literature (and other
arts, like Perseus in the Hall of Calyxa) as envy of their
blessedness spurs others to imitate. The telling of tales is left
to those who, like Bellerophon and Polyeidus, feel profoundly
the urge to wonder but who cannot in their own identities
achieve the wonderful. It is they who created the oral texts by
assuming the identities of others, by, to use Barth's phrase,
"becoming the tale." Hence, from the earliest stages, the
writer is both Bellerophon, the failed hero, and Polyeidus,
the eternal shape changer.

Barth most frequently creates the spirit of literature as a
disembodied voice speaking mysteriously through others,
often through a series of others within the same story ("Echo,"
"Menelaiad," "Bellerophoniad," and—in somewhat different
ways—"Title" and "Life-Story"). The voice describes itself at
the end of the "Menelaiad":

> When I understood that Proteus somewhere on the beach be-
> came Menelaus holding the Old Man of the Sea, Menelaus
> ceased. Then I understood further how Proteus thus also was
> as such no more, being as possibly Menelaus's attempt to hold
> him, the tale of that vain attempt, the voice that tells it. Ajax is
> dead, Agamemnon, all my friends, but I can't die, worse luck;
> Menelaus's carcass is long wormed, yet his voice yarns on
> through everything, to itself. Not my voice, I am this voice, no
> more, the rest has changed, rechanged, gone. The voice too,
> even that changes, becomes hoarser, loses its magnetism,
> grows scratchy, incoherent, blank. (*Funhouse*, p. 167)

The person who physically tells or writes the story becomes
the transmitter of that voice, a ventriloquist's dummy in the
sense that the voice speaks through him, but more than that

because the abstraction of the story can be made flesh only when told by an individual human being, subject to all the personal and historic conditioning of his being. The spirit of the story will go on and on, enduring longer than men but less than stones and stars. (Like a good German idealist, Barth is taking the long view here; later, when we consider the personal history of the artist, we shall see him, like a good American pragmatist, taking the short view.)

Thus far I have avoided a third significant character in the "Bellerophoniad": Pegasus, Bellerophon's faithful flying steed and the traditional symbol of inspiration. As Bellerophon has settled into becoming a good and wise ruler (what Fowles might call one of the "decent second-rate"), Pegasus has lost his ability to fly. When Bellerophon wants to redo his adventures, he is distraught because the bepastured Pegasus can barely hop a buttercup. The problem, he learns, is that he has forgotten that Pegasus—inspiration—was originally a gift from both Athena and Aphrodite; his calm and careful recent life has given sufficient homage to the former but totally ignored the latter. Pegasus's weakness is a direct consequence of Bellerophon's failing sexual energy. After he recognizes the problem, the more energetically he mounts the women he encounters, the higher his mount is able to soar. Art is not, as the medieval theologians and the modern Freudians have told us, a matter of sexual sublimation; it is a gift that comes only with joint service to both Athena and Aphrodite.

Sometime during or after the eons that pass as Bellerophon and Polyeidus fall to earth and after countless heroes and tales, a young storyteller is abandoned on a Mediterranean island. He had previously been a lover and a poet and a storyteller. He is too detached from the world to enter wholeheartedly into the things it considers important—too aware of the comedy to take things seriously and too aware of the tragedy to dismiss them. Blessed with a certain charm and much imagination, he learns that he can please audiences with new versions of old tales, pleasant allegories, songs, and all the usual stock and trade of the bard. Like Ambrose centuries later, he can create funhouses, the stories and songs, for others, but he cannot himself function well within the funhouse—which happens to be the locale of the tale of Agamemnon and Merope and Clytemnestra. The teller of tales finds himself lost within the intrigues of the tale he is living and abandoned on an island with his amphorae and his goats. His agonizing problem is loneliness, the special loneliness of the artist who has no one with whom to share his art. What good, he wonders, are stories of

> Zeus's lecheries and Hera's revenge, to a man on a rock? No past musings seemed relevant to my new estate, about which I found such a deal to say, memory couldn't keep pace. Moreover, the want of any audience but asphodel, goat, and tern played its part after all in the despairs that threatened me: a man sings better to himself if he can imagine someone's listening. In time therefore I devised solutions to both problems. Artist through, I'd been wont since boyhood when pissing on beach or bank to make designs and clever symbols with my water. From this source, as from Pegasus's idle hooftap on Mount Helicon, sprang now a torrent of inspiration: using tanned skins in place of a sand-beach, a seagull-feather for my tool, and a mixture of wine, blood, and squid-ink for a medium, I developed a kind of coded markings to record the utterance of mind and heart. By drawing out these chains of symbols I could so preserve and display my tale, it was unnecessary to remember it. I could therefore compose more and faster; I came largely to exchange song for written speech, and when the gods vouchsafed me a further great idea, that of launching my productions worldward in the empty amphorae, they loosed from my dammed soul a Deucalion-flood of literature. (*Funhouse*, pp. 192–93)

In Barth's allegory, then, writing begins in yearning, a yearning both for the preservation of one's imagined offspring and for contact with other human beings. We are back, in a very real way, to the desire to be wonderful, but with a change. The artist may not himself be wonderful, but may at least be the medium through which the wonderful passes.

Although Barth's allegory of the spirit of literature is mostly comic, even in describing despair, the mood of the prose changes appreciably when the despair is that special yearning of the writer for an audience. Some time after casting his amphorae on the waters, the anonymous minstrel discovers

> a parchment marked with ink, . . . on the foreshore. . . . The script was run, in places blank; I couldn't decipher it, or if I did, recognize it as my own, though it may have been.
>
> No matter: a new notion came, as much from the lacunae as from the rest, that roused in me first an echo of my former interest in things, in the end a resolve which if bone-cool was ditto deep: I had thought myself the only stranded spirit, and had survived by sending messages to whom they might concern; now I began to imagine that the world contained another like myself. Indeed, it might be astrew with islèd souls, become minstrels perforce, and the sea a-clink with literature! Alternatively, one or several of my messages may have got through: the document I held might be no ciphered call for aid but a reply, whether from the world or some marooned fellow-inksman: that rescue was on the way; that there was no rescue, for anyone, but my SOS's had been judged to be not without artistic merit by some who'd happened on them; that I should forget about my plight, a mere scribblers' hazard, and sing about goats and flowers instead, the delights of island life, or the goings-on among the strandees of that larger isle the world.
>
> I never ceased to allow the likelihood that the indecipherable ciphers were my own; that the sea had fertilized me as it were with my own seed. No matter, the principle was the same: that I could be thus messaged, even by that stranger my former self, whether or not the fact tied me to the world, inspired me to address it once again. (*Funhouse*, p. 196)

Similarily, the narrator of "Life-Story," sickened by the contemporary malaise of cleverness for the sake of cleverness, introversion for the sake of hypochondria, says of the Author:

> Read him fast or slow, intermittently, continuously, repeatedly, backward, not at all, he won't know it; he only guesses someone's reading or composing his sentences, such as this one, because he's reading or composing sentences such as this one; . . . . (*Funhouse*, p. 128)

The particular anguish of the writer is the obsession with creation and the deep-rooted fear that the creation may be both meaningless and unappreciated—an anguish Barth himself felt in his long struggle to win a readership. Perhaps this is why the bottle messages that recur in Barth's work are so important to their finders. The bottle message that Ambrose finds, presumably eons after it has been set awash by the anonymous bard, at least hints at the companionship he so desperately needs. And although the artist may feel the anguish most deeply because of his passion to communicate, there is a sense in which we are all on those isolated islands the anonymous poet described, communicating only uncertainly, sporadically, ambiguously. It is no wonder that Ambrose takes heart from the messageless text that is at once initiation into the society of the elect and carte blanche, at once confirmation of his own specialness and an announcement that he is (like Barth's other shape changers) a man without his own fate. Late in *Letters*, Ambrose will cast his own water-message into the sea.

As we have seen, for Ambrose the fatelessness constitutes the additional burden of being an artist, the one who lives through others, who must become the other in order to craft his works. That is why, on one level, Bellerophon is a kind of proto-artist, why the anonymous minstrel must be marooned, Menelaus be a disembodied voice, and Ambrose unable in his own identity to participate in the funhouse. It is also, on another level, the meaning of the Author's dream in *Letters*. In the short view, literature (small l, finally) results from the individual's longing to break through his isolation, and his fear of doing so. Although the anonymous minstrel who invents writing does not emphasize the anguish of the longing, preferring a light tone for the retelling of his early years, he makes it clear that like Menelaus—who also desired to find his identity in another and who became, with Proteus, a disembodied voice telling a tale—he felt himself not as good as other youths his age, somehow less able. Being apart from the ordinary world, he is in a position that is both painful and privileged. The pain is that he cannot be Aegisthus, who wins all that the minstrel loses, any more than Bellerophon can be Perseus or Ambrose, Peter. But the reason that the minstrel is an artist and Bellerophon and Menelaus only proto-artists is that the former recognizes the advantages of his privileged position. His detachment—described as an ability to view the world either tragically or comically and hence another instance of the tragic view—permits him to compensate for his losses in the real world by his vision of its richness and its imaginative possibilities. Like the youthful Ambrose, he may not reap the purely human pleasures of the funhouse, but there is much if not perfect compensation in his awareness of its workings and his ultimate mastery of them.

Throughout *Letters* Barth lets us follow Ambrose through the emergence of his second phase, his second cycle, in which he renounces finally his formalism, turns the graphic calendar design of *Letters* over to the Author, and says, "Adieu, Art" (*Letters*, p. 764). The mature Ambrose, a moderately successful writer nominated for the Maryland Laureateship, is writing a script for an avant garde production of a movie of the Author's "latest novel"—which the Author discovers means not his most recently published novel, but any present or future novel that is his latest. Practically, as the movie progresses under the direction of Prinz (a Burlingame-Cooke!), the filming separates itself further and further from the Author's writing in what becomes a war between the picture and the word, between the director and the scenarist. Words or text disappear from the movie as the disembodied voice becomes the voiceless picture. Ambrose also helps the Author with *Letters,* suggesting that the original plan to include in it the *Chimera* stories be rejected, and offering other advice. In the midst of a life of personal chaos, he seems to be gathering the strength to take some control of his fate. Within the movie he becomes not only writer, but actor, arguing loudly for the role he wants (contrast the situation of Jacob Horner, who is unable to create a role in which he can star). Outside the movie, the former youth too shy to smooch in the funhouse becomes the imperious lover of the widely experienced Germaine Bree (Lady Amherst)—lover of famous persons, former wife of Casteen, and historian—leading her through a regimen of intercourse that is staggering in its intensity and comedy. I suspect that Barth is making a quite telling point when he has Ambrose bid adieu to art and, in the same P.S., formally propose to his lover. He enters his new cycle, leaving art behind and entering history. When one no longer feels the anguish of isolation, there is no longer the need for art; when one becomes a part of history, one no longer writes imaginary histories. It is not that Pegasus can no longer fly, as the final bits of advice Ambrose gives the author prove, but that his flight is no longer needed.

The Sot-Weed Factor presents us with still another view of the artist; because of the discrepancy between Ebenezer's desire and his ability, it is a view more comic than that in the *Funhouse* stories. Like Ambrose, Ebenezer is an outsider; unlike Ambrose, he never quite gets inside. While other English youths are learning to replace their fathers, learning and half learning the traditional subjects in the traditional ways, Ebenezer plays word games, practices shape changing by "disguising his assumed identity in the presence of adults" (*Factor,* p. 6), and begins to live more in his imagination than in the world's reality. He knows

> very well, for instance, that "France is shaped like a teapot," but he could scarcely accept the fact that there was actually in

existence *at that instant* such a place as France, where people were speaking French and eating snails whether he thought about them or not, and that despite the virtual infinitude of imaginable shapes, this France would have to go on resembling a teapot forever. (P. 8)

Until the final dramatized scene in *The Sot-Weed Factor*, Ebenezer remains an Ambrose who has never had that complex experience in the funhouse, that intense realization that "if you knew all the stories behind all the people on the boardwalk, you'd see that *nothing* was what it looked like" (*Funhouse*, p. 91) and the loneliness of the knowledge that because he does understand, he "must construct funhouses for others and be their secret operator—though he would rather be among the lovers for whom funhouses are designed" (p. 97). As is appropriate for the Barthian artist, Ebenezer discovers his calling in a moment of failure in life. Unable to enjoy the favors of Joan Toast because he mistakes his lust for undying love, Ebenezer discovers his double vocation: he will be a virgin poet. Much of what Barth has to say about art in *The Sot-Weed Factor* arises dramatically because Ebenezer's physical innocence so perfectly matches his mental innocence. (If we remember the lesson of Bellerophon—that service to Aphrodite is necessary for inspiration—we will understand why Ebenezer's Pegasus never soars.)

Ebenezer becomes a poet in the same naive way that the young Giles becomes a grant tutor; it is not an addition to his character, not something to be learned or earned, not something he does. As he tells Burlingame (disguised as Lord Baltimore), he is a poet in the same sense that others are gentlemen. Yet quite early in the novel, Barth makes us aware that there is at least one other kind of artist. Joan Toast's pimp, McEvoy, is a fiddler—not a maestro, but good enough to earn his way by his talents. After McEvoy tries to blackmail Ebenezer, an act which will result in Ebenezer being sent to Maryland, McEvoy asks:

"Ye'll go to Maryland for a whore?"

"I'd not cross the street for a whore," Ebenezer said firmly, "but I shall cross the ocean for a principle! To you, haply, Joan Toast is a whore; to me she is a principle."

"To me she is a woman," replied McEvoy. "To you she's a hallucination." . . .

"What manner of artist [are] *you*," retorted McEvoy, "that can't see through it? And are ye in sooth a virgin, as Joan Toast swears?" (*Factor*, pp. 63–64)

After this, it should come as no surprise that Ebenezer begins his epic of Maryland before embarking from England; a part of the fun of those sections of the book when he is composing his epic is the discrepancy between his grandiose descriptions and the tawdry reality. When Ebenezer is surprised, on occasion, by reality, Burlingame is there to tell him playfully that

" 'Tis the genius of the poet to transcend his material: and it wants small eloquence to argue that the meaner the subject, the greater must be the transcension." (*Factor*, pp. 386–87)

Ebenezer's innocence—and Barth reminds us that "innocence" is but another word for "ignorance"—is a willful blindness to the conditions that surround him. As long as that blindness persists, he cannot be, to use a phrase from Barth's Library of Congress speech, "responsive to his times." His one successful poem, *The Marylandiad*, is written only after his recognition that his blindness has caused the ruin of those he sought to protect. After a dream vision (actually an opium dream) displaying the vanity and futility of scaling Parnassus, he determines that he will recycle his grandiose notes for the epic into a

"fiction! I'll be a tradesman, say—nay, a factor that comes to Maryland on's business, with every good opinion of the country, and is swindled of his goods and property. All my trials I'll reconceive to suit the plot and alter just enough to pass the printer!" (*Factor*, p. 458)

The irony of this is as wonderful as the implications. Ebenezer's now discarded epic was the total fabrication, the imaginative fiction; what he calls the "fiction" is—with names altered, etc., to protect the innocent—the history. Viewed more generally, Ebenezer cannot achieve even the limited stature as an artist that he does manage so long as he merely fabricates: the beasties of the funhouse have to be simulacra of the beasties outside, else literature is merely verbiage.

Barth makes the point quite openly in an interview with Glaser-Wörher in a comment about characterization. "I find almost everybody I know," he says,

> including myself, rather protean finally and difficult to lay hold of. . . . And if I didn't believe that were true of almost everybody I know and love I wouldn't be interested in fiction because I would be utterly self-regarding and I don't think I am. (P. 219)

I think we can generalize Barth's comment here to say that the interest of art is not merely its heartless technique—and Ebenezer's innocence is heartless in the most radical sense because it can love the object only as it imagines it to be—but its impassioned recognition of the conditions under which, in which, and through which individuals live.

In a final irony, Ebenezer's *Marylandiad* wins for him what he once thought he wanted, the recognition that the Laureateship of Maryland confers. Yet it does so in a surprising way. The satire that has replaced the epic expresses all of Ebenezer's bitterness, his disillusion with Maryland and its people; the poem is read, accepted, and approved because its very satire is interpreted as proof of the culture of the state, for how could barbarism cultivate such artful self-criticism? His fame leaves Ebenezer more isolated than before, perhaps for the first time in his life deeply aware of the real difference between himself and his fellows.

If the personal lot of the artist is not a happy one, his professional lot has its own difficulties. Perhaps the most obvious of those are described in Ebenezer's vision of Parnassus. Although a delight to read, it is too long to quote here so I shall have to summarize. The would-be Laureate imagines himself at the foot of two peaks and is told that Parnassus is the one on the right; when he mentions that the answer would be different if he approached from the other side, he is told, "Right is right and be damned to ye"—which leaves him in the existential predicament of having a choice to make but no basis for making it. The peaks are guarded by "ugly men with clubs," presumably critics, who "mashed climbers' fingers"; on higher levels they have hatchets or bodkins. Those who help the ascent at one stage attack at the next. In other areas on the peaks are "groups of women who, whether in the manner of Circe or Calypso, invited the climbers from their objective"; in other areas, treadmills and false signposts lead to precipices, deserts, jungles, jails, and lunatic asylums. Those who are not driven off are sheltered by "heavy pink mists" (insubstantial fads?), "the bulk of the peak on which they sat" (tradition?), or the grapes and China oranges that they fling to the envious mob below (toadying to reviewers and readers?)

Ebenezer is finally transported up to a safe place; he finds himself looking down at the other climbers and talking to an old man with Burlingame-like characteristics:

> "'Sbody, but aren't they silly-looking?" he exclaimed. "And how ill-mannered, pushing and breaking wind on one another!"
>
> "They've little else to do," the old man answered.
>
> "But there's naught here to climb for: you've said that yourself!"
>
> "Aye, nor aught anywhere else, either. They'd as well climb mountains as sit and die."
>
> "I'm going to jump!" Ebenezer declared suddenly. "I've no wish to see these things a moment more!"
>
> "No reason why ye oughtn't, nor any why ye ought."
>
> The Laureate made no further move to jump, but sat on the edge of the peak and sighed. "'Tis all most frightfully empty, is't not?"

"Empty indeed," the old man said, "but there's naught o'
good or bad in that. Why sigh?"

"Why not?" asked Ebenezer.

"But why?" repeated the old man.

"Why not?"

"Why not indeed?" the old man sighed. (*Factor*, pp. 453–
56)

The dream-vision is, as we have seen, prophetic. Although
the reception of *The Marylandiad* may not raise Ebenezer to
the heights of Parnassus, it does secure for him a certain ele-
vation. But once there, he finds his work misunderstood, his
success meaningless. Like Perseus, Bellerophon, Giles, and
even Barth himself, success means either stagnation or beginning anew, recycling.

If Ebenezer is fated to learn the same lesson as heroes from
his mythological past and the Author from his future, it is
because Barth seems to believe that things do not change
nearly as much as we would like to believe. A part of Barth's
immense strength as a writer, both technically and thematically, is the peculiar way in which he is "responsive to his
time"; as we have seen when discussing more general issues,
it means standing both within and without one's times, having
an awareness of and passion about issues, while preserving a
certain detachment—that cause or result of the tragic view.
His attitude toward literature in general and the novel in particular is similarly "responsive," perhaps nowhere more than
in "Life-Story," which is both a modernistic tour de force and
a harsh critique of some of our more fashionable assumptions
about life and literature.

On one level, "Life-Story" (and its companion piece, "Title") is a compendium of clichés of contemporary fiction. It is
one of those involuted stories of a writer writing a story about
himself writing a story, becoming a fictional character in his
own fiction, and wondering whether his life is indeed a fiction. Like a good metafiction, the story speculates on its own
style, philosophizes about the reader, leads both reader and

writer through the frustrations of fiction-making as it explains them, is self-conscious of its place in the spectrum of literature in general, meditates on the author-story relationship, considers the possibility of the author's sanity, bemoans the death of the novel and of society, and makes all those other requisite gestures to our age of confusion, anxiety, and purposelessness.

On a second level, "Life-Story" has a ring of truth to it. The writer's speculations are legitimate speculations for one in the midst of a story that is not going well. The concerns about getting to the next sentence, about the fate of literature, about the reader, about getting too autobiographical, the daydreams and interruptions, the sense that the story the author wants to write is not the story he is writing—all the doubts and fears and frustrations Barth puts into "Life-Story" help make it add up to much more than a series of modernistic clichés and transform it into a moving account of a person's consciousness as he tries to do something he considers necessary. The story acquires added resonance from other stories in *Lost in the Funhouse* that dramatize the problems of authorship.

What is so peculiarly Barthian about "Life-Story," however, is an additional level, an ability to refuse to take the issues seriously while taking them seriously, the sense that the anonymous poet had that life is too comic for tears and too tragic for laughter. After acknowledging that "his fictions were preoccupied with these fears [of exposing too much of his personal life] among the other, more serious preoccupations," he inanely exclaims, "Hot dog" (p. 124). The rhetoric, ranging from the banal to the pretentious, constantly undercuts the treatment of the author and his story as unfortunate victims. Further undercutting the portrayal of the suffering writer is the ease of his life. The story ends as his wife says,

> "Happy birthday" . . . kissing him et cetera to obstruct his view of the end of the sentence he was nearing the end of, playfully refusing to be nay-said so that in fact he did at last as

did his fictional character end his ending story endless by in-
terruption, cap his pen. . [*sic*] (P. 129)

And so we may assume that the discontent of the writer, as
often happens with Barth's heroes and artists, was at least in
part the result of a birthday signaling a change in his life. The
discontent is real; it is as real as the discontent of Perseus and
Bellerophon and the Genie, but the form it takes is pure
twentieth-century *Weltschmerz.*

In what is almost certainly a broadside against some of the
more dehumanized and self-pitying clichés of avant garde fiction, the voice in "Title"—presumably a short story dissatisfied with the way it is developing—delivers a very sharp
sermon:

> the fact is that people still lead lives, mean and bleak and brief
> as they are, briefer than you think, and people have characters
> and motives that we divine more or less inaccurately from
> their appearance, speech, behavior, and the rest, . . . people
> still fall in love, and out, yes, in and out, and out and in, and
> they please each other, and hurt each other, isn't that the
> truth, and they do these things in more or less conventionally
> dramatic fashion, unfashionable or not, . . . and what goes on
> between them is still not only the most interesting but the
> most important thing in the bloody murderous world.
> (*Funhouse*, p. 113)

The point is clear enough, and it is almost certainly Barth's
own rather than a dramatic convenience. The attitude behind
the sermon explains in part Barth's penchant for humanizing
the myths he borrows; even his demigods still fall in love, still
hurt and are hurt, and still bemoan the brevity of their lives.

Perhaps Barth gives his best version of his concern with
current fiction to our Author as paraphrased by Lady Amherst:

> A[mbrose] assures me that you do not yourself take with much
> seriousness those Death-of-the-Novel or End-of-Letters chaps,
> but that you *do* take seriously the climate that takes such ques-

tions seriously; you exploit that apocalyptic climate, he maintains, to reinspect the origins of narrative fiction in the oral
tradition. (*Letters*, p. 438)

Yes, Barth's fictions seem to say, human beings in our part of
the twentieth century do feel anxiety, nausea, purposelessness, helplessness. Writers perhaps feel them more acutely
than most persons because their craft requires that they explore the way their fellow humans feel.

The writer, according to Barth, has still another problem;
he

> knows the history of the medium he's working in as well as the
> present urgent concerns of his mind and spirit, and he tries to
> express each in a way reflective of the other. There's a kind of
> entelechy involved. An artist should be aware of the effects
> that have been wrought in his genre and of the kinds of things
> that have been said so that he will appreciate the problems of
> saying anything freshly and originally at this late hour.. . .
> This catches him in something of a paradox: the more he
> knows the better an artist he can theoretically become, and
> yet the knowledge he acquires is overwhelming—it places
> him in competition with the accumulated best of human histo-
> ry. . . . The feat becomes harder and harder to pull off, but at
> the same time it becomes more and more admirable to man-
> age it successfully. (*Barth*, pp. 210–11)

The modern artist is caught in the same bind Perseus was: the
great adventures are over, the great books written; the artist
can no more repeat the works of others than Perseus can repeat his own feats, for to do so turns him into Bellerophon,
the imitation hero. Like all serious writers, the modern writer
must still write of people who "fall in love, and out, . . . and
hurt each other" and must do so in "more or less conventionally dramatic fashion, unfashionable or not," for what goes
on between people "is still not only the most interesting but
the most important thing in the bloody murderous world."
Not to write of "the most important thing in the bloody mur-

derous world" is to write work that is passionless; to neither
know nor use the conventions of one's medium is to write
without technique. From either side, the writer has upon his
spirit the whole weight of the past of his art. Hence, quite
probably, a large part of the reason for the tone of "Title" and
"Life-story."

How does the modern writer manage the burden? Barth
has two general answers—the tragic view and recycling. The
tragic view, as we've seen, is chiefly a certain detachment, an
acknowledgement of both sides of a proposition and a refusal
to despair in the fact of lack of certainty; it permits Barth that
mixture of playfulness and seriousness that is the hallmark of
his work. It permits him to acknowledge the reality of the
feelings that the pressures of his age are unique—that there
has never been another period in which achievement was so
difficult and universal doom so certain—while simultaneously
admitting that the feeling of uniqueness is unwarranted. The
scene in which the anonymous minstrel, living in a past so
remote that he is privileged to invent both writing and fiction,
laments that all the good work has been done is a splendid
example of the implications of Barth's tragic view of literature.
Having seen what he has seen in Agamemnon's court, having
spent most of his life writing poems and telling stories, marooned on a desert island with neither audience nor new subjects, his lament is perfectly understandable; we can sympathize because his feelings have the kind of reality feelings
attain in a plausibly motivated fiction. Yet we are simultaneously aware of the countless stories which will have been
told since that dawn of fiction. In *Letters*, Barth lets Lady
Amherst remind us that Samuel Richardson—writing just as
the novel was to become the major literary form in Western
literature—"was the first to speak of the death of the novel"
(p. 439). This kind of double vision permits Barth to be responsive—in the fullest sense of that word—to the modern
feeling that all the best has been done, without feeling responsible for it, either in the sense of having to share it completely or of having to atone for it. (The result of Barth's dou-

ble vision is what Derrida would call an "erasure," an expression that "erases" or cancels itself in such a way that the result is neither a negation of the reference nor an affirmation of it, but rather a reminder that we have outlived the Aristotelian world of "and-or" and entered the modern world of "both-and.") The tragic view of art, at least as it operates in Barth's fictions, permits the artist to have those qualities that Barth seems to feel essential: a feeling of uniqueness, a tremendous responsibility to craft both as model and as equipment for the communication of passion, a sense of personal and professional isolation, a desire to be thought marvelous—without accepting the loss of creativity those feelings tend to engender. It is true that the novel is dying; it is equally true that the novel has been dying since its birth, a fact which makes it still more human. Whatever the truth of Barth's tragic view, it is a supremely effective defense mechanism because it acknowledges the validity of the author's plight even as it undercuts it. *The Ocean of the Stream of Stories*, to use that wonderful old title of our oldest anthology of narrative, is in no more danger of drying up for the contemporary author than it was for the anonymous bard. Barth's tragic view permits his fictions to show, sometimes quite movingly, the oppressiveness of the burden of being a modern even as they remind us that all times are modern for the persons who live through them.

We have seen that recycling may be considered a means of dramatizing the tragic view, but its importance in Barth's understanding of modern narrative deserves a more detailed look. Most modern writers who are sensitive to the burden of the past attempt, when they describe their works, to emphasize their break with the past; Durrell's claim to have found the "classic form of the modern novel" is typical. Yet in Durrell's case, we know that the work succeeds not because the break is complete, not because he has shrugged off the burden, but because he has managed to carry it so gracefully—to tell, in The Quartet, several rousing good stories complete with an abundance of all the good things that novels have tra-

ditionally done. Barth, with his passion for recycling, prefers
to emphasize the use of the burden, the adjusting to it, rather
than the escape from it. If we remember Barth's notion that
basics do not change greatly, his reuse of older forms and
myths is fitting. As he remarks in the afterword to *Roderick
Random:*

> Adventure and adversity—hazarding forth and overcoming—
> are what the enduring attractiveness of *Roderick Random*
> comes to. Those ancient, most profoundly lifelike human
> sports, the obstacle race and the scavenger hunt, are also the
> oldest appealingest matter for the storyteller.[11]

The two metaphors, the obstacle race and the scavenger hunt,
provide both forms and subjects for narrative, from the labors
of Hercules to the most recent adventure story.

A list of the forms that Barth has recycled would be long and
impressive, ranging from Greek tragedy (the "Oedipus Tal-
iped" section of *Giles Goat-Boy* and, nondramatically, the story
of Giles itself) to such minor forms as the dream-vision and the
swearing contest in *The Sot-Weed Factor.* It would be tempting
to make rather large claims for what Barth does to renew the
old forms, to talk about grafting a version of existentialist philosophy on the old-fashioned historical novel (*The Sot-Weed
Factor*) or experimenting with oral performance techniques in
a set of linked stories (*Lost in the Funhouse*), or turning the
mythos of the hero into a contemporary *roman à clef.* It would
be equally tempting to describe the brilliance of Barth's inclusion of minor forms within his work—the multiple functions of
the dream-vision, for example, in *The Sot-Weed Factor.* The
example of most of Barth's work after *The End of the Road,*
though, makes an impressive point: old forms neither die nor
fade away. They may go dormant (and their sleep is likely to be
deepest in the generation immediately following their greatest
success—hence Barth's avoidance of literary realism), but they
can come to life again in the hands of a master. *The Sot-Weed
Factor* succeeds not because it is an existentialist-historical

comedy (which is a specific way of saying that it does not succeed merely because it combines the modern and the traditional), but because Barth's imagination can invent a thousand
details that make Ebenezer come alive in the way that Charlie
Chaplin came alive as a clown, as one of those rich stereotypes
that open the imagination of the reader to the complex possibilities of humankind. And it comes alive because of Barth's
virtuoso technique—both in the sense of providing the skill to
win our credence for Ebenezer and his companions and in the
sense of the mastery of an astonishing variety of skills that keep
the knowledgeable reader delighted. The contests between
Burlingame and Cooke, for example, have a kind of energy and
technical flourish that interests on the sheer level of "how-
long-can-he-keep-it-up?" The journey of the sperm in "Night-
Sea Journey" is essentially an obstacle course with the narrator,
the sperm, commenting upon the frustrations of the race—
ranging from the deaths of his companions to the purposelessness of it, speculations about its conclusion, and so on.
By a wonderfully full and intricate pattern of metaphor, the
sperm bobbing and fighting its way through the birth canal
becomes the anonymous minstrel's story-filled amphorae bobbing their way through the seas. And by a simple act of jux-
taposition, the sperm becomes Ambrose, who is born in the
next story. As Ambrose matures, we discover he has the same
qualities of self-doubt, perseverance, impassioned confusion
about whether he is wonderful or common, and need for reas-
surance that characterize the sperm. A more detailed analysis
could relate "Night-Sea Journey" to the theme of love as it
appears, for example, in "Menelaiad," or to the analogy Barth
frequently makes between sex and art; the human loneliness of
the sperm even provides a pointed yet undeveloped contrast
between the inception of the true artist and Jerome Bray's
inhuman techniques for fertilizing the women he victimizes.
However, the point here is not to explicate the implications of
"Night-Sea Journey," but to hint quietly at the immense skill of
Barth in recycling a form as old as the story-cycle. The old

forms do not work for Barth simply because he has the courage to use them, and certainly not because he is too uninventive to imagine any other; they work for him for the same reason that any form has ever worked for any artist—because of the imagination that can envision a full and exciting world and the skill that can realize it. It is not, if we remember the lesson of Perseus, the recycling that is important; to recycle meaningfully, Perseus has still to be Perseus, still to be the hero. For Barth's recycling of old forms to succeed, Barth has to be Barth, to be the immensely inventive and skilled fictionalist.

Barth's recycling includes content rather than form (if I may use a distinction that is as superficially useful as it is ultimately indefensible). Although it would be useful to speak of at least three levels of Barth's recycling of content—the recycling of his personal experiences in his fictions, the recycling of his past fictions (most notably in *Letters*), and the recycling of myth—I shall discuss only the latter in some detail, though the problems raised on each of the levels are especially interesting and deserve separate articles. If we imagine a continuum ranging from the minimal alteration of one's experience in strictly autobiographical fiction, through a sort of halfway point in Joyce's *Ulysses*, say, to such highly generalized use of it in Faulkner's novels, it seems clear that Barth's appearance as Author in "The Dunyazadiad" and *Letters* constitutes a unique use of the personal. The recycling of characters in *Letters* gives that novel the feel of an immensely long symphonic coda and poses fascinating questions about the interrelationship of texts.

Barth somewhere makes the very interesting observation that the modern use of myth, as typified by Joyce, consists of demonstrating that contemporary human beings recapitulate the mythic patterns—e.g., Stephen Bloom as Telemachus is only the most obvious of hundreds of possible examples. Barth prefers to reverse the use, to show the mythic figure as contemporary (or at least sharing the concerns of contemporary—and all—persons) rather than showing the contemporary as mythic. Perseus, the intrepid hero, becomes in Barth's recycling of the myth not merely the hero as hero, but the hero as human. His problems are internalized; his real task is not merely external (to slay Medusa) but internal (to discover whether he still is a hero, and still deserves the admiration he receives). What makes the reversal work, however, is not simply the concept, but its execution: the exaggeratedly prosaic language of many of the sections, the almost clichéd presentation of the symptoms of male menopause, the unheroic typicality of Perseus's thinking—all these combine to turn Perseus from stock mythic hero to a certain version of stock modern man. The following passage is typical; Perseus is explaining the reasons for his second journey to Calyxa:

"You saw how it was, . . . the kids were grown and restless; Andromeda and I had become different people; our marriage was on the rocks. The kingdom took care of itself; my fame was sure enough—but I'd lost my shine with my golden locks: twenty years it was since I'd headed Medusa; I was twenty kilos overweight and bored stiff. With half a life to go, I felt fettered and coffered as ever by Danae's womb, the brass-bound chest, Polydectes's tasks. In fact—please keep your face straight—I became convinced I was petrifying, and asked my doctor if it mightn't be the late effects of radiation from Medusa. 'Just aging of the old joints,' the fool declared, correctly, told me to forget about the Gorgon, give up ouzo, get more exercise. But hare-hunts can't hold a candle to monstermachy: I stayed up too late, drank too many, traded shameless on my authority to bore each night a captive audience with the story of my life. 'Change of scene, then,' the doctor ordered: 'bit of a sea-trip, do you oodles.' He even winked: 'Take the Missus along: second honeymoon, et cetera.'" (*Chimera*, p. 79)

And so Perseus recycles himself as he is recycled by Barth. The myth lives anew not because deep down within us a Perseus may be lurking, but because on the surface Perseus is very much like us, or at any rate like people whom we can recognize.

I suspect that Barth's inversion of the use of myth is psychologically more valid than the standard use; more cautiously, it does seem certain that the approaches work for different kinds of readers. Whatever the historical realities, the gulf between me and the standard Perseus is too great for comprehension on any but an intellectual level, despite the claims of the Jungians. When I recognize that Stephen Bloom is an avatar of Telemachus, I must admit delight (and it is real delight, and one of the legitimate delights of art), but a delight which is intellectual rather than emotional. The Telemachus of myth is a kind of abstraction, his steadfastness of purpose limits him too greatly, cuts off too many potential areas of experience, for me to admit that the myth adds directly any significant emotional depth to *Ulysses*. For those who are not sympathetic, Barth's treatment of his heroes may seem to trivialize them; for those of us who are sympathetic, his treatment brings them within human range without diminishing their wonder. Although it is not quite fair to Joyce and other modern writers who use myth in the orthodox ways, it is *almost* fair to remark that, whereas the standard use attempts to achieve power through the importation of a ready-made symbol system, Barth attempts to transform that system within the fiction. One consequence, incidentally, is that Joyce and Barth require quite different kinds of attention. As a glance at the Joyce bibliography shows, much of the labor in interpreting Joyce is the tracking down and elaboration of scholarly materials—versions of the myth, word usage, etc.—as a preliminary to understanding. Although such work is occasionally helpful in appreciating Barth's work, it is seldom indispensable. Joyce demands a learned and intelligent reader, Barth merely an intelligent reader.

The Barthian use of myth also establishes a fortunate base for one of the things Barth does best—comedy. The fundamental incongruity between expectation and result, between, in this case, the general reverence for the mythic hero and the ordinariness of the hero's concerns, is the stuff of which laughter can be made. But, of course, as soon as we mention incongruity we have returned to the Barthian tragic view, a view which insists on seeing both the heroic and the commonplace simultaneously and on denying neither. Appropriately, three of Barth's most humourous recyclings of myth ("Menelaiad," "Persied," and "Dunyazadiad") integrate into themselves both the ordinariness of love and its awesomely powerful mystery. The burden of the past under which so many contemporary artists groan is, Barth's fictions show, less an impediment than a bundle of treasures that can be used by the gifted and diligent. As Barth observes in an interview with Prince:

> The idea of writing a novel which imitates the form of the Novel, or which imitates some other form of document, is not so decadent as it sounds at first blush. In fact, that's where the genre began—with Cervantes pretending that he's Homete Benengeli, Alonzo Quijano pretending that he's Don Quixote; Fielding parodying Richardson, Richardson imitating letters, and so forth. The novel seems to have its origins in documental imitation, really. . . . [In the modern penchant for imitation] one simply feels that the novel is coming full circle. (*Introduction*, p. 33)

If the contemporary novel is artifice, it is because art has always been artifice.

But is it merely artifice? We have seen Barth's annoyance when critics accuse him of being a mere technician, but the charge is at least superficially understandable if not finally justifiable. Barth seldom misses an opportunity to play a literary game; he will rewrite *Oedipus Rex*, turn himself into a genie, pun outrageously, create literary set pieces in larger works, weave a dense texture of allusion between his texts, have narrators self-consciously break into a story with concerns over such trivia as the use of italics, play off sets of formal and subject expectations against each other, distort time sequences, toy with the rhythm of the Lord's Prayer—in short, fill his funhouses to the brim with surprises, half-familiar figures, dead ends, mirrors, wind machines, odd perspectives, and all the gimmicks that in the hands of lesser artists remain gimmicks. He has also provided ammunition for his critics in his statements about the function of art, both within and outside his fictions. In *The Sot-Weed Factor*, Ebenezer Cooke, terrified, has beshat himself and gone into hiding. He contemplates his predicament; remembering that he is a scholar, he searches through his learning for help. History and philosophy fail.

> He did not even consider physics, astronomy, and the other areas of natural philosophy, . . . nor did he crack his memory on the plastic arts, for he knew full well no Phidias nor Michelangelo would deign to immortalize a state like his, whatever their attraction for human misery. No, he resolved at last, it was to literature he must turn for help, and should sooner, for literature alone of all the arts and sciences took as her province the entire range of man's experience and behavior—from cradle to grave and beyond, from emperor to hedge-whore, from the burning of cities to the breaking of wind—and human problems of every magnitude: in literature alone one might find catalogued with equal care the ancestors of Noah, the ships of the Achaians—
>
> "And the bum-swipes of Gargantua!" he exclaimed aloud.

Gargantua has reported that the best of bumswipes is the neck of a live white goose, an expedient Ebenezer finds most impractical. He concludes, "with heavy heart," that literature,

> for though it afforded one a certain sophistication about life and a release from one's single mortal destiny, it did not, except accidentally, afford solutions to practical problems. (*Factor*, pp. 173)

If such passages about the futility of literature are taken seriously by Barth's critics, it is in part because he has repeatedly maintained that his interest in fiction is in its "artifice" (*Introduction*, pp. xvii–xviii) and denied that it has any *essential* effect on society (*Barth*, p. 217). Yet we could hardly expect the founder and champion of the tragic view to have so one-sided a view. How, then, to justify the almost obsessive interest in games?

In an important section of the Prince interview, Barth defined fiction

> as a kind of true representation of the distortion we all make of life. In other words, it's a representation of a distortion; not a representation of life itself, but a representation of a representation of life. If you acknowledge that premise to begin with, there's no reason in the world why you can't do all sorts of things that otherwise could be objected to on philosophical or other grounds. . . . If you acknowledge that you're doing it as an imitation of the way we in fact characterize each other in life, then you're not pretending to an illegitimate omniscience—you're not pretending that the novel is something it isn't. Art *is* artificial, after all. (*Introduction*, p. 30)

To generalize, art neither tells nor creates truth in the classical, mimetic sense; its basis is not any kind of reality—common sense, historical, philosophical, whatever—but rather the artificial structure, the distortion, that is our only way of dealing with it. Put another way, Barth knows from the start what Lessing's Anna Wulf must go through madness to learn—that no number of notebooks, novels, screenplays, adaptations, dreams, or memories will ever capture the reality without distortion. Whereas Lessing prefers to concentrate on the terrifying aspects of the uncertainty, Barth prefers to emphasize the benign. A Lessing, at least before *Briefing for a Descent into Hell*, might have been concerned with the Truth of the Perseus myth; Barth is eager to acknowledge that any telling of it we can or might recover—even Perseus's own—is already a distortion of what might have happened.

But is a distortion of a distortion worth doing? I suspect Barth's first answer to that question would be something like, "It's all we have." He might then refer to Todd Andrews's rationale for suicide, which is equally a rationale for continued living, and point out that his impassioned "Yes, it is worthwhile" is a totally unjustifiable preference, one of those decisions that is immensely significant in the here and now, however insignificant it might be ultimately. I suspect further that Barth's best answer would come from the anonymous minstrel, although Ambrose and Menelaus make much the same point, as do in less direct ways many of Barth's other characters. The answer is that unless we can share our distortions, we are marooned, isolated on our small isles and desperate for another voice. That desperation, that lack of sharing what we make of reality, is for Barth the birth of fiction; on a more important level, it is also the birth of love. If life and art are the same funhouse, to pass through life alone is a terror that will never be alleviated so long as we are alone. Barth's fictions invite us to share. We in the twentieth century are not lone, lorn, isolated creatures, alienated and anxious, not so much because our feeling is a distortion of reality, but because, as Barth is able to persuade us, those feelings have been shared by humans throughout history. The fictions remind us that in a world in which theoretically we are not supposed to be able to communicate, human beings have communicated with great success; that if all values are ultimately relative, the most basic values are relative only to the degree that humanity as a species is ephemeral. Perhaps, most specially Barthian, his work reminds us that in an absurd world we might as well choose life; and his wit, his inventiveness, his basic good sense, should help convince us that, precisely because it makes no difference in the long run, the choice of laughter and life makes all the difference in the short span we have.

Chapter 6

Conclusion

A critic writing a conclusion to a study such as this is in much the same position as Anna Wulf as she looks back upon the events that inspired her first novel. There is that awareness that the experience was vastly more complex than the telling of it and, in addition, the sense that to write a conclusion is to pretend to finalize in words what ought never be finalized in experience. Conclusions tend to say, "This is the way it was, is now, and ever shall be. Amen." And if, as critic or reader, we have learned anything from our authors, it must be that we can never recapture the way it was, that our knowledge of how it is now is unreliable, and our knowledge of how it will be merely one of some vast number of alternate visions. We know that texts—whether artistic or critical—consume themselves, deconstruct, and do other things more melodramatic than critics a generation ago would have dreamed. And we know that we can no more read the same book twice than Eugene Gant can go home again, and for much the same reason. Our knowledge of our world, Barth has told us, is entirely at the mercy of our memory, and our memory slavishly follows whim and interest. In one way or another, each of our authors has said much the same. Fowles would distinguish between memories created freely and those created by contemporary stereotyping (but perhaps the former is merely another name for whim, the latter for interest). Durrell would probably agree without much qualification, and perhaps give the line to Pursewarden. White would have some reservation, perhaps, about the inaccuracy of memory, at least among his *zaddikhim*, although he would certainly acknowledge that the creation of a mandala to share the memory is one of humankind's most rare, and precious, and difficult achievements. And, even though probably put off by the lightness of tone of Barth or Durrell, the creator of Anna Wulf would have to agree.

Except for a change of tense (which is more illusory than real, because prefaces are usually written after the text), the problem of the conclusion is precisely the problem of the preface that Derrida worried through. To say what one will say, or has said, but in different words and a different form from the original—is that possible? Isn't it, to use an older vocabulary, to commit the heresy of the paraphrase? If I present my conclusions as a series of generalizations about the material I have looked at, I am distorting, abstracting, generalizing, deconstructing, and consuming my own text. I could, for example, at this stage launch into a structuralist analysis of the narratological features of the *Künstlerroman*, with an appendix on the self-reflexive novel. But to do that would be to *not* discuss specific content questions—for example, the role of the artist in society, the definition of art, the relation of art to morality, and so on. And those generalizations about the concerns of aesthetics could be made only while subordinating or ignoring questions about the peculiar cultural conditions that provoked the particular descriptions of artists and their plight we get in the fictions. If I choose to do all three, then I have the problem of which to put first, second, third; the last will make the strongest impression, and therefore ought to be the most important. . . .

What I have drifted into here is, of course, a mild fit of self-reflexive criticism. If I were to continue in this vein, I might begin the same kind of analysis I made of Barth's "Life Story" —pointing out its self-reflexive nature, mentioning the current critical preoccupations it occupies itself with, and so on; then I might go on to mention that, yes, although this is the fashion in criticism—or a fashion—the problems are nevertheless real problems; and then, as I did with the Barth story, show that I am both denying and admitting the problem in the way I treat it.

To be self-reflexive for just a moment more. As I was writing the preceding paragraphs, I was not certain whether I was producing a poor imitation of Derrida, or of Fowles (as he worries about the position of the endings of *The French Lieutenant's Woman*), or of Barth, or of Barthes. And that is the significant point—our novelists, our philosophers, and our critics have lost their innocence. A critic imbued with the contemporary habits of mind and feeling will be as reluctant to bind the subject of his studies as Fowles is to lock his budding aristoi into any particular fate. Like the narrator of *The French Lieutenant's Woman*, who gradually changes his public persona from preacher to impresario, the persona of the philosopher and critic has changed from discoverer of TRUTH to arranger of fictions. We can no longer deceive ourselves into believing that we have the authority to tell the definitive truth about the *Künstlerroman* or the portrait of the contemporary artist or the *Zeitgeist;* we can only bring together a set of authors, play the spotlight as we will, and hope that by seeing things in part from our perspective, the reader will have taken one of those little steps to the left or the right that Durrell describes as so indispensable to a healthy relationship with reality.

Perhaps the most surprising feature about the writers we have looked at is their uniform belief that it is, in this era of troubles, possible to have a healthy relationship with reality. As Lessing especially—and each of the others in his own way—makes abundantly clear, the odds are against it. The loss of that comforting sense that Wordsworth had—that nature ne'er betrayed the heart that loved her—is precisely the change that recycles our contemporary novelists. In order to substantiate their faith in nature and in humanity, the artists we have considered have to struggle considerably harder than did Wordsworth. Nature, for Wordsworth's friend Coleridge, was God's mighty alphabet—a message of literally infinite meaning and hope, eternally there for the reading. For the artist after relativity, alternate logics and mathematical systems, and indeterminancy, nature is less an alphabet than a code that translates only into another code, in an infinite regress of shifting perspectives; it is no wonder that so many of the artists our novelists have described suffer from a kind of spiritual vertigo. The maturing artist—Darley on his way to the nudge, Anna Wulf suffering through her writer's block, Alf Dubbo trying to paint what he sees and feels, Daniel Martin working up his courage to write an honest book, or the voices of Ambrose in *Lost in the Funhouse*—is much like Durrell's Keats in his journalistic phase: each lives with the anxiety that Truth is always around the next corner, that one more bit of experience will provide the wisdom to read the mighty alphabet. And all the experience, and all the dealings with people, and all the dealings with nature, and all the contemporary wise men, tell the artist that there is no Truth.

But if, by the kind of miracle that White and Durrell and Lessing dream in their more optimistic moments, one were actually to experience Truth? If Ambrose's water-message did indeed offer a message that we could read? Then, unfortunately, the letters would transform themselves within our memories. Whim and interest would falsify the message; Lessing's projectionist, Fowles's nemo, would replay it in our minds with such shifting variety that we would know the loss better than the reality.

But if, another miracle, we should truly remember the first miracle? How to express it? How to have enough human compassion, enough courage, enough honest love, to paint the truth of Rhoda's hump or to dance Waldo's sterility? How to choose the words, when we know that the eye sees in three dimensions and that words make only cartoons? How to have the courage to contradict the cultural stereotype that mandates tales of universal misery to writers who must admit that much of their lives has been spent in comparative warmth and comfort and ease and security and success and, sometimes, even happiness? Or that tells them that their forms are played out, their messages delivered long ago?

I suspect, if our authors were to answer the questions in a word, it would be "faith." And I am certain that none of our authors would agree about the implications of that word.

For Durrell, the word would probably be pronounced with a smile. In some ways the most romantically optimistic of our authors, he believes that we can discover the Heraldic Universe if we are attentive and loving enough—which means that if we can abandon our egos sufficiently to listen and look and feel and love and reserve judgment and imagine, the nudge will come. If the artist matures wisely—shuts off no possible aspect of reality and keeps practicing at the nets—he can preserve that vision of the Heraldic Universe until artists have lost their "vanity and laziness" and the audience its "self-indulgent blindness." When, as readers and writers our imaginations are healthy, our imaginations shall enact Utopia.

For Lessing, the faith is in the gods, in universal physical / spiritual forces, in DNA, in . . . , but "I gotta use words," as she says in *Briefing for a Descent into Hell*, and words deconstruct thought and feeling. Lessing's faith is perhaps the most desperate we have encountered. It assumes that contemporary humanity is as doomed as its Cro-Magnon cousins. Our best instrument of communication is words, and we have seen in detail Lessing's despair over language. So long as words are our best hope of communication—which means not the mere transferral of an approximation of our thoughts and feelings, but a transferral so full that the experiences can in fact be shared—we are locked within ourselves, a species of individuals competing as individuals, as political blocs, as classes, as societies, as races. We will not work each for the other unless we feel each with the other, so our selfishness speeds the decline of the technology upon which our overpopulated planet depends for survival. If we do not interact with full understanding, we will interact with bombs. But for Lessing, there is that faith in the something—a universal power, order, spirit—that is even now preparing for the new humanity. Whether that new species is the emerging beings hinted at in Canopus in Argos, avatars of Mercury like Charles Watson, or Martha Quest's empaths, Lessing has an unshakeable faith that some part of humanity will make the change. Meanwhile, the true modern artist suffers, and the suffering is double. Lessing's vision is so radical, so contrary to our communal sense, that faith in it can come only after all else is lost—and to lose all that our culture has taught us is to experience absolute madness. It is, to paraphrase Saul Green, to go as low as we can go. Lessing is the contemporary mistress of the dark night of the soul, of the harrowing of hell, of that complete loss whose only cure is complete and radical faith. This is the experience that Lessing's modern artist must undergo to be a complete artist; it is but the first half of the artist's double suffering. The second is the artist's awareness that however fine, however true and beautiful the art produced, it will become obsolete the moment the vision becomes reality. In Lessing's vision, artists are not the unacknowledged legislators of the world they have been led to believe they are. They are at best boulder pushers, minor prophets who help humanity make small steps, help preserve a vision of love and courage, and perhaps point the way.

White, if I read him correctly, would be very little inclined to explain his faith. It is, quite simply, the inexplicable certainty that stones and chairs and bread and birds and beasts and even people are loveable, and that in fact love is the only proper response to everything except the occasional fool who refuses to love or be loved. Because the faith is inexplicable, White wisely refuses to write about it at length—an occasional passage in *Flaws in the Glass*, for instance, mostly to say or to show that it is inexplicable. He prefers to show its effects. I suspect White would be somewhat impatient with the utopian visions of Durrell and Lessing, because there is in White's character if not his theology very much of the classic Protestant. Salvation, for White, is an individual thing. Its precondition, love, is a gift, an act of grace, the power to achieve it given to the individual by something very much like what Fowles would call hazard—White's characters do not ever fall from grace, nor ever attain it on their own. White does not question its why or how; he scrutinizes its consequences. Its result is not inevitably happiness or even chiefly happiness, but rather a depth and quality of experience that transcends individual happiness. His saints may suffer greatly and dramatically, like Voss and Himmelfarb, or they may suffer a life of small slights and stupidities, like Mary Hare and Arthur, but on some level each recognizes that the suffering is but the price to be paid for the ecstasy of love. That love—or, to return to the word I used earlier, reverence—is the only force that lets us escape the isolation of the self. It enables us to see the other as it is; and therein, for White, lies the power of art. It is no accident that the apparently retarded Arthur writes poetry and dances meaningfully, or that Aunt Theodora would write poems if she could, or that Voss appreciates poetry, or that even minor characters appear at the ends of *The Tree of Man* and *Riders in the Chariot* to make art. The professional artist, for White, is simply the saint whose gift drives him to master the technique necessary to do at will what the simpler saint does spontaneously. In either case, the work of art is a mandala primarily for the artist, only secondarily for the audience. Hurtle Duffield paints and Kathy Volkov plays piano for themselves, just as Alf paints because he is driven to get it right and an unknown workman dances at the end of *Riders* because he is impelled by a spontaneous overflow of powerful feeling. If Mr. Cutbrush, the solitary masturbator, can realize some pride in himself as a result of Hurtle's art, or if the neighborhood feels a bit warmer as old Topp plays his flute, that is but a by-product of the artist's rapt attention. The artist, true to White's Protestant ethic, merely realizes as best he can the grace he has been given. If his life or his work should prove an example to others, that too is part of the ineluctable, ineffable workings of grace.

In Fowles's worlds the requisite faith is less a gift of grace than an act of will; the saviors are not *zaddikhim* but aristoi, not God-chosen but self-chosen. Fowles's equivalent of grace is hazard, the blind chance that makes some persons more intelligent or more wise or more strong or more beautiful than others, that places in the way of some but not others a Conchis or a Sarah—an example of and an opportunity for self-determination. The elect have pride but not vanity; that is, their self-worth is not the reflected value others place upon them but their own just estimate of their value. The vain person is time-bound, for he looks to the world about him for his worth. Like David Williams, he writes careful essays and paints careful paintings that offend no one; or, like Sam, Charles Smithson's servant, he estimates his own value by his position in society, and so connives to better that position. If, like Breasley and Conchis, the aristoi are blessed with sufficient talent and wealth, they can safely buy their corner away from the world; if not so blessed, like Sarah, they have to manipulate, but the manipulation is not—like Mrs. Poulteney's—to control others but to be free of the control of others. If the aristos does manipulate, and does sometimes inflict injury, the cost is worth it, for even to the injured the aristoi become at the least, an example, at the most, a guru. The social function of the aristoi—realized on a grand scale by Conchis—is to aid in the creation of other aristoi, to provide for others the opportunity and the example for choice. Without that opportunity, freedom is not possible, and art is meaningless. For just as the meaning of freedom is to have the power to stand outside of time, to escape the determining forces of one's own age, so the meaning of art is to be an event beyond time, an event, as Fowles calls it, "for all time." Until we can each be artists, or aristoi, if such is ever possible, the responsibility of art is to remind us that in a universe that cares nothing for humanity, individuals have been free, and may still be free, and that freedom is worth the cost.

Fowles's uncaring universe that permits the possibility of freedom—or, perhaps, permits freedom precisely because it is uncaring—differs little in general concept from Barth's world, in which ultimately nothing matters, but immediately everything matters. The faith of both Fowles and Barth recognizes that we live neither in nor for eternity; we live in and for a now, a series of moments in which we must choose to be who we are and what we are. Like Durrell (and the historic John Keats), Barth tells us that what the imagination seizes as truth must indeed be true. Free choice, in a sense, is the dramatization of the imagination, the acting out of our vision. Barth's heroes and his artists must learn the power of "as if," the power to write their own scripts and, as the doctor advises Jacob Horner, take starring roles in their own dramas. When Barth's major characters are at their most unfortunate, most abused by fate and most unhappy—whether they be Jacob Horner, Todd Andrews, Ebenezer Cooke, Giles, or Bellerophon—they are quite literally acting in dramas written and directed by others. That is why, for example, Ambrose is given, by his water-message, carte blanche, and why the advice given Giles and Ebenezer must be ambiguous or contradictory. For Ambrose to be given the message for which he longs, that special secret from his father, or Giles to be given more than a pattern without content, would be to deny them their personal as if. It would be as contrary to the laws that govern Barth's universe as it would be for Fowles to have Sarah reveal herself, or to close *The Magus* with the promise that Nicholas and Alison will live happily ever after. We are to create our as if, Barth tells us, not only in a world in which ultimately nothing makes a difference, but in a world into which we are born alone and lonely and with the haunting fear that we are not wonderful, that we are a part of that nothing that counts for nothing. Like all of our novelists, Barth would see the first step toward maturity as the ability to love. Although tonally there is all the difference in the world, at bottom there is little difference between Burlingame's Cosmophilism, his love of all things, and, say, Patrick White's reverence for all things. Both are equally serious, equally fundamental in their authors' worlds. The two characters in Barth's work who mature most and who are presented—for the most part—most sympathetically are Todd Andrews and Ambrose Mensch; each reaches maturity at the moment he acknowledges his love. In Barth's world, it is only the "unending power of love" that can stay our loneliness and preserve our wonder. Heroism and art—whether it be the real heroism of Perseus or the playful swashbuckling of Burlingame, the tales the genie tells Scheherezade or the fictions of Ambrose—are the consolations we occupy ourselves with until we know the wonder of love. And that is perhaps the final message of the Bellerophon and Perseus legends. Bellerophon, incapable of love, merges with the shape changer, the disembodied voice of narrative, the teller of all tales and the hero of none. Perseus busies himself with heroism, then with rule, then with heroism, but finds peace only when united eternally with Medusa. But until our individual apotheosis, the best we can do is to stave off some of the effect of our loneliness and, hopefully that of others, with messages that may or may not be read. All other ways are, the Shah tells us, "deathy." And Barth's faith is that we do have the ability to choose life, and that perhaps the funhouses of art may even convince us that life is worthwhile.

I think it not surprising that after sixty thousand or so words, we find that our writers have found the same uses for art that artists and readers have always found—self-realization, discovery, example, communication. Human needs, after all, change more slowly than intellectual fashions. And, our writers tell us, because the needs are universal, the ability to satisfy them must be universal. The use of the ability awaits only our courage, only our daring to heed what Quakers would call our inner voice, what Durrell and Barth would call our imagination, what Lessing would call our vision, Fowles our Daimon, and White . . . ? Perhaps, most wise of all, White is least specific, for to fix it too precisely in words is to make it no longer ours. Whether it be the communal vision of Lessing or the extremely personal vision of White, the infinite sadness of the expression of the bust Conchis keeps at his villa or Barth's insistence on joy, the ways are various; and each of our authors manages both to present his or her personal vision and to admit the possibility of others. In their works there is at once no logic to their faith—for faith cannot submit to logic—and the best of all logics: the fact that the alternatives are unbearable. They tell us that we must love the world we live in, despite its confusions, its imperfections, its horrors; and that we must love ourselves, despite our confusions, our imperfections, and the horrors of our loneliness. And we must love both equally, and we must express that love. The power of art is to remind us of that as nothing else can.

Notes

(After the initial citation, references to works used will be given in the text by short title and page number.)

Chapter One: Lawrence Durrell

1. Lawrence Durrell, The Alexandria Quartet: *Justine, Balthazar, Mountolive, Clea* (New York: E. P. Dutton, 1961; vols. pub. 1957, 1958, 1958, 1960 respectively), p. 221.

2. Lawrence Durrell, *A Key to Modern British Poetry* (Norman: University of Oklahoma Press, 1952), *Justine*, p. 40.

3. Harry T. Moore, ed., *The World of Lawrence Durrell* (New York: E. P. Dutton, 1964; 1962), p. 165.

4. Lawrence Durrell, *Tunc* (New York: E. P. Dutton, 1968), p. 264.

5. Lawrence Durrell, *Nunquam* (New York: E. P. Dutton, 1970), pp. 98–99.

6. Lawrence Durrell, *The Black Book* (New York: E. P. Dutton, 1960; 1938), p. 166.

7. Lawrence Durrell, *Lawrence Durrell and Henry Miller: A Private Correspondence*, ed., George Wickes (New York: E. P. Dutton, 1963), pp. 104–5.

8. Lawrence Durrell, *The Big Supposer: A Dialogue with Marc Alyn*, trans. Francine Baker (New York: Grove Press, 1972), p. 46.

9. G. S. Fraser, *Lawrence Durrell: A Critical Study* (London: Faber and Faber, 1968), pp. 8–9.

10. Lawrence Durrell, *Livia; or, Buried Alive* (New York: Viking Press, 1979), p. 115.

11. Lawrence Durrell, *The Dark Labyrinth* (New York: E. P. Dutton 1962; orig. *Cefalu*, 1947), p. 114.

12. Lawrence Durrell, *Spirit of Place: Letters and Essays on Travel*, ed. Alan G. Thomas (New York: E. P. Dutton, 1969), p. 50.

13. In *Sebastian, or Ruling Passions*, Durrell has one of his characters tell us that "'Einstein's non-discrete field, Groddeck's "It," and Pursewarden's "heraldic universe" were all one and the same concept and would easily answer to the formulations of Patanjali.'" (New York: Viking Press, 1984), p. 28.

14. Lawrence Durrell, *A Smile in the Mind's Eye* (New York: Universe Books, 1982), p. 49.

15. Lawrence Durrell, *Monsieur, or the Prince of Darkness* (New York: Viking Press, 1974), p. 292.

Chapter Two: Doris Lessing

1. Doris Lessing, *A Small Personal Voice: Essays, Reviews, Interviews*, ed. Paul Schlueter (New York: Alfred A. Knopf, 1974), p. 100.

2. Doris Lessing, *The Four-Gated City*, vol. 5 of *Children of Violence* (New York: Alfred A. Knopf, 1969), p. 520.

3. Doris Lessing, *The Golden Notebook* (New York: Simon and Schuster, 1962), p. 20.

4. Mary Ann Singleton, *The City and the Veld: The Fiction of Doris Lessing* (Lewisburg, PA: Bucknell University Press, 1977), pp. 103–4.

5. Doris Lessing, *Briefing for a Descent into Hell* (New York: Alfred A. Knopf, 1971), p. 123.

6. Doris Lessing, *A Proper Marriage*, vol. 2 of *Children of Violence* (New York: New American Library, 1970; 1952), pp. 61–62

7. Doris Lessing, *A Ripple from the Storm*, vol. 3 of *Children of Violence* (New York: New American Library, 1970; 1958), p. 70.

8. Doris Lessing, *A Man and Two Women* (New York: Simon and Schuster, 1963), p. 97.

Chapter Three: Patrick White

1. Patrick White, *Flaws in the Glass: A Self-Portrait* (New York: Viking Press, 1982), p. 70.

2. Patrick White, *The Tree of Man* (New York: Viking Press, 1955), pp. 63–64.

3. Patrick White, *The Aunt's Story* (New York: Viking Press, 1948), p. 46.

4. Patrick White, *Riders in the Chariot* (New York: Viking Press, 1961), p. 8.

5. Patrick White, *Voss* (New York: Viking Press, 1957), p. 132.

6. Patrick White, *The Solid Mandala* (New York: Viking Press, 1966), pp. 189–90.

7. Patrick White, *The Eye of the Storm* (New York: Viking Press, 1973), p. 409.

8. Geoffrey Dutton, *Patrick White* (Melbourne: Landsdowne Press, 1963, p. 32.

9. Patrick White, *The Vivisector* (New York: Viking Press, 1970), p. 12.

Chapter Four: John Fowles

1. John Fowles, *Daniel Martin* (Boston: Little, Brown & Co., 1977), p. 526.

2. John Fowles, *The French Lieutenant's Woman* (Boston: Little, Brown & Co., 1969), pp. 460–61.

3. John Fowles, *The Ebony Tower* (Boston: Little, Brown & Co., 1974), p. 107.

4. John Fowles, *The Aristos: A Self-Portrait in Ideas* (Boston: Little, Brown & Co., 1970; 1964), p. 115.

5. John Fowles, *The Magus* (Boston: Little, Brown & Co., 1977; 1965), p. 10.

6. John Fowles, *Mantissa* (Boston: Little, Brown & Co., 1982), p. 26.

7. John Fowles, *The Collector* (Boston: Little, Brown & Co., 1963), p. 88.

Chapter Five: John Barth

1. John Barth, *Chimera* (New York: Random House, 1972), p. 59.

2. John Barth, *Lost in the Funhouse* (Garden City, NY: Doubleday, 1968), p. 85.

3. John Barth, *The End of the Road* (Garden City, NY: Doubleday, 1958), p. 76.

4. John Barth, *Giles Goat-Boy; or, The Revised New Syllabus* (Garden City, NY: Doubleday, 1966), p. 86.

5. John Barth, *Letters* (New York: G. P. Putnam's Sons, 1979), p. 167.

6. David Morrell, *John Barth: An Introduction* (University Park: Pennsylvania State University Press, 1976), p. 102.

7. Evelyn Glaser-Wöhrer, *An Analysis of John Barth's Weltanschauung: His View of Life and Literature*, Salzburger Studien Zur Anglistik und Amerikanistik, Band 5 (Salzburg: Institute für Englische Sprache und Literatur, Universität Salzburg, 1977), p. 220.

8. John Barth, *The Sot-Weed Factor* (Garden City, NY: Doubleday, 1967; 1960), p. 739.

9. John Barth, *Lost in the Funhouse: Fiction for Print, Tape, Live Voice*, rev. ed. (Harmondsworth, Middlesex: Penguin Books, 1972), p. 9.

10. John Barth, *The Floating Opera* (Garden City, NY: Doubleday, 1967; 1956), p. 111.

11. John Barth, Afterword, *The Adventures of Roderick Random*, by Tobias Smollett (New York: Signet, 1964), p. 479.

Bibliography

The following bibliography is by no means complete. The reader interested in approaching our five novelists from directions different from the one taken here will find the standard bibliographic sources listed below; computer printouts quickly update bibliographic sources more than a few months old.

I have arranged the major primary sources chronologically by author in order to help the reader gain at least a superficial sense of the span and shape of the writers' careers. When I have used an edition other than the first, the bibliographical information for the edition used is given at the end of the standard entry. Essays, interviews, and such by each novelist appear in alphabetical order after the major listings.

The secondary sources listed are those I found most helpful in clarifying my own thought about the topics at hand. As often as not, they suggest alternate interpretations that the reader might want to explore.

The final bibliographical section lists a number of the major studies that, although not specifically concerned chiefly with the novelists studied here, help set the terms for the study of contemporary fiction and the role of the artist in society. In a sense, they are often the background, the other voice in the dialogue.

Lawrence Durrell

MAJOR WORKS

1935. *Pied Piper of Lovers.* London: Cassell.

1937. *Panic Spring: A Romance.* London: Faber and Faber. Pseudonym Charles Norden.

1938. *The Black Book: An Agon.* Paris: Obelisk Press. New York: E. P. Dutton, 1960.

1945. *Prospero's Cell: A Guide to the Landscape and Manners of the Island of Corcyra.* London: Faber and Faber.

1946. *Cities, Plains and People.* London: Faber and Faber.

1947. *Cefalu: A Novel.* London: Editions Poetry London. Reprinted as *The Dark Labyrinth.* New York: E. P. Dutton, 1962.

1948. *On Seeming to Presume.* London: Faber and Faber.

1952. *Key to Modern Poetry.* London: Peter Nevill. Reprinted as *A Key to Modern British Poetry.* Norman: University of Oklahoma Press, 1952.

1953. *Reflections on a Marine Venus: A Companion to the Landscape of Rhodes.* London: Faber and Faber.

1956. *Selected Poems.* New York: Grove Press.

1957. *Bitter Lemons.* London: Faber and Faber.

_____. *Esprit de Corps: Sketches from Diplomatic Life.* London: Faber and Faber.

_____. *Justine: A Novel.* London: Faber and Faber. New York: E. P. Dutton, 1961.

_____. *White Eagles over Serbia.* London: Faber and Faber.

1958. *Balthazar: A Novel.* London: Faber and Faber. New York: E. P. Dutton, 1961.

———. *Mountolive: A Novel.* London: Faber and Faber. New York: E. P. Dutton, 1961.

———. *Stiff Upper Lip: Life among the Diplomats.* London: Faber and Faber.

1959: *Art and Outrage: A Correspondence about Henry Miller between Alfred Perlès and Lawrence Durrell.* London: Putnam.

1960. *Clea: A Novel.* London: Faber and Faber. New York: E. P. Dutton, 1961.

———. *Collected Poems.* London: Faber and Faber.

1962. *The Poetry of Lawrence Durrell.* New York: E. P. Dutton.

———. *An Irish Faustus: A Morality in Nine Scenes.* London: Faber and Faber.

1964. *Selected Poems, 1935–1963.* London: Faber and Faber.

———. *Acte: A Play.* London: Faber and Faber.

1966. *Sauve Qui Peut.* London: Faber and Faber.

1968. *Collected Poems.* New York: E. P. Dutton.

———. *Tunc: A Novel.* New York: E. P. Dutton.

1969. *Spirit of Place: Letters and Essays on Travel.* Edited by Alan G. Thomas. London: Faber and Faber.

1970. *Nunquam: A Novel.* New York: E. P. Dutton.

———. *Faustus: A Poem.* London: n.p.

1971. *The Red Limbo Lingo: A Poetry Notebook.* New York: E. P. Dutton.

1973. *The Big Supposer: A Dialogue with Marc Alyn.* Translated by Francine Barker. London: Abelard-Schuman. New York: Grove Press, 1975.

1975. *Monsieur; or, the Prince of Darkness.* New York: Viking Press.

1977. *Sicilian Carousel.* New York: Viking Press.

———. *Selected Poems.* Selected and Introduction by Alan Ross. London: Faber and Faber.

1978. *The Greek Islands.* London: Faber and Faber.

———. *Livia; or, Buried Alive.* London: Faber and Faber. New York: Viking Press, 1979.

1980. *A Smile in the Mind's Eye.* London: Wildwood House. New York: Universe Books, 1982.

1981. *The Richard Aldington-Lawrence Durrell Correspondence.* Edited by Ian S. MacNiven and Harry T. Moore. New York: Viking Press.

1982. *Constance; or, Solitary Practices*. New York: Viking Press.
1984. *Sebastian; or, Ruling Passions*. New York: Viking Press.

MINOR WORKS: TRANSLATIONS, INTERVIEWS, PREFACES, ETC.

The Curious History of Pope Joan. From the Greek of Emmanuel Royidis. New York: E. P. Dutton, 1948; 1961.

Goulianos, Joan. "A Conversation with Lawrence Durrell about Art, Analysis, and Politics." *Modern Fiction Studies* 17 (1971): 159–66.

A Henry Miller Reader. Edited with an introduction by Durrell. New York: New Directions, 1959.

Henig, Suzanne. "Interview with Lawrence Durrell." *Virginia Woolf Quarterly* 2 (1980): 4–12.

Introduction to *The Book of the It*, by Georg Groddeck. New York: Random House, 1961.

"Lawrence Durrell." In *Writers at Work: The Paris Review Interviews*. Second Series. Introduction by Van Wyck Brooks. New York: Viking Press, 1963, pp. 257–82.

Lyons, Eugene, and Antrim, Harry. "An Interview with Lawrence Durrell." *Shenandoah* 22, no. 3 (1971): 42–58.

Preface to *Children of the Albatross*, by Anais Nin. London: Peter Owen, 1959.

Preface to *The Perennial Avantgarde*, by Gerald Sykes. Englewood Cliffs, NJ: Prentice Hall, 1971.

Preface to *Poems,* by William Wordsworth. Harmondsworth, Middlesex: Penguin Books, 1972.

Preface to *Sexus,* by Henry Miller. New York: Grove Press, 1962.

Wickes, George, ed. *Lawrence Durrell and Henry Miller: A Private Correspondence*. New York: E. P. Dutton, 1963.

Young, Kenneth. "A Dialogue with Durrell." *Encounter* 13 (6 December 1959): 61–88.

SECONDARY SOURCES

Baldanza, Frank. "Durrell's Word Continuum." *Critique* 4, no. 2, (Spring–Summer 1961): 3–17.

Bode, Carl. "Durrell's Way to Alexandria." *College English* 22 (May 1961): 531–38.

Burns, J. Christopher. "Durrell's Heraldic Universe." *Modern Fiction Studies* 13 (1967): 375–88.

Cartwright, Michael. "Playwright as Miracle Worker: An Irish Faustus." Deus Loci 3, no. 4 (1980): 3–11.

Creed, Walter G. "The Muse of Science and *The Alexandria Quartet.*" Norwood, PA: Academic Monographs, 1977.

Durrell, Gerald. *Birds, Beasts and Relatives.* New York: Viking Press, 1969.

———. *My Family and Other Animals.* New York: Viking Press, 1956.

Fraiberg, Louis. "Durrell's Dissonant Quartet." In *Contemporary British Novelists,* edited by Charles Shapiro. Carbondale: Southern Illinois University Press, 1965, pp. 16–35.

Franklin, Steve. "Space-Time and Creativity in Lawrence Durrell's *Alexandria Quartet.*" *Perspectives on Contemporary Literature* 5 (1979): 55–61.

Fraser, G. S. *Lawrence Durrell.* Writers and Their Work, no. 216. London: The Longman Group for the British Council, 1970.

———. *Lawrence Durrell: A Critical Study.* London: Faber and Faber, 1968. Rev. 1973. Bibliography by Alan G. Thomas.

Friedman, Alan Warren. *Lawrence Durrell and "The Alexandria Quartet": Art for Love's Sake.* Norman: University of Oklahoma Press, 1970.

———. "Key to Lawrence Durrell." *Wisconsin Studies in Contemporary Literature* 8 (Winter 1967): 31–42.

Glicksberg, Charles I. "The Fictional World of Lawrence Durrell." *Bucknell Review* 11, no. 2 (March 1963): 118–33.

———. *The Self in Modern Literature.* University Park: Pennsylvania State University Press, 1963.

Godshalk, William Leigh. "Aspects of Lawrence Durrell." *Journal of Modern Literature* 1 (1971): 439–45.

———. "Some Sources of Durrell's *Alexandria Quartet.*" *Modern Fiction Studies* 13 (1967): 361–74.

Gossman, Ann. "Some Characters in Search of a Mirror." *Critique* 8, no. 3 (Spring–Summer 1966): 79–89.

Hagopian, John V. "The Resolution of *The Alexandria Quartet.*" *Critique* 7, no. 1 (Spring 1964): 97–106.

Hutchens, Eleanor H. "The Heraldic Universe in Durrell's *Alexandria Quartet.*" *College English* 24, no. 1 (October 1962): 56–61.

Jones, Leslie W. "'Selected Fictions': The Intersection of Life and Art in *The Alexandria Quartet.*" *Deus Loci* 2, no. 1 (1978): 11–23.

Kermode, Frank. "Durrell and Others." In *Puzzles and Epiphanies.* New York: Chilmark Press, 1962, pp. 214–27.

Koser, Grove. "Some Contributions to the Lawrence Durrell Bibliography." *Deus Loci* 3, no. 3 (1980): 11–20.

Kruppa, Joseph A. "Durrell's *Alexandria Quartet* and the 'Implosion' of the Modern Consciousness." *Modern Fiction Studies* 13 (1967): 401–16.

Lewis, Nancy W. "Two Thematic Applications of Einsteinian Field Structure in *The Alexandria Quartet.*" *Deus Loci* 5, no. 1 (Fall 1981): 242–43.

MacNiven, Ian S. "A Map of Durrell's Inner World?" *Deus Loci* 4, no. 4 (June 1981): 7–10.

———. "Steps to *Livia:* The State of Durrell's Fiction." *Deus Loci* 5, no. 1 (Fall 1981): 330–47.

Miller, Henry. *The Colossus of Maroussi.* San Francisco: Colt Press, 1941. New York: New Directions, 1958.

Moore, Harry T. ed. *The World of Lawrence Durrell.* Carbondale: Southern Illinois University Press, 1962.

Moros, Mona Louis. "Elements of the Autobiographical in *The Alexandria Quartet.*" *Modern Fiction Studies* 13 (1967): 343–60.

Pierce, Carol Marshal. "'Wrinkled Deep in Time': *The Alexandria Quartet* as Many-Layered Palimpsest." *Deus Loci* 2, no. 4 (1979): 11–28.

Proser, Matthew N. "Darley's Dilemma: The Problem of Structure in Durrell's *Alexandria Quartet.*" *Critique* 4, no. 2 (Spring–Summer 1961): 18–28.

Read, Phyllis J. "The Illusion of Personality: Cyclical Time in Durrell's *Alexandria Quartet.*" *Modern Fiction Studies* 13 (1967): 389–400.

Robinson, W. R. "Intellect and Imagination in *The Alexandria Quartet.*" *Shenandoah* 18, no. 4 (Summer 1965): 55–68.

Russo, John Paul. "Love in Lawrence Durrell." *Prairie Schooner* 44, no. 4 (Winter 1969–70): 396–407.

Scholes, Robert. "Lawrence Durrell and The Return to Alexandria." In *The Fabulators.* New York: Oxford University Press, 1967, pp. 17–26. Also in his *Fabulation and Metafiction.* Urbana: University of Illinois Press, 1979, pp. 29–36.

Steiner, George. "Lawrence Durrell: The Baroque Novel." *Yale Review* 49, no. 4 (June 1960): 488–95.

Stromberg, Robert L. "The Contribution of Relativity to the Inconsistency of Form in *The Alexandria Quartet*." *Deus Loci* 5, no. 1 (Fall 1981): 246–56.

Taylor, Chet. "Dissonance and Digression: The Ill-fitting Fusion of Philosophy and Form in Lawrence Durrell's *Alexandria Quartet*." *Modern Fiction Studies* 17 (1971): 167–79.

Thomas, Alan G., and Brigham, James A. *Lawrence Durrell: An Illustrated Checklist*. Carbondale: Southern Illinois Press, 1983.

Unterecker, John. "Lawrence Durrell." in *Six Contemporary British Novelists*, edited by George Stade. New York: Columbia University Press, 1976, pp. 219–270.

_____. *Lawrence Durrell*. Columbia Essays on Modern Writers, no. 6. New York: Columbia University Press, 1960.

Wedin, Warren. "The Artist as Narrator in *The Alexandria Quartet*." *Twentieth Century Literature* 5 (1972): 144–53.

Weigel, J. A. *Lawrence Durrell*. New York: Twayne, 1965.

Doris Lessing

MAJOR FICTIONS

1950. *The Grass Is Singing*. New York: T. Y. Crowell.

1951. *This Was the Old Chief's Country*. London: Michael Joseph,

1952. *Martha Quest. Children of Violence*, vol. 1. London: Michael Joseph. New York: New American Library, 1970.

1953. *Five: Short Novels*. London: Michael Joseph.

1954. *A Proper Marriage*. Children of Violence, vol. 2. London: Michael Joseph. New York: New American Library, 1970.

1956. *Retreat to Innocence*. London: Michael Joseph.

1957. *The Habit of Loving*. New York: Ballantine Books.

_____. *Going Home*. London: Michael Joseph.

1958. *A Ripple from the Storm*. Children of Violence, vol. 3. London: Michael Joseph. New York: New American Library, 1970.

_____. "Mr. Dollinger." Unpublished play.

1959. *Each His Own Wilderness*. In *New English Dramatists: Three Plays*, edited by E. Martin Browne. Harmondsworth, Middlesex: Penguin Books, 1959.

————. *Fourteen Poems*. Northwood, Middlesex: Scorpion Press.

1960. "The Truth about Billy Newton." Unpublished play.

————. *In Pursuit of the English: A Documentary*. London: MacGibbon and Kee.

1962. *The Golden Notebook*. New York: Simon and Schuster.

————. *Play with a Tiger: A Play in Three Acts*. London: Michael Joseph.

1963. *A Man and Two Women*. New York: Simon and Schuster.

1964. *African Stories*. New York: Simon and Schuster.

1965. *Landlocked*. Children of Violence, vol. 4. London: MacGibbon and Kee. New York: New American Library, 1970.

1966. *The Black Madonna*. London: Panther Books.

————. *Winter in July*. London: Panther Books.

————. *Particularly Cats*. New York: Simon and Schuster.

1969. *The Four-Gated City*. Children of Violence, vol. 5. New York: Alfred A. Knopf.

1971. *Briefing for a Descent into Hell*. New York: Alfred A. Knopf.

1972. *The Temptation of Jack Orkney and Other Stories*. New York: Alfred A. Knopf. Published in England as *The Story of a Non-marrying Man and Other Stories*. London: Jonathan Cape.

1973. *The Summer Before the Dark*. New York: Alfred A. Knopf.

————. *This Was the Old Chief's Country. Doris Lessing's Collected African Stories*, vol. 2. London: Michael Joseph.

————. *The Sun Between Their Feet. Doris Lessing's Collected African Stories*, vol. 2. London: Michael Joseph.

1974. *The Memoirs of a Survivor*. London: Octagon Press.

————. *A Small Personal Voice: Essays, Reviews, Interviews*. Edited by Paul Schlueter. New York: Alfred A. Knopf.

1975. *Sunrise on the Veld*. Cambridge: Cambridge University Press.

1977. *A Mild Attack of Locusts*. Cambridge: Cambridge University Press.

1978. *To Room Nineteen: Her Collected Stories*, vol. 1. London: Jonathan Cape.

————. *The Temptation of Jack Orkney: Her Collected Stories*, vol. 2. London: Jonathan Cape.

————. *Stories*. New York: Alfred A. Knopf, 1978.

1979. *Re: Colonised Planet 5: Shikasta*. Canopus in Argos: Archives, vol. 1. New York: Alfred A. Knopf.

1980. *The Sirian Experiments*. Canopus in Argos: Archives, vol. 2. New York: Alfred A. Knopf.

_____. *The Marriages between Zones Three, Four, and Five*. Canopus in Argos: Archives, vol. 3. New York: Alfred A. Knopf.

1982. *The Making of the Representative for Planet 8*. Canopus in Argos: Archives, vol. 4. New York: Alfred A. Knopf.

1983. *The Sentimental Agents in the Volyan Empire*. Canopus in Argos: Archives, vol. 5. New York: Alfred A. Knopf.

INTERVIEWS

Howe, Florence. "A Conversation with Doris Lessing." *The Nation*, 6 March 1967, pp. 311–13.

Newquist, Roy. *Counterpoint*. New York: Rand McNally Co., 1964, pp. 413–24.

SECONDARY SOURCES

Barnouw, Dagmar. "Disorderly Company: From *The Golden Notebook* to *The Four-Gated City*." *Contemporary Literature* 14 (1973): 491–514.

Bazin, Nancy Topping. "The Moment of Revelation in *Martha Quest* and Comparable Moments by Two Modernists." *Modern Fiction Studies* 26 (1980): 87–96.

Berets, Ralph. "A Jungian Interpretation of the Dream Sequence in Doris Lessing's *The Summer Before the Dark*." *Modern Fiction Studies* 26 (1980): 117–29.

Brewster, Dorothy. *Doris Lessing*. New York: Twayne, 1965.

Burkom, Selma R. *Doris Lessing: A Checklist of Primary and Secondary Sources*. Troy, NY: Whitston Pub., 1973.

_____. "Only Connect: Form and Content in the Works of Doris Lessing." *Critique* 11 (1968): 51–68.

Carey, John L. "Art and Reality in *The Golden Notebook*." *Contemporary Literature* 14 (1973): 437–56.

Cohen, Mary. "Out of the Chaos, a New Kind of Strength: Doris Lessing's *The Golden Notebook*." In *The Authority of Experience*, edited by Arlyn Diamond and Lee R. Edwards. Amherst: University of Massachusetts Press, 1977, pp. 160–78.

Craig, Joanne. "*The Golden Notebook*: The Novelist as Heroine." *University of Windsor Review* 10 (Fall–Winter 1974): 55–66.

Drabble, Margaret. "Doris Lessing: Cassandra in a World under Siege." *Ramparts* 10 (February 1972): 50–54.

Draine, Betsy. "Changing Frames: Doris Lessing's *Memoirs of a Survivor.*" *Studies in the Novel* 11 (Spring 1979): 51–63.

_____. "Nostalgia and Irony: The Postmodern Order of *The Golden Notebook.*" *Modern Fiction Studies* 26 (1980): 31–48.

_____. *Substance under Pressure: Artistic Coherence and Evolving Form in the Novels of Doris Lessing.* Madison: University of Wisconsin Press, 1983.

Ezergailis, Inta. *Women Writers: The Divided Self, Analysis of Novels by Christa Wolf, Ingeborg Bachmann, Doris Lessing, and Others.* Bonn: Bouvier Verlag Herbert Grundmann, 1982.

Fouroli, Caryn. "Doris Lessing's 'Game': Referential Language and Fictional Form." *Twentieth Century Literature* 27, no. 2 (Summer 1981): 146–165.

Gindin, James. *Postwar British Fiction: New Accents and Attitudes.* Berkeley: University of California Press, 1962, pp. 65–86.

Halliday, Patricia Ann Young. "The Pursuit of Wholeness in the Work of Doris Lessing: Dualities, Multiplicities, and the Resolution of Patterns in Illumination." Dissertation, University of Minnesota, 1973.

Holmquist, Ingrid. *From Society to Nature: A Study of Doris Lessing's Children of Violence.* Gothenburg Studies in English. Goteborg, Sweden: Acta Universitatis Gothoburgensis, 1980.

Howe, Florence. "Doris Lessing's Free Women." *The Nation,* 11 January 1965, pp. 34–37.

Hynes, Joseph. "The Construction of *The Golden Notebook.*" *Iowa Review* 4 (Summer 1973): 100–113.

Johnson, Sally H. "Form and Philosophy in the Novels of Doris Lessing." Dissertation, University of Connecticut, 1976.

Kaplan, Sydney Janet. "Doris Lessing." *Feminine Consciousness in the Modern Novel.* Urbana: University of Illinois Press, 1975, pp. 136–73.

_____. *Passionate Portrayal of Things to Come: Doris Lessing's Recent Fiction.* Totowa, NJ: Barnes and Noble, 1982.

Karl, Frederick R. "Doris Lessing in the Sixties: The New Anatomy of Melancholy." *Contemporary Literature* 13 (Winter 1972): 15–33.

_____. "The Four-Gaited Beast of the Apocalypse: Doris Lessing's *The Four-Gated City.* In *Old Lines, New Forces,* edited by

Robert K. Morris. London: Associated University Presses, 1976, pp. 181–99.

King, Holly Beth. "Criticism of Doris Lessing: A Selected Checklist." *Modern Fiction Studies* 26 (1980): 167–75.

Lightfoot, Marjorie J. "Breakthrough in *The Golden Notebook*." *Studies in the Novel* 7 (Summer 1975): 277–85.

———. " 'Fiction' vs. 'Reality': Clues and Conclusions in *The Golden Notebook*." *Modern British Literature* 2 (Fall 1977): 182–88.

Magie, Michael L. "Doris Lessing and Romanticism." *College English* 38 (February 1977): 531–52.

Marchino, Lois. "The Search for Self in the Novels of Doris Lessing." *Studies in the Novel* 4 (Summer 1972): 252–62.

Marder, Herbert. "The Paradox of Form in *The Golden Notebook*." *Modern Fiction Studies* 26 (1980): 49–54.

Mulkeen, Anne M. "Twentieth-Century Realism: The 'Grid' Structure of *The Golden Notebook*." *Studies in the Novel* 4 (Summer 1972): 262–75.

Perrakis, Phyllis Sternberg. "Doris Lessing's *The Golden Notebook*: Separation and Symbiosis." *American Imago* 38, no. 4 (Winter 1981): 407–28.

Pratt, Annis, and Dembo, L. S., eds. *Doris Lessing: Critical Studies*. Madison: University of Wisconsin Press, 1974.

Rigney, Barbara Hill. *Lillith's Daughters: Women and Religion in Contemporary Fiction*. Madison: University of Wisconsin Press, 1982.

Rose, Ellen Cronan. "The End of the Game: New Directions in Doris Lessing's Fiction." *The Journal of Narrative Technique* 6 (Winter 1976): 66–75.

Rubenstein, Roberta. "Briefing on Inner Space: Doris Lessing and R. D. Laing." *Psychoanalytic Review* 63 (Spring 1976): 83–95.

———. *The Novelistic Vision of Doris Lessing: Breaking the Forms of Consciousness*. Urbana: University of Illinois Press, 1979.

———. "Outer Space, Inner Space: Doris Lessing's Metaphor of Science Fiction." *World Literature Written in English* 14 (April 1975): 187–98.

Ryf, Robert S. "Beyond Ideology: Doris Lessing's Mature Vision." *Modern Fiction Studies* 21 (Summer 1975): 193–201.

Scanlan, Margaret. "Memory and Continuity in the Series Novel: The Example of *Children of Violence*." *Modern Fiction Studies* 26 (1980): 75–85.

Schlueter, Paul. "The Free Woman's Commitment." In *Contemporary British Novelists,* edited by Charles Shapiro. Carbondale: Southern Illinois University Press, 1965, pp. 48–62.

———. *The Novels of Doris Lessing.* Carbondale: Southern Illinois University Press, 1973.

Seligman, Dee. *Doris Lessing: An Annotated Bibliography of Criticism.* Westport, CN: Greenwood Press, 1981.

———. "The Four-Faced Novelist." *Modern Fiction Studies* 26 (1980): 3–16.

Shapiro, Charles. *The Novels of Doris Lessing.* Carbondale: Southern Illinois University Press, 1969.

Singleton, Mary Ann. *The City and the Veld: The Fiction of Doris Lessing.* Lewisburg: Bucknell University Press, 1977.

Spacks, Patricia Meyer. *The Female Imagination.* New York: Alfred A. Knopf, 1975.

———. "Only Personal: Some Function of Fiction." *Yale Review* 65 (June 1976): 528–44.

Spiegel, Rotraut. *Doris Lessing: The Problem of Alienation and the Form of Fiction.* Neue studien zur Anglistik und Amerikanistic, no. 19. Berne, Switzerland: 1980.

Sprague, Claire. "Doubletalk and Doubles Talk in *The Golden Notebook.*" *Papers on Language and Literature* 18, no. 2 (Spring 1982): 181–97.

———. "Without Contraries Is No Progression: Doris Lessing's *The Four-Gated City.*" *Modern Fiction Studies* 26 (1980): 99–116.

Stizel, Judith. "Reading Doris Lessing." *College English* 40 (January 1979): 498–505.

Taylor, Jenny, ed. *Notebooks / Memoirs / Archives: Reading and Rereading Doris Lessing.* London: Routledge and Kegan Paul, 1982.

Thorpe, Michael. *Doris Lessing.* Burnt Mill, Essex: Longman House, 1973.

Tiger, Virginia. "Doris Lessing." *Contemporary Literature* 21 (1980): 286–90.

Vlastos, Marion. "Doris Lessing and R. D. Laing: Psychopolitics and Prophecy." *PMLA* 91 (March 1976): 245–57.

Walker, Melissa G. "Doris Lessing's *The Four-Gated City:* Consciousness and Community—A Different History." *Southern Review* 17, no. 1 (January 1981): 97–120.

Watson, Barbara Bellow. "Leaving the Safety of Myth: Doris Lessing's *The Golden Notebook.*" In *Old Lines, New Forces,* edited by Robert K. Morris. London: Associated University Presses, 1976, pp. 12–37.

Patrick White

MAJOR WORKS

1939. *Happy Valley.* London: Harrap.
1941. *The Living and the Dead.* London: Routledge and Kegan Paul.
1948. *The Aunt's Story.* London: Routledge and Kegan Paul.
1955. *The Tree of Man.* New York: Viking Press.
1957. *Voss.* New York: Viking Press.
1961. *Riders in the Chariot.* New York: Viking Press.
1964. *The Burnt Ones.* New York: Viking Press.
1966. *The Solid Mandala.* New York: Viking Press.
1970. *The Vivesector.* New York: Viking Press.
1973. *The Eye of the Storm.* New York: Viking Press.
1974. *The Cockatoos: Shorter Novels and Stories.* London: Jonathan Cape. New York: Viking Press, 1975.
1976. *A Fringe of Leaves.* New York: Viking Press.
1979. *The Twyborn Affair.* New York: Viking Press.
1982. *Flaws in the Glass: A Self-Portrait.* New York: Viking Press.

SECONDARY SOURCES

Argyle, Barry. *Patrick White.* New York: Barnes and Noble, 1967.
Baker, Robert S. "Romantic Onanism in Patrick White's *The Vivesector.*" *Texas Studies in Literature and Language* 21 (1979): 203–25
Beatson, Peter. *The Eye in the Mandala: Patrick White: A Vision of Man and God.* New York: Barnes and Noble, 1976.
Brady, Veronica. "The Novelist and the New World: Patrick White's *Voss.*" *Texas Studies in Literature and Language* 21 (1979): 169–85.
Brissenden, R. F. "On the Edge of the Empire: Some Thoughts on Recent Australian Fiction." *Sewanee Review* 87 (1979): 142–57.
_____. *Patrick White.* London: Longman's, Green, 1966.

Chapman, Edgar L. "The Mandala Design of Patrick White's *Riders in the Chariot*." *Texas Studies in Literature and Language* 21 (1979): 186–202.

Core, George. "A Terrible Majesty: The Novels of Patrick White." *The Hollins Critic* 11, no. 1 (1974): 1–16.

Dutton, Geoffrey. *Patrick White*. Melbourne: Landsdowne Press, 1963.

Garebian, Keith. "The Desert and the Garden: The Theme of Completeness in *Voss*." *Modern Fiction Studies* 22 (1976–77): 557–59.

Ghose, Zulfikar. "The One Comprehensive Vision." *Texas Studies in Literature and Language* 21 (1979): 260–79.

Harries, Lyndon. "The Peculiar Gifts of Patrick White." *Contemporary Literature* 19 (1978): 459–71.

Johnson, Manly. "*Twyborn:* The Abbess, the Bulbel, and the Bawdy House." *Modern Fiction Studies* 27, no. 1 (Spring 1981): 159–68.

Lawson, Alan. "Meaning and Experience: A Review-Essay on Some Recurrent Problems in Patrick White Criticism." *Texas Studies in Literature and Language* 21 (1979): 280–95.

Mackenzie, Manfred. "The Consciousness of 'Twin Consciousness': Patrick White's *The Solid Mandala*." *Novel* 2 (1969): 241–54.

———. "Tradition and Patrick White's Individual Talent." *Texas Studies in Literature and Language* 21 (1979): 147–68.

Morley, Patricia. *The Mystery of Unity: Theme and Technique in the Novels of Patrick White*. Montreal: McGill-Queen's University Press, 1972.

Scheick, William J. "A Bibliography of Writings about Patrick White, 1972–1978." *Texas Studies in Literature and Language* 21 (1979): 296–303.

———. "The Gothic Grace and Rainbow Aesthetic of Patrick White's Fiction: An Introduction." *Texas Studies in Literature and Language* 21 (1979): 131–46.

Walsh, William. "Fiction as Metaphor: The Novels of Patrick White." *Sewanee Review* 79 (1974): 197–211.

———. "Patrick White." In his *A Manifold Voice: Studies in Commonwealth Literature*. New York: Barnes and Noble, 1970, pp. 86–124.

———. "Patrick White: The Religious Connection." *Sewanee Review* 85 (1977): 509–11.

Warren, Thomas L. "Patrick White: The Early Novels." *Modern Fiction Studies* 27, no. 1 (Spring 1981): 121–39.

Whitman, Robert F. "The Dream Plays of Patrick White." *Texas Studies in Literature and Language* 21 (1979): 240–59.

Wood, Susan A. "The Power and Failure of 'Vision' in Patrick White's *Voss.*" *Modern Fiction Studies* 27, no. 1 (Spring 1981): 141–58.

John Fowles

MAJOR WORKS

1963. *The Collector.* Boston: Little, Brown.

1964. *The Aristos: A Self-Portrait in Ideas.* Boston: Little, Brown. Rev. ed. 1968.

1965. *The Magus.* Boston: Little, Brown. Rev. ed. 1977.

1969. *The French Lieutenant's Woman.* Boston: Little, Brown.

1973. *Poems.* Toronto: Macmillan.

1974. *Shipwreck.* London: Jonathan Cape.

———. *The Ebony Tower.* Boston: Little, Brown.

1977. *Daniel Martin.* Boston: Little, Brown.

1978. *Islands.* Boston: Little, Brown.

———. *Steepholm: A Case History in the Study of Evolution.* With R. Legg. London: Kenneth Allsop Trust.

1979. *The Tree.* London: Aurum Press.

1980. *The Enigma of Stonehenge.* London: Jonathan Cape.

1982. *Mantissa.* Boston: Little, Brown.

ESSAYS, INTERVIEWS, TRANSLATIONS, ETC

Campbell, James. "An Interview with John Fowles." *Contemporary Literature* 17, no. 4 (1976): 455–69.

de Durfort, Claire. *Ourika.* Translated by Fowles. Austin, TX: W. Thomas Taylor, 1977.

Fowles, John. Afterword to *The Wanderer,* by Henri Alain-Fournier. Translated by Lowell Bair. New York: New American Library, 1971.

———. Foreword to *Hawker of Morwenstow: Portrait of a Victorian Eccentric,* by Piers Brendon. London: Jonathan Cape, 1975.

———. Foreword and Afterword to *The Hound of the Baskervilles,* by Sir Arthur Conan Doyle. London: John Murray and Jonathan Cape, 1974.

————. Foreword to *The Lais of Marie de France*, by Marie de France. Translated and with an introduction by Robert Hanning and Joan Ferrante. New York: E. P. Dutton, 1978.

————. "Hardy and the Hag." In *Thomas Hardy after Fifty Years*, edited by Lance St. John Butler. London: Macmillan, 1977, pp. 28–42.

————. "Is the Novel Dead?" *Books* 1 (Autumn 1970): 2–5.

————. "I Write Therefore I Am." *Evergreen Review* 8 (August–September 1964): 16–17, 89–90.

————. "My Recollections of Kafka." *Mosaic* 3 (Summer 1970): 31–41.

————. "Notes on Writing a Novel." *Harper's Magazine* 237 (July 1968): 88–97.

————. "On Being English but Not British." *Texas Quarterly* 7 (Autumn 1964): 154–62.

————. "Why I Rewrote the Magus." *Saturday Review* 18 (February 1978): 25–30.

Gussow, Mel. "Talk with John Fowles." *New York Times Book Review*, 13 November 1977, pp. 3, 84–5.

Halpern, Daniel. "A Sort of Exile in Lyme Regis." *London Magazine* 10 (March 1971): 34–46.

North, David. "Interview with Author John Fowles." *Macleans* 14 (November 1977): 4, 6, 8.

Singh, Raman K. "An Encounter with John Fowles." *Journal of Modern Literature* 8, no. 2 (1980–81): 181–202.

SECONDARY SOURCES

Adam, Ian; Brantlinger, Patrick; and Rothblatt, Sheldon. "*The French Lieutenant's Woman*: A Discussion." *Victorian Studies* 15 (March 1972): 339–56.

Allen, Walter. "The Achievement of John Fowles." *Encounter* 35 (August 1970): 64–67.

Alter, Robert. "*Daniel Martin* and the Mimetic Task." *Genre* 14, no. 1 (Spring 1981): 65–78.

Bagchee, Syhamal. "*The Collector*: The Paradoxical Imagination of John Fowles." *Journal of Modern Literature* 8, no. 2 (1980–81): 219–34.

Baker, James R. "Fowles and the Struggle of the English Aristoi." *Journal of Modern Literature* 8. no. 2 (1980–81): 163–80.

Barnum, Carol M. "John Fowles's *Daniel Martin:* A Vision of Whole Sight." *Literary Review* 25, no. 2 (Fall 1981): 64–79.

———. "The Quest Motif in John Fowles's *The Ebony Tower:* Theme and Variations." *Texas Studies in Language and Literature* 23, no. 2 (Spring 1981): 138–57.

Bellamy, Michael O. "John Fowles's Version of Pastoral: Private Valleys and the Parity of Existence." *Critique* 21, no. 2 (1979): 72–84.

Berets, Ralph, "*The Magus:* A study in the Creation of a Personal Myth." *Twentieth Century Literature* 19 (April 1973): 89–98.

Binns, Ronald. "John Fowles: Radical Romancer." *Critical Quarterly* 15 (Winter 1973): 317–34.

Boccia, Michael. "'Visions and Revisions': John Fowles's New Version of *The Magus.*" *Journal of Modern Literature* 8, no. 2 (1980–81): 235–46.

Boomsma, Patricia J. "'Whole Sight': Fowles, Lukács, and *Daniel Martin.*" *Journal of Modern Literature* 8, no. 2 (1980–81): 325–36.

Bradbury, Malcolm. "John Fowles' *The Magus.*" In *Sense and Sensibility in Modern Literature,* edited by Brom Weber. Carbondale: Southern Illinois University Press, 1970, pp. 26–38.

———. "The Novelist as Impressario: John Fowles and His Magus." In his *Possibilities: Essays on the State of the Novel.* London: Oxford University Press, 1973, pp. 256–71.

Burden, Robert. "The Novel Interrogates Itself: Parody as Self-consciousness in Contemporary English Fiction." In *The Contemporary English Novel,* edited by Malcolm Bradbury and D. Palmer. Stratford-upon-Avon Studies, 18. London: Edward Arnold, 1979, pp. 133–55.

Conradi, Peter. *John Fowles.* London and New York: Methuen, 1982.

Churchill, Thomas. "Waterhouse, Storey, and Fowles: Which Way Out of the Room?" *Critique* 10 (Summer 1968): 72–87.

Detweiler, Robert. "The Unity of John Fowles's Fiction." *Notes on Contemporary Literature* 1 (March 1971): 3–4.

Docherty, Thomas. "A Constant Reality: The Presentation of Character in the Fiction of John Fowles." *Novel* 14, no. 2 (Winter 1981): 118–34.

Eddins, Dwight. "John Fowles: Existence as Authorship." *Contemporary Literature* 17 (Spring 1976): 204–22.

Evarts, Prescott. Jr., "Fowles' *The French Lieutenant's Woman* as Tragedy." *Critique* 13 (1972): 57–69.

———. "John Fowles: A Checklist." *Critique* 13 (1972): 105–107.

Ferris, Ina. "Realist Intention and Mythic Impulse in *Daniel Martin*." *Journal of Narrative Technique* 12, no. 2 (Spring 1982): 146–53.

Glaserfeld, Ernst von. "Reflections on John Fowles's *The Magus* and the Construction of Reality." *Georgia Review* 33 (1979): 444–48.

Hagopian, John V. "Bad Faith in *The French Lieutenant's Woman*." *Contemporary Literature* 32, no. 2 (Spring 1982): 190–201.

Hill, Roy Mack. "Power and Hazard: John Fowles's Theory of Play." *Journal of Modern Literature* 8, no. 2 (1980–81): 211–18.

Holmes, Frederick M. "The Novel, Illusion, and Reality: The Paradox of Omniscience in *The French Lieutenant's Woman*." *Journal of Narrative Technique* 11, no. 3 (Fall 1981): 184–98.

Huffaker, Robert. *John Fowles.* Boston: Twayne Publishers, 1980.

Kaplan, Fred. "Victorian Modernists: Fowles and Nabokov." *Journal of Narrative Technique* 3 (May 1973): 108–20.

Kennedy, Alan. "John Fowles's Sense of an Ending." In his *The Protean Self: Dramatic Action in Contemporary Fiction.* London: Macmillan, 1974, pp. 251–60.

Klemptner, Susan Strehle. "The Counterpoles of John Fowles's *Daniel Martin*." *Critique* 21, no. 2 (1979): 59–71.

Laughlin, Rosemary M. "Faces of Power in the Novels of John Fowles." *Critique* 13 (1972): 71–88.

Lever, Karen M. "The Education of John Fowles." *Critique* 21, no. 2 (1979): 85–99.

Magalaner, Marvin. "The Fool's Journey: John Fowles's *The Magus* (1966)." In *Old Lines, New Forces: Essays on the Contemporary British Novel, 1960–1976*, edited by Robert K. Morris. London: Associated University Presses, 1976, pp. 81–92.

Mansfield, Elizabeth. "A Sequence of Endings: The Manuscript of *The French Lieutenant's Woman*." *Journal of Modern Literature* 8, no. 2 (1980–81): 275–86.

McDaniel, Ellen. "*The Magus*: Fowles's Tarot Quest." *Journal of Modern Literature* 8, no. 2 (1980–81): 247–60.

McSweeney, Kerry. "John Fowles's Variations in *The Ebony Tower*." *Journal of Modern Literature* 8, no. 2 (1980–81): 303–24.

———. "Withering into the Truth: John Fowles and *Daniel Martin*." *Critical Quarterly* 20 (Winter 1978): 31–38.

Myers, Karen Magee. "John Fowles: An Annotated Bibliography, 1963–1976." *Bulletin of Bibliography* 32 (July–September 1976): 162–69.

Nadeau, Robert L. "Fowles and Physics: A Study of *The Magus: A Revised Version.*" *Journal of Modern Literature* 8, no. 2 (1980–1981): 261–74.

O'Haen, Theo. *Text to Reader: A Communicative Approach to Fowles, Barth, Cortázar, and Boon.* Amsterdam: Benjamins, 1983.

Olshen, Barry. *John Fowles.* New York: Frederick Ungar, 1978.

———. "John Fowles's *The Magus:* An Allegory of Self-Realization." *Journal of Popular Culture* 9 (Spring 1976): 916–25.

———, and Olshen, Toni. *John Fowles: A Reference Guide.* Boston: G. K. Hall, 1980.

Palmer, William J. *The Fiction of John Fowles.* Columbia: University of Missouri Press, 1974.

Rackham, Jeff. "John Fowles: The Existential Labyrinth." *Critique* 13 (1972): 89–103.

Rankin, Elizabeth D. "Cryptic Coloration in *The French Lieutenant's Woman.*" *Journal of Narrative Technique* 3 (September 1973): 193–207.

Rose, Gilbert J. *The French Lieutenant's Woman:* The Unconscious Significance of a Novel to Its Author." *American Imago* 29 (Summer 1972): 165–79.

Rubenstein, Roberta. "Myth, Mystery, and Irony: John Fowles's *The Magus.*" *Contemporary Literature* 16 (Summer 1975): 328–39.

Runyon, Randolph. *Fowles / Irving / Barthes: Canonical Variations on an Apocryphal Theme.* Columbus: Ohio State University Press, 1981.

Scholes, Robert. "John Fowles as Romancer." In *Fabulation and Metafiction.* Urbana: University of Illinois Press, 1979, pp. 37–46.

———. "The Orgastic Fiction of John Fowles." *Hollins Critic* 6 (December 1969): 1–12.

Thorpe, Michael. *John Fowles.* Windsor, Berkshire, England: Profile Books, 1982.

Wolfe, Peter. *John Fowles: Magus and Moralist.* Lewisburg, PA: Bucknell University Press, 1976.

Wymard, Eleanor B. "A New Version of 'the Midas Touch': *Daniel Martin* and *The World According to Garp.*" *Modern Fiction Studies* 27, no. 2 (Summer 1981): 284–86.

John Barth

MAJOR FICTIONS

1956. *The Floating Opera*. New York: Appleton-Century-Crofts.
Rev. ed. Garden City: Doubleday, 1967.

1958. *The End of the Road*. Garden City: Doubleday.

1960. *The Sot-Weed Factor*. Garden City: Doubleday.

1966. *Giles Goat-Boy; or, The Revised New Syllabus*. Garden City:
Doubleday.

1968. *Lost in the Funhouse: Fiction for Print, Tape, Live Voice*. Garden City: Doubleday. Rev. ed. Harmondsworth, Middlesex: Penguin Books, 1972.

1972. *Chimera*. New York: Random House.

1979. *Letters: A Novel*. New York: G. P. Putnam's Sons.

1982. *Sabbatical: A Romance*. New York: G. P. Putnam's Sons.

ESSAYS, INTERVIEWS, ETC.

Barth, John. Afterword. *The Adventures of Roderick Random*, by
Tobias Smollett. New York: Signet Books, 1964, pp. 469–79.

_____. "My Two Muses." *Johns Hopkins Magazine* 12 (April 1961):
9–13.

_____. "The Literature of Exhaustion." *Atlantic Monthly* 220 (Au-
gust 1967): 29–34.

Bellamy, Joe David. "John Barth." In his *The New Fiction: Interviews with Innovative American Writers*. Urbana: University of
Illinois Press, 1974, pp. 1–18.

Enck, John J. "John Barth: An Interview." *Wisconsin Studies in Contemporary Literature* 6 (1965): 3–14.

Gado, Frank, ed. "John Barth." In *First Person: Conversations on
Writers and Writing*. Schenectady, NY: Union College Press,
1973, pp. 110–41.

LeClair, Thom, and McCaffery, Larry. "A Dialogue: John Barth and
John Hawkes." In their *Anything Can Happen: Interviews with
Contemporary American Novelists*. Urbana: University of Illinois
Press, 1983, pp. 9–19.

Meras, Phyllis. "John Barth: A Truffle No Longer." *New York Times
Book Review*, 7 August 1966, p. 22.

Price, Alan. "An Interview with John Barth." *Prism*, Spring 1968,
pp. 50–51.

Reilly, Charlie. "An Interview with John Barth." *Contemporary Literature* 22, no. 1 (Winter 1981): 1–23.

SECONDARY SOURCES

Bienstock, Beverly Gray. "Lingering on the Autognostic Verge: John Barth's *Lost in the Funhouse.*" *Modern Fiction Studies* 19, no. 1 (1973): 69–78.

Bluestone, George. "John Wain and John Barth: The Angry and the Accurate." *Massachusetts Review* 1, no. 3 (1960): 582–89.

Bradbury, John M. "Absurd Insurrection: The Barth-Percy Affair." *South Atlantic Quarterly* 18, no. 3 (1969): 319–29.

Christensen, Inger. "John Barth's Metafictional Redemption." In her *The Meaning of Metafiction: A Critical Study of Selected Novels by Sterne, Nabokov, Barth and Beckett.* Bergen: Universitetsforlaget, 1981, pp. 57–96.

Davis, Cynthia. " 'The Key to the Treasure': Narrative Movements and Effects in *Chimera.*" *Journal of Narrative Technique* 5, no. 2 (1975): 105–15.

Decker, Sharon Davie. "Passionate Virtuosity: The Fiction of John Barth." Dissertation, University of Virginia, 1972.

Diser, Philip E. "The Historical Ebenezer Cooke." *Critique* 10, no. 3 (1968): 48–59.

Farwell, Harold. "John Barth's Tenuous Affirmation: 'The Absurd Unending Possibility of Love.' " *Georgia Review* 20 (1974): 290–306.

Gillespie, Gerald. " 'Lost in the Funhouse': Short Story Text in its Cyclic Context." *Studies in Short Fiction* 12 (1975): 223–30.

Glaser-Wöhrer, Evelyn. *An Analysis of John Barth's Weltanschauung: His View of Life and Literature.* Salzburger Studien zur Anglistik und Amerikanistik, Band 5. Salzburg: Institut für Englische Sprache und Literatur, Universität Salzburg, 1977.

Godshalk, William L. "Cabell and Barth: Our Comic Athletes." In *The Comic Imagination in American Literature*, Edited by Louis D. Rubin, Jr. New Brunswick, NJ: Rutgers University Press, 1973, pp. 275–83.

Graff, Gerald. "Under Our Belt and Off Our Back: Barth's *Letters* and Postmodern Fiction." *TriQuarterly* 52 (Fall 1981): 150–64.

Gross, Beverly. "The Anti-Novels of John Barth." *Chicago Review* 20, no. 3 (1968): 95–109.

Harris, Charles B. "George's Illumination: Unity in *Giles Goat-Boy.*" *Studies in the Novel* 8 (1976): 172–84.

———. "John Barth and the Critics: An Overview." *Mississippi Quarterly* 32 (1979): 269–83.

———. "Todd Andrews: Ontological Insecurity, and *The Floating Opera.*" *Critique* 18, no. 2 (1976): 51–8.

Hauck, Richard Boyd. "These Fruitful Fruitless Odysseys: John Barth." In his *A Cheerful Nihilism: Confident and "The Absurd" in American Humorous Fiction.* Bloomington: Indiana University Press, 1971, pp. 201–36.

Hendin, Josephine. "John Barth's Fictions for Survival." *Harper's Magazine* 247, (September 1973): 102–6.

Henkle, Roger B. "Symposium Highlights: Wrestling (American Style) with Proteus." *Novel* 3 (1970): 197–207.

Joseph, Gerhard. *John Barth.* University of Minnesota Pamphlets on American Writers, no. 91. Minneapolis: University of Minnesota Press, 1970.

Kennard, Jean E. "John Barth: Imitations of Imitations." In his *Number and Nightmare: Forms of Fantasy in Contemporary Fiction.* Hamden, CT: Archon Books, 1975, pp. 57–81.

Kiernan, Robert F. "John Barth's Artist in the Fun House." *Studies in Short Fiction* 10, no. 4 (1973): 273–80.

Klinkowitz, Jerome. "John Barth Reconsidered." *Partisan Review* 49, no. 3 (1982), 407–411.

———. Preface and "Prologue", "The Death of the Death of the Novel." In his *Literary Disruptions: The Making of a Post-contemporary Fiction.* Urbana: University of Illinois Press, 1975, pp. ix–x, 1–32.

Knapp, Edgar H. "Found in the Barthhouse: Novelist as Savior." *Modern Fiction Studies* 14, no. 4 (1968–69): 446–51.

Kostelanetz, Richard. "The New American Fiction." In his *The New American Arts.* New York: Horizon Press, 1965, pp. 194–236.

Kyle, Carol A. "The Unity of Anatomy: The Structure of Barth's *Lost in the Funhouse.*" *Critique* 13, no. 3 (1972): 31–43.

LeClair, Thomas. "Death and Black Humor." *Critique* 17, no. 1 (1975): 5–40.

———. "John Barth's *The Floating Opera:* Death and the Craft of Fiction." *Texas Studies in Literature and Language* 14, no. 4 (1973): 711–30.

McCaffery, Larry. "Barth's *Letters* and the Literature of Replenishment." *Chicago Review* 31, no. 4 (1980): 75–82.

McConnell, Frank D. "John Barth and the Key to the Treasure." In his *Four Postwar American Novelists: Bellow, Mailer, Barth, and Pynchon*. Chicago: University of Chicago Press, 1977, pp. 108–58.

McDonald, James L. "Barth's Syllabus: The Frame of *Giles Goat-Boy*. *Critique* 13, no. 3 (1972): 5–10.

Majdiak, Daniel. "Barth and the Representation of Life." *Criticism* 13 (1970): 51–67.

Marta, Jan. "John Barth's Portrait of the Artist as a Fiction: Modernism through the Looking Glass." *Canadian Review of Comparative Literature / Revue Canadienne de Litterature Comparée* 9, no. 2 (June 1982): 208–22.

Morrell, David. "Ebenezer Cooke. Sot-Weed Factor Redivivus: The Genesis of John Barth's *The Sot-Weed Factor*." *Bulletin of the Midwest Modern Language Association* 8, no. 1 (1975): 32–47.

———. *John Barth: An Introduction*. University Park: Pennsylvania State University Press, 1976.

Morris, Christopher D. "Barth and Lacan: The World of the Moebius Strip." *Critique* 17, no. 1 (1975): 69–77.

Noland, Richard W. "John Barth and the Novel of Comic Nihilism." *Wisconsin Studies in Contemporary Literature* 7 (1966): 239–57.

Pütz, Manfred. "John Barth: The Pitfall of Mythopoesis." In his *The Story of Identity: American Fiction of the Sixties*. Stuttgart: J. B. Metzlersche Verlagsbuchhandlung, 1979, pp. 61–104.

Powell, Jerry. "John Barth's *Chimera:* A creative Response to the Literature of Exhaustion." *Critique* 18, no. 2 (1976): 59–72.

Rovit, Earl. "The Novel as Parody: John Barth." *Critique* 6, no. 2 (Fall 1963): 77–85.

Runyon, Randolph. *Fowles / Irving / Barthes: Canonical Variations on an Apocryphal Theme*. Columbus: Ohio State University Press, for Miami University, 1981, pp. 110–14.

Schloss, Carol, and Tololyan, Khachig. "The Siren in the Funhouse: Barth's Courting of the Reader." *Journal of Narrative Technique* 11, no. 1 (Winter 1981): 64–74.

Scholes, Robert. "Fabulation and Epic Vision." In his *The Fabulators*. New York: Oxford University Press, 1967, pp. 135–73.

———. "John Barth's *Goat-Boy*." In his *Fabulation and Metafiction*. Urbana: University of Illinois Press, 1979, pp. 75–102.

————. "The Range of Metafiction: Barth, Barthelme, Coover, Gass." In his *Fabulation and Metafiction*. Urbana: University of Illinois Press, 1979, pp. 114–23.

Schulz, Max F. "Barth, *Letters*, and the Great Tradition." *Genre* 14, no. 1 (Spring 1981), 95–115.

————. "The Metaphysics of Multiciplicity: and, the Thousand and One Masks of John Barth." In his *Black Humor Fiction of the Sixties: A Pluralistic Definition of Man and His World*. Athens: Ohio University Press, 1973, pp. 17–42.

Slethaug, Gordon E. "Barth's Refutation of the Idea of Progress." *Critique* 13, no. 3 (1972): 11–29.

Stark, John O. "John Barth." In his *The Literature of Exhaustion: Borges, Nabokov, and Barth*. Durham: Duke University Press, 1974, pp. 118–75.

Stubbs, John C. "John Barth as a Novelist of Ideas: The Themes of Value and Identity." *Critique* 8, no. 2 (1965–66): 101–16.

Tanner, Tony. "The Hoax That Joke Bilked." *Partisan Review* 34, no. 1 (1967): 102–9.

————. "What Is the Case?" In his *City of Words: American Fiction, 1950–1970*. New York: Harper and Row, 1971, pp. 230–59.

Tatham, Campbell. "John Barth and the Aesthetics of Artifice." *Contemporary Literature* 12, no. 1 (1971): 60–73.

Tharpe, Jac. *John Barth: The Comic Sublimity of Paradox*. Carbondale: Southern Illinois University Press, 1974.

Tilton, John W. "*Giles Goat-Boy:* An Interpretation." *Bucknell Review* 28, no. 1 (Spring 1970): 92–119.

————. "*Giles Goat-Boy:* Man's Precarious Purchase on Reality." In his *Cosmic Satire the Contemporary Novel*. Lewisburg, PA: Bucknell University Press, 1977, pp. 43–68.

Trachtenberg, Alan. "Barth and Hawkes: Two Fabulists." *Critique* 6, no. 2 (1963): 4–18.

Vine, Richard Allan. *John Barth: An Annotated Bibliography.* Scarecrow Author Bibliographies, no. 31, Metuchen, NJ: Scarecrow Press, 1977.

Waldmeir, Joseph J. *Critical Essays on John Barth*. Critical series in American Literature. Boston: Hall, 1980.

Warrick, Patricia, "The Circuitous Journey of Consciousness in Barth's *Chimera.*" *Critique* 18, no. 2 (1976): 73–85.

Weixlmann, Joseph. *John Barth. A Descriptive Primary and Anno-*

tated Secondary Bibliography, Including a Descriptive Catalogue of Manuscript Holdings in United States Libraries. New York: Garland Publishing Co., 1976.

Zamora, Lois Parkinson. "The Structural Games in the Fiction of John Barth and Julio Cortázar." *Perspectives in Contemporary Literature* 6 (1980): 28–36.

General Criticism

Aldridge, John. *The Devil in the Fire: Retrospective Essays on American Literature and Culture, 1951–1971.* New York: Harper Magazine Press, 1972.

Allen, Mary. *The Necessary Blankness: Women in American Fiction of the Sixties.* Urbana: University of Illinois Press, 1976.

Allen, Walter. *The Modern Novel in Britain and the United States.* New York: E. P. Dutton and Co., 1964.

Alter, Robert. *Partial Magic: The Novel as a Self-Conscious Genre.* Berkeley and Los Angeles: University of California Press, 1975.

Barrett, William. *Time of Need: Forms of Imagination in the Twentieth Century.* New York: Harper and Row, 1972.

Baumbach, Jonathan. *The Landscape of Nightmare: Studies in the American Novel.* New York: New York University Press, 1965.

Beebe, Maurice. *Ivory Towers and Sacred Founts: The Artist as Hero in Fiction from Goethe to Joyce.* New York: New York University Press, 1964.

Bergonzi, Bernard. *The Situation of the Novel.* Pittsburgh: University of Pittsburgh Press, 1970.

Berthoff, Warner. *Fictions and Events: Essays in Criticism and Literary History.* New York: E. P. Dutton, 1971.

Bienstock, Beverly Gray. "The Self-Conscious Artist in Contemporary American Fiction." Dissertation, University of California, 1973.

Bradbury, Malcolm and Palmer, David. *The Contemporary English Novel.* Stratford-upon-Avon Studies, 18. London: Edward Arnold, 1979.

———. *The Modern American Novel.* New York: Oxford University Press, 1983.

———. *Possibilities: Essays on the State of the Novel.* London: Oxford University Press, 1973.

Bryant, Jerry H. *The Open Decision: The Contemporary American Novel and Its Intellectual Background*. New York: Free Press, 1970.

Burns, Alan, and Sugnet, Charles, eds. *The Imagination on Trial: British and American Writers Discuss Their Working Methods*. London: Allison and Busby, 1981.

Carter, Everett. *The American Idea: The Literary Reaction to American Optimism*. Chapel Hill: University of North Carolina Press, 1976.

Christensen, Inger. *The Meaning of Metafiction: A Critical Study of Selected Novels by Sterne, Nabokov, Barth and Beckett*. Bergen: Universitetsforlaget, 1981.

Dickstein, Morris. *Gates of Eden: American Culture in the Sixties*. New York: Basic Books, 1977.

Federman, Raymond, ed. *Surfiction: Fiction Now . . . and Tomorrow*. Chicago: Swallow Press, 1975.

Fraser, G. S. *The Modern Writer and His World*. Rev. ed. Baltimore: Penguin Books, 1964.

Friedman, Alan F. *Multivalence: The Moral Quality of Form in the Modern Novel*. Baton Rouge: Louisiana State University Press, 1978.

Galloway, David. *The Absurd Hero in American Fiction: Updike, Styron, Bellow, Salinger*. Austin: University of Texas Press, 1966.

Gindin, James. *Postwar British Fiction: New Accents and Attitudes*. Berkeley: University of California Press, 1962.

Glicksberg, Charles I. *The Self in Modern Literature*. University Park: Pennsylvania State University Press, 1963.

———. *Tragic Vision in Twentieth-Century Literature*. Carbondale: Southern Illinois University Press, 1963.

Hardy, Barbara. *Tellers and Listeners: The Narrative Imagination*. London: Athlone, 1975.

Harris, Charles B. *Contemporary American Novelists of the Absurd*. New Haven, CT: New College and University Press, 1971.

Hassan, Ihab. *Paracriticisms: Seven Speculations of the Times*. Urbana: University of Illinois Press, 1975.

———. *Radical Innocence: Studies in the Contemporary American Novel*. Princeton: Princeton University Press, 1961.

———. *The Right Promethean Fire: Imagination, Science, and Cultural Change*. Urbana: University of Illinois Press, 1980.

Hauck, Richard Boyd. *A Cheerful Nihilism: Confidence and "The Absurd" in American Humorous Fiction.* Bloomington: Indiana University Press, 1971.

Hough, Graham. *Reflections on a Literary Revolution.* Washington: Catholic University of America Press, 1960.

Kaplan, Frederick R. *A Reader's Guide to the Contemporary English Novel.* Rev. ed. New York: Farrar, Straus and Giroux, 1972.

Kaplan, Sydney Janet. *Feminine Consciousness in the Modern British Novel.* Urbana: University of Illinois Press, 1975.

Karl, Frederick R. *A Reader's Guide to the Contemporary English Novel.* London: Thames and Hudson, 1963.

Kellman, Steven G. *The Self-Begetting Novel.* New York: Columbia University Press, 1980.

Kennedy, Alan. *Meaning and Signs in Fiction.* London: Macmillan, 1978.

Kermode, Frank. *Puzzles and Epiphanies: Essays and Reviews, 1958–1961.* New York: Chilmark Press, 1972.

———. *The Sense of an Ending: Studies in the Theory of Fiction.* New York: Oxford University Press, 1967.

Klinkowitz, Jerome. *The Life of Fiction.* Urbana: University of Illinois Press, 1977.

Lebowitz, Naomi. *Humanism and the Absurd in the Modern Novel.* Evanston, IL: Northwestern University Press, 1971.

Lefevre, André. *Literary Knowledge: A Polemical and Programmatic Essay on Its Nature, Growth, Relevance and Transmission.* Netherlands: Royal Vangorcum, 1977.

Lodge, David. *The Modes of Modern Writing: Metaphor, Metonymy, and the Typology of Modern Literature.* Ithaca, NY: Cornell University Press, 1977.

———. *The Novelist at the Crossroads.* Ithaca, NY: Cornell University Press, 1971.

McConnell, Frank P. *Four Postwar American Novelists: Bellow, Mailer, Barth, and Pynchon.* Chicago: University of Chicago Press, 1977.

McCormick, John. *Fiction as Knowledge: The Modern Post-Romantic Novel.* New Brunswick, NJ: Rutgers University Press, 1975.

Marcuse, Herbert. *One-Dimensional Man: Studies in the Ideology of Advanced Industrial Society.* Boston: Beacon, 1964.

Marx, Leo. *The Machine in the Garden: Technology and the Pastoral Idea in America*. New York: Oxford University Press, 1964.

Mellard, James M. *The Exploded Form: The Modernist Novel in America*. Urbana: University of Illinois Press, 1980.

Olderman, Raymond M. *Beyond the Waste Land: A Study of the American Novel in the Nineteen Sixties*. New York: Free Press, 1970.

Poirier, Richard. *The Performing Self*. New York: Oxford University Press, 1971.

Rabinovitz, Rubin. *The Reaction Against Experiment in the English Novel, 1950–1960*. New York: Columbia University Press, 1967.

Scholes, Robert. *Fabulation and Metafiction*. Urbana: University of Illinois Press, 1979.

_____. *The Fabulators*. New York: Oxford University Press, 1967.

Schulz, Max F. *Black Humor Fiction of the Sixties: A Pluralistic Definition of Man and His World*. Athens: Ohio University Press, 1973.

Shapiro, Charles, ed. *Contemporary British Novelists*. Carbondale: Southern Illinois Press, 1965.

Sontag, Susan. *Against Interpretation*. New York: Farrar, Straus and Giroux, 1966.

_____. *Styles of Radical Will*. New York: Farrar, Straus and Giroux, 1969.

Stade, George, ed. *Six Contemporary British Novelists*. New York: Columbia University Press, 1976.

Stark, John O. *The Literature of Exhaustion: Borges, Nabokov, and Barth*. Durham, NC: Duke University Press, 1974.

Stevick, Philip. *Alternative Pleasures: Postrealist Fiction and the Tradition*. Urbana: University of Illinois Press, 1981.

Stewart, Grace. *A New Mythos: The Novels of the Artist as Heroine*. St. Albans, VT: Eden Press, 1978.

Tanner, Tony. *City of Words: American Fiction, 1950–1970*. New York: Harper and Row, Publishers, 1971.

Toliver, Harold. *Animate Illusions: Explorations of Narrative Structure*. Lincoln: University of Nebraska Press, 1974.

Walker, David. "Subversion of Narrative in the Work of André Gide and John Fowles." In *Comparative Criticism: A Yearbook*, vol. 2. Cambridge, 1980, pp. 187–212.

Weber, Brom, ed. *Sense and Sensibility in Twentieth-Century Writing*. Carbondale: Southern Illinois University Press, 1970.

Weinberg, Helen. *The New Novel in America: The Kafkan Mode in Contemporary Fiction.* Ithaca, N.Y.: Cornell University Press, 1970.

Zavarzadeh, Mas'ud. *The Mythopoeic Reality.* Urbana: University of Illinois Press, 1976.

Index